My VITA, If You Will

THE UNCOLLECTED

Ed McClanahan

My **VITA**, *If You Will*

FOREWORD BY ROBERT STONE

EDITED AND WITH AN ESSAY BY TOM MARKSBURY

COUNTERPOINT

The author wishes to thank the editors and publishers of *Ace*, *Contact*,
Esquire, *The Geography of Hope: A Tribute to Wallace Stegner* (Sierra Club
Books, 1996), *The Journal of Kentucky Studies*, *Kentucky Voices*, *The Last
Supplement to the Whole Earth Catalog*, *Limestone*, *Louisville Magazine*,
Place, *Playboy*, *Playboy's Music Scene* (Playboy Press, 1972), *Rolling Stone*, *Spit
in the Ocean*, and *The Writer*, where some of these works have appeared in
slightly different form. "Furthurmore" is an afterword to the 1997 Gnomon
Press reissue of *Famous People I Have Known*; it also appeared in *Wild Duck
Review*. "New Speedway Boogie" lyric by Robert Hunter, copyright © Ice
Nine Publishing Company. Used by permission.

Library of Congress Cataloging-in-Publication Data
McClanahan, Ed.
    My *vita*, if you will : the uncollected Ed McClanahan / foreword by
Robert Stone ; edited and with an essay by Tom Marksbury.
      p.   cm.
    ISBN 1-887178-77-5 (alk. paper)
    I. Marksbury, Tom.   II. Title.
PS3563.C3397A6 1998
813'.54—dc21   98-34792
                                                    CIP

ISBN: 978-1-88717-877-8

Book design by David Bullen
Composition by Wilsted & Taylor Publishing Services

Printed in the United States of America

COUNTERPOINT

2560 Ninth Street Suite 318
Berkeley, CA 94710
counterpointpress.com

In memory of Mr. Kelsie Mertz,

one of a kind

contents

foreword

IN THE AUTUMN of 1962, I found myself seated in a California classroom across from a man in a two-tone cotton jacket and wraparound sunglasses. I noted that his shoes actually seemed to be made of blue suede. These were the days when native costume was still to be seen worn by the inhabitants of out-of-the-way regions, and the man was an alarming phenomenon in his. He seemed to combine in person and outfit some ghastly time past and an unimaginably weird time future. As for the region his regalia represented—it turned out to be located somewhere south of his frontal lobes.

Except perhaps for the shoes, which may be one of the atrocious false memories with which aggrieved offspring send their parents to protective custody in the penitentiary, my first impression proved correct over time. Ed McClanahan (for it was he) would regale me with tales of growing up over a pool-room in Rosemary Clooney's hometown of Maysville, Kentucky. He sounded nothing like Ms. Clooney; more of a cross between Big Mike Fink, the murderous river bandit, and Red Barber, the Dodgers' home park announcer.

He would also take me to Perry Lane in Menlo Park, where Ken Kesey and his friends lived at the time, and with whom Ed consorted. In fact it was through Ed that I became acquainted with the group of lifelong friends who have become known, rather ludicrously, as the Merry Pranksters.

On Perry Lane we assisted noted figures of the day in psychic research: the incisionless mind-transplant, the human cat's cradle, the imaginary inflatable, and the bone-dry kelp forest were all products of our laboratory in the California of the Mind.

Ed would celebrate the close of a hard night's research at dawn by doing his inimitable imitation of a Jacques Brel finale at the Folies Bergère in low Kentuckian on the steps of Dinkelspiel Auditorium, a spectacle that haunts those who witnessed it to this day.

Our best moments, our most profound inquiries into the nature of existence, however, remain forgotten, confirming the old adage that if you can remember California in the sixties, you weren't there. Ed's work will be remembered when the rest of us have forgotten who we are.

In those days Ed often read from his writings, either in the Stanford workshop above the library or at one of the cottages that abounded in the days before Silicon Valley made the hills of the San Francisco Peninsula an unaffordable ghetto of wealthy wizards, and in which we Stanford graduate students made our homes. His writing then, as now, was whimsical and absurdist, outrageous, extreme, and most pleasurable. But it was more than that; it was also writing with close observation, sympathy, and a tragic vision that underlay his comedy.

As his reputation grows, and more and more readers become aware of McClanahan's work, those of us who knew him in the old days take a particular pride in America's increasing familiarity with its distinctively native son. But we are not surprised.

It gives me singular pleasure to introduce the uncollected works collected here, which represent Ed at the peak of his comic vision. Funny and moving, alternately comically grandiloquent and genuinely eloquent, this is the writing of a true American original. Ladies and gentlemen—Ed McClanahan.

Robert Stone

"Hit's all in one piece, O my honeys!"

Brother Ransbottom

Robert Hazel died in 1993 after a long and distinguished career as a poet and teacher of writing. I wrote this memoir in 1996 as my contribution to *An American Romantic: Perspectives on Robert Hazel* (edited by John and Linda Kuehl), which is still in preparation. "Bob's Lost Years" also appeared in *Ace* magazine.

Bob's Lost Years: A Memoir of Robert Hazel

In 1956 or '57, when I was Bob Hazel's student at the University of Kentucky (where I was desultorily plodding my way through graduate school), Bob and I were eating lunch one day in his UK office when I launched into some anecdote about the dreadful job I'd once briefly held as a school bus driver. You oughta write about that, Bob said; there's a *story* in it. I stashed the suggestion away in the back of my mind and mulled it over now and then, but didn't act upon it. I couldn't have known it then, of course, but (as I'll explain in good time) Bob's idea would reverberate down through my life for the ensuing forty years.

I think it's interesting that the romantic impulse that served Bob so well as a poet betrayed him so brazenly as a novelist. His novels—*The Lost Year* (1953), *A Field Full of People*

(1954), and *Early Spring* (1971)—are paeans to Art, the Noble Savage, Alcohol, Self-Destruction, and the venerable Hard, Gemlike Flame. (The fact that I make a rather inglorious appearance in *Early Spring* as a grad student named Crutley Buster Glans has nothing to do, cross my heart, with the fact that I think it's the weakest of the three.) Utterly devoid of the merest taint of ironic distance, these novels otherwise have too much of everything: too much maudlin poetic sensibility, too many billboard-sized symbols, too much nameless, free-floating despair . . . Needless to say, I admired *Lost Year* and *Field Full of People* extravagantly and sought to emulate them in my own fiction at every turn.

Bob's presence loomed monumentally large during my two years at UK. He was a fine classroom teacher, with a relaxed, noncensorious manner that made his classes feel like small, subversive cells within the stuffy confines of the English Department and that belied his demanding—but never condescending—attention to the quality of our work. But it was his out-of-school style that most impressed me.

He was dashingly handsome, he'd already published two novels and lots of poems, he could talk knowledgeably (or, at any rate, persuasively) about abstract expressionist painting and French symbolist poetry, he'd hung out in Greenwich Village with Saul Bellow and Jackson Pollock and had gotten drunk at the Whitehorse Tavern with (or, at any rate, in the presence of) Dylan Thomas. He and his beautiful young wife, Pat (with whom his male students routinely and hopelessly fell in love), invited us to their home for cookouts and beer, insisted that we call them by their first names, went out drinking with us, and treated us like the nascent literary whizbangs we imagined ourselves to be. For me, at least, they were as gods.

I bilked UK out of an M.A. in 1958 and went west to Oregon State College (now University) in Corvallis to teach freshman comp (I'd much rather drive a school bus) and, eventually, creative writing. I modeled my writing classes after Bob's: first names de rigueur, smokin' in the classroom recommended if not required, a give-it-a-try-and-you'll-get-by grading policy. After school, my students and I drank beer at the joints on Two Street, and I told them about my friend Bob Hazel, who knew Saul Bellow and Dylan Thomas.

I wrote my first "successful" story in 1960, my second year at Oregon State. It was published in the spring 1961 issue of *Contact,* a nationally distributed quarterly that was a sort of clone of the *Evergreen Review.* The story, "The Little-Known Bird of the Inner Eye," is overwrought and overwritten, word-drunk, fraught with Freudian innuendo and egregious symbolism—in short, it has Bob's indelible footprints all over it. Even the photograph of myself in *Contact*—dark, brooding, doomed, existential soul that I was—is a carbon copy of the picture of Bob on the jacket of *The Lost Year.*

In 1962, on the untested strength of an early draft of the novella that was to become, twenty-two years later, my novel *The Natural Man,* I became the fourth Bob Hazel by-product in a five-year span (following my UK friends Wendell Berry, James Baker Hall, and Gurney Norman) to win a Stegner Fellowship to Stanford.

Now Bob was in rather a bad way by that time. He and Pat had busted up, and Bob had got himself fired at UK (girl trouble, as will hardly surprise those who knew him) and was living in Louisville in seedy circumstances, drinking a good deal—a life remarkably similar to that of the doomed young Byronic hero of *The Lost Year.* Since I was leaving Oregon State, I persuaded our department chairman to hire Bob as my replacement. I'm sure it must have been humiliating for Bob to have to take a cheesy instructorship that was being sloughed off by one of his former students, but I guess he had no choice. Anyhow, he'd never been west before, and he took an instant, all-purpose loathing to everything west of East Saint Louis. (I seem to recall that his car vapor-locked in the Rockies and that he had to be *towed* over the Continental Divide. How's that for ready-to-wear foreshadowing?) Then, in typical Bob Hazel death-wish fashion, no sooner had he arrived in Corvallis than he began—there is no delicate way to say this—putting the moves on the department chairman's own student secretary.

I don't know whether Bob quit or got fired again, but after two academic quarters he was on his way back east; I imagine him bounding this time over the Continental Divide with all four wheels off the ground. Not long after his return, he landed a much more appropriate job at NYU, and his teaching career was back on track.

Meanwhile, down at Stanford, I had begun my year on the fellowship by embarking on what I thought would be a short story about—what else?—the school bus driver of yore. The short story turned out to be a 125-page novella; I spent the entire year writing it. It wasn't very good, and in that form, happily for me, it never found a publisher. But of course I kept thinking about it and tinkering with it over the years—paring it down to ninety pages in the process, so I figure I've unwritten this story at the rate of about one page a year over the past thirty-five years—and now it's my favorite of the three novellas in my brand-new book *A Congress of Wonders.*

On balance, I consider Bob Hazel's influence on my life and on my work immeasurably salutary. Bob was—still is— a major hero of mine. The sort of writing he inspired wasn't all just posturing, bravado, soul-baring existential despair, and (in my case) assonance, alliteration, and a serious three-adjective habit. That audacious wind-in-the-hair passion and brash, risk-taking, lyrical derring-do (these old habits are hard to break) liberated something in my head, in my heart, and in my voice and made an altogether different writer of me. During the relatively short time I was close to him, I was still very much a work in progress—it would be many years before my style began to jell into whatever it wanted to become—but without Bob the work in progress could have had no denouement.

Remarkably, Bob's presence in my life extends right into this very moment, in which I am being pestered at my desk by my year-old Great Dane puppy, Boggles, who is named after a big boxer pup that Bob and the gorgeous Pat had raised and, after their bust-up (ca. 1959), given to my parents, who had room for him at their big country home, where he—Boggles the First—became so profoundly attached to my father that when my father died in 1962, so, within months, did Boggles.

Endnote

Bob Hazel was one of a phalanx of great writing teachers who profoundly influenced my work and my life.

I spent my freshman year (1951–52) at Washington and Lee University, home of the World's Longest Concrete Footbridge, in Lexington, Virginia. Almost from the first moment, I hated it. Back then, W&L was an all-male enclave with the stated mission—they actually put this in their catalog—of grinding out a product they called the Southern Gentleman, which apparently wore a seersucker suit and a rep-striped tie at all times and steadfastly eschewed the society of the inferior races and classes. I knew right away that I absolutely did not want to be one. What *I* wanted, vaguely, was to wear turtleneck sweaters and grow a beard and be some kind of boho, maybe even—hey! a writer!

Back home in Kentucky over Christmas break, Ned Stiles,

my best buddy from high school days, pointed out (rather smugly, in my opinion) that at *his* university—Miami of Ohio—you could wear whatever you damn well pleased, and there were actual non-Caucasians in nonmenial positions on the campus, and *girls,* honest-to-God flesh-and-blood *girls*—he already knew several of them *personally,* Ned claimed, and planned to get to know several others at the earliest opportunity—and then he added the portentous clincher: Miami, he said, offered a course in something called "creative writing." My fate was sealed; come next fall, I was transferring to Miami.

Professor Walter Havighurst, who at the time constituted Miami's creative-writing department in its entirety, wore tweeds instead of turtlenecks and had a salt-and-pepper mustache instead of a beard, but he looked every inch a writer, all the same. Tall and dignified and distingué, he had the faintly bemused, self-assured air of a man with a Pulitzer in his hip pocket. That impression, unfortunately, was a bit deceptive; Dr. Havighurst was a very fine writer, but because he was a midwesterner and a regionalist, his work never received the recognition it deserved.

But he was a masterful teacher. Our textbook was one of those old prewar anthologies of classic short stories—Chekhov, de Maupassant, Poe, Crane, Joyce, and company, with maybe something by that young sprout Hemingway thrown in as a sop to the avant-garde—and of all the teachers I've had before or since, Dr. Havighurst was the best at dismantling those stories and explaining how they worked. And when he critiqued our own writing, his quiet authority was to us as a marble monument is to a graffiti artist: we longed above all else to make our mark upon it.

That proved a daunting task: on the first three assignments—a character sketch, a dialogue exercise, and an exercise in what we used to call "tone"—I racked up a trio of C-minuses. For the fourth assignment—a story with flash-backs—I produced "Fear and Hope and a Gutter," an attempt at noir realism of which I was immensely proud—especially of all those *ands* in the title, which I thought were awfully classy. But Dr. Havighurst was no pushover, and he had an unerring eye for pretension and preciousness; my story pulled a C-plus. Perversely, I've included it elsewhere in this volume.

But after two more C-pluses, my next effort, a funky little dialect story called "Me and George," brought home . . . a B-minus! Jubilant, I immediately submitted the story to *Atlantic Monthly*—but not before I'd hastily sent in a subscription, on the theory that no self-respecting magazine would buy some-thing from someone who didn't even read it. (Amazingly, I got a very nice rejection note—on account of my subscrip-tion, I figured.) In any event, I had seen my last C-plus, at least in creative-writing class.

Thanks to Dr. Havighurst, in the summer of 1955, after my graduation from Miami, I scored a fellowship to a writers' conference at the University of Colorado in Boulder. My roommate there was a young Stanford undergraduate named Vic Lovell, who was destined to figure importantly in my life in any number of ways, first of all by telling me that *his* uni-versity offered not only God's own plenty of beards and tur-tlenecks and girls but also a whole *master's* degree in creative writing! Within the hour I was on the phone to the Stanford registrar's office, requesting an application.

(Now for a little sidelight: during the Boulder conference I happened across a copy of volume three of *New World Writ-ing,* the most exciting literary journal of the day. In that issue, cheek by jowl with Margaret Mead, Dylan Thomas, Alberto Moravia, Malcolm Lowry, and a couple of dozen other major writers, was a young writer named Hollis Summers, who was from, of all places, Eminence, Kentucky, and was teaching at, of all places, the University of Kentucky. His short story, "How They Chose the Dead," was a gem; my new friend Vic and I spent hours, as I recall, debating its meaning. Little did I suppose then that—well, more on this momentarily. As we McLeprechauns always sez, I precedes meself.)

The fiction workshop at Boulder was directed by the poet and novelist May Sarton. She was very encouraging; she praised my story "Postcard" in class and actually called me a "real writer" right out loud! I was ecstatic. When, during a pit stop on my way home to Kentucky after the conference, a friendly barkeep asked what line of work I was in, I gave myself what seemed to me the coolest title this side of, say, "Movie Star" or "Soldier of Fortune": "Oh," I told him, with a shrug of elaborately feigned nonchalance, "I'm just a Free-lance Writer."

And so when I arrived at Stanford that September, I was still pretty full of myself . . . until the subsequent Wednesday afternoon, which found me cowering in what I realized, too late, was perhaps the most high-powered creative-writing class in all of academe, the Stanford English Department's CW 501, a fabled graduate workshop in which four places were permanently reserved for holders of the coveted Wallace E. Stegner Fellowships in Creative Writing.

Mr. Stegner himself was on leave that year, so the stewardship of the program fell to his longtime associate and close friend, English professor and novelist Richard Scowcroft, who opened the workshop with a reading of an alarmingly fine story called "Hey Sailor, What Ship?" by the rising star of the current crop of Stegner Fellows, a petite, handsome woman named Tillie Olsen. She was unknown and unpublished at the time, but in a few short years my formidable classmate would become famous as the author of *Tell Me a*

Riddle, a landmark collection of stories (including, incidentally, "Hey Sailor, What Ship?") that remains to this day a feminist icon. But that afternoon, as I sat there listening to the eminent Dr. Scowcroft read the soon-to-be-eminent Tillie Olsen, my heart sank; it was my first day of grad school, and already I was out of my depth.

I had that about right. Dr. Scowcroft (or Dick, as I would come to know him in later years) was and is a lovely man, maybe the sweetest, kindest, most forbearing teacher I've ever known, but the only impression I managed to make on him that term was sartorial, not literary: when our paths merged again in 1962, he confessed that the only thing he could recall about me were the shades and cycle boots I'd taken to wearing when I got to Stanford. Thanks to Dick Scowcroft's generosity, I didn't drop all the way back into the C-plus ranks, but I was definitely on the bubble.

In the winter quarter, another éminence grise, the great literary critic Malcolm Cowley, took the reins of the workshop as a guest professor. We were obliged to submit samples of our work to gain admission, and to my dismay, he (quite rightly) didn't want to let me in; but I begged and wheedled and whined and groveled to such an embarrassing extent that at last, with a sigh of resignation, he succumbed. Nonetheless, although I didn't write a whit better for his workshop than I had for Dr. Scowcroft's, Mr. Cowley took a liking to me; his critiques of the twaddle I was submitting to him were models of restraint. Best of all, I had a conference with him at his university apartment, and his wife—a beautiful gray-haired lady named, I think, Miriam—served me what appeared to be a very small drink of water with one of those little round green things on a toothpick in it. My first martini—and, believe it or not, my first olive.

I'd also signed up that term for Mr. Cowley's course in

modern criticism, which turned out to be the all-time best literature course I've ever experienced. We read Proust and Henry James and Hemingway, but the main event was Faulkner. Viking Press had published, in 1946, *The Portable William Faulkner,* edited by Mr. Cowley; the collection had almost single-handedly restored Faulkner's literary reputation—which had been undeservedly compromised by his screen-writing career and the steamy-potboiler notoriety of some of his novels, notably *Sanctuary*—and laid the groundwork for his 1950 Nobel prize. Mr. Cowley had a hatful of wonderful personal anecdotes about Faulkner—not one of which, dammit, can I now recall—and listening to them was to be in the presence of greatness . . . squared.

But not even Mr. Cowley could save me—and my Stanford graduate career—from myself. By the end of that quarter, I knew it was time to hang it up. I slunk back to Kentucky with my tail between my legs, hired on as a laborer with a construction crew, took up drinking beer—*lots* of beer—with my fellow proles, and generally resigned myself to a life nasty, brutish, and (the good news) short, amongst the Natural Men. If the literary world was gonna be all that goddamn snooty, I'd just deprive it of the light of my genius and sit back and watch it wither on the vine.

Larry, the honcho of the construction outfit I was working for, was such a cheapskate he wouldn't buy us hard hats. He'd contracted to dismantle a four-story steel storage shed, and one day early that summer, he dropped a one-inch steel nut and bounced it off my head from forty feet above. If he'd sneaked up behind me and rapped me sharply on the noggin with a ball-peen hammer, it couldn't have been more effective. I went down like I'd been shot, and a few minutes later when I came to, with a halo of little cuckoo birds circling my head, I was already reassessing my career options. Within the next few days, I was at the University of Kentucky in Lexington, registering for a couple of graduate English lit summer school classes.

I logged countless hours that summer sitting in a ratty old tavern (named, rather elementally, the Tavern), drinking beer and reading Shakespeare—to such an unseemly degree that the bartender began addressing me as "Hamlet" or, alternatively, "Snakeshit." (The latter term of affection turns up elsewhere in this volume.)

My unusual study habits notwithstanding, I acquitted myself well enough in summer school to bring me back for the fall semester and one more try at nailing that old sheepskin to the wall. But not even that lick on the skull had quite killed off my tiny inner writer; the very first class I signed up for that fall was Hollis Summers's creative-writing workshop.

Dr. Summers, a man of elegant, almost patrician manners who dressed carefully and always employed a cigarette holder, was a demanding teacher and a punctilious editor of his students' manuscripts, with a scrupulous eye for detail and a penchant for writing copious marginal notes intrusively questioning a person's own personal grammar and diction and spelling and whatnot. In other words, he was picky, picky, picky. Why such a fastidious gent would put up with a pseudo-surly mope like me—I was still in my shades-and-cycle-boots phase—remains an astonishment to me. Maybe he saw me as a challenge, some sort of overdue campus beautification project.

But put up with me he was about to, in spades, for I was destined to spend the next two years struggling to wrest my M.A. from the reluctant clutches of the UK English Department, and I'd soon be passing a good deal of my on-campus time lollygagging about the office Dr. Summers shared with another favorite professor of mine, Bill Jansen, a folklorist.

They and Dr. Summers's junior colleague Bob Hazel (remember him?) basically carried me through the dismal groves of academe for two years: they gave me A's in their courses, and Drs. S. and J. both served on my master's oral exam committee—twice, because I flunked the goddamn thing the first time. (Not their fault; they lobbed me softball questions, at which, in a panic, I went down swinging wildly.) Bob—the first teacher I ever formed a first-name friendship with— made me the editor of *Stylus,* the campus lit mag, and encouraged me to publish myself in it.

I was even beginning to benefit from Dr. Summers's finicky marginal notes. Not that my writing was getting better; indeed, I was mostly just recycling my old Miami and Stanford stories, trying to find some new angle on them. But I was becoming a better reader of my own prose, better at identifying those passages where some mysterious but essential element has been omitted, and the language just sits there on the page in a gob, like dough that won't rise because the baker has forgotten the yeast.

What was really happening, although I didn't quite know it yet, was that I was shutting down my Freelance Writer operation to take up an apprenticeship in the creative-writing teacher game.

But that's another story.

My first nationally published story; it appeared in *Contact* 8 (Spring 1961), a quarterly based in San Francisco.

The Little-Known Bird
of the Inner Eye

He does not know that I exist. Or if he does, he must see me the way a wild canary sees a bird-watcher, through the big end of the field glasses, a tiny thing a million miles away, while the canary becomes, to the watcher, enormous, framed in a double-vision circle bigger than the earth.

But once he did. For three whole days he knew me, and we even almost talked once.

I am again on that street for the first time. It is one of those warm, gray Northwest fall days that bear with them a feeling of rain, even though it will not rain for several weeks yet. The town assails me with decay. Vacant houses, empty shop windows, the stinking corpse of a dog wheelmarked in a gutter, fat flies at its eyeballs, the blind eyes of people on the streets, faces rotten with worry, despair. And behind the low roofs the looming barrenness of the gray hills, stump-pocked, pressing their dead weight against the town. Fruit cannot drop through this thick air. . . .

Yet I had come for beauty to this place where there were hardly even shadows (for lack of trees to cast them). Had carefully in Kansas made my choice of places (1927 *World Atlas:* "... heartland of the great Pacific Northwest timber country ... abounds with lush forests ..."), had driven truck and fed a starving cement mixer, saved money, fought my father ("I don't see why the goddamn hell you can't be an artist right here in ..." "I'll go back to college next year. What you can't see is this is something I have got to do. It's my own goddamn money ...").

And got here, too, smelling of buses, riding the last of those only yesterday into this vast dead orchard haunted by the ghosts of long-gone trees. I had stood and watched the bus roar off and leave me in this place far worse than Kansas, and said to myself I'd by God stay till spring no matter what.

In my suitcase, sharing space with my clothes, were traveler's checks, and chisels, sketch pads, brushes, and one fine new welding torch. My pride in those things got me through the day, though their weight to carry made me take the first room I could find, a long, dusty loft above a garage, with rafters, a greasy sink, and one small window. But by afternoon it also had a hot plate, some plastic dishes, whitewashed walls, a chair and table (with my torch a centerpiece), a used mattress (soon to make some logger's lusty daughter happy?), and a rented acetylene tank with needled eyes that followed me about the room. At night I tried some sketches, gave it up, and slept off two days of buses, dreaming of blond-breasted girls who loved me for the beard already started. But now today, and this street, as warm and moist as the gut of the dead dog. I seek an open door, and find one, beneath quivering neon: Orville's Eye-Deal.

The room is long, narrow, dark, lighted only by a second neon sign, red, Heidelberg Beer, above the big mirror behind the bar. There, a fat man in a white shirt reads a newspaper.

His white shirt becomes, in the mirror, red from the neon. He does not look up until he hears the bar stool scrape on the bare floor as I sit down.

"Heidelberg," I tell him. In the dark coolness of the room my sweat turns cold, and I can smell its cooling.

As he hands me the beer I see the word *Orville* stitched in careful script above the pocket of his shirt. He looks pleasant in his fatness, and when he grins he shows bad teeth.

"You ain't been in before," he tells me.

"No. I just got in town yesterday. From Kansas."

"Well, if you're smart you'll get right back out again. Kansas? I wish I had me Kansas and this place had a feather up its ass. Then we'd both be tickled. You ain't here to look for work?"

"No." I hesitate, wondering how to say it so it will sound as if I said it often. Then, "I'm an artist. A sculptor."

(Too much pride there: I should have practiced saying it. But Orville only laughs.) "Hell of a place for an artist to come to. When I come here twelve years ago it was a pretty place. But now there ain't no trees. Or hardly any. They was seven thousand people here in this town then, and now there ain't but two thousand, and they ain't here for long. It takes trees to run a lumber town."

"Well, I hope it lasts till spring. Because that's as long as I'll be here."

Orville grins. "I expect it will. But don't bet on it. I'm goin' to the can. You holler if anybody comes in. Holler Orville." He disappears through a door at the far end of the bar. I study my image in the mirror. The glass glows translucent red from the beer sign, and the reflection of my face absorbs the redness and is absorbed by it. I study it more closely, squinting, suddenly aware of something else there in the red, a movement, something alive. And then I see them, just above the image of my right shoulder, a pair of tiny yellow eyes, bright with fear, a triangle of a face too small to be a face, chinless, straggled gray goat-beard beneath a slit of mouth, nose that is a beak and not a nose at all, the eyes, the eyes that glisten yellow-white in the shadow of the old hat pulled down to cover as much as possible, and all the rest is redly glowing. He is not really there behind me at all but here inside my head, looking out through my own eyeballs at my reflection in the glass.

I turn on my stool—slowly, slowly—to face him, and he *is* really there, near the wall, a creature so small within the great mackinaw coat and heavy logger's boots that it does not seem possible he could even carry them, let alone wear them. As I look at him his eyes glisten even brighter, and I see a slight movement somewhere within the enormous coat, as if the frail body is not wearing it but hiding in it.

"Hello," I say, in a voice so gentle that I can hardly believe it is my own. "Would you like a beer?"

The eyes turn pure gold, and the mouth twitches once, twice, and there is a sound not human but almost visible, like a musical note hanging there gleaming in the dark silence, a coo, a trill, filled with fear as the song of the emperor's nightingale, and I suddenly stare blankly at the bare wall where he had stood. He is gone, almost without my realizing his going, the great boots taking him strangely soundless through the open door and gone, the boots filled not with human feet but spindly-fingered things that clutch electric wires all night, head tucked under wing, the sandpiper feet that flee the giant waves on the hard sand.

A voice behind me. Orville, returning silent from the can. "Bet you never seen one like him before," laughing.

"No," I tell him, turning back to my beer. "Who is he?"

"Name is Freddy, I don't know what else. Been around here ever since I can remember, all his life, I guess. They say he comes from a family all normal sized, he's the only one of the bunch that's like that."

"What's he do for a living?"

"He's got a little place out towards the coast, where the log-gers ain't got to yet, just a little old shack made out of logs and mud, with pasture for two, three cows and a little garden space. He's got an old pickup truck, too, and he comes to town pretty near every afternoon. He most always comes in here, but it's a funny thing, he don't never drink anything, a beer or anything. Just stands around, off back in the corner where he don't get stepped on by the loggers when they're in here after they get off work. They are a pretty rough bunch, but they don't seem to bother him any, they let him alone, and so it's kind of like he wants to be where they're at even if they are so big and it scares him. Would you have another beer?"

I did. I had another beer, and then another, and several more, and the loggers came to fill the long room with noises and hard hats, and in the men's room a heavy-muscled logger showed me where his buddy with the clap had pulled the water pipes loose from the wall above the urinal, and Freddy did not come back that day. I walked home in the gray twi-light, the dead hills smoked with hot fog, and no bird sang. That night I made red sketches, dozens of them, yet even as I made them I knew he was not there, that when he left he took himself along, left nothing behind to copy down with crayons.

But the next afternoon I was back in Orville's, and so was Freddy, crouching furtive and fearful amid the muscles and hard hats, handful of trembling terror caressed gently by the rough noises of loggers drinking, loggers saying soft as they came in "Hello Freddy" in which was unsaid, *I helped cut down the tree your nest was maybe in today, and damn I'm sorry,* and then they drank and laughed and did not look at him again. And they teased him only once, when a giant all shoul-ders and beard and belly said through foam, "Aaaah, c'mon, Freddy, have a beer!" I watched the golden glitter, the tiny twitch, the sudden absence—too quick to call it disappearance—of him from the room. "Now see what you done, big sunnabitch. You run him off now. You know he don't never." The last another logger, or two, or three, all edge-voiced angry at their friend, who said, "Well, sheeit," but looked sorry and said no more. So I went home too.

The next day, then. Just me and Orville, for a while. Orville saying (wiping glasses), "It's a funny thing how they are about him. They don't like for one another to tease him. I see them get in fights over it sometimes. It's just how they are about him."

Soon after Orville said that, Freddy was there, just there, coming not through the door but emerging, tiny red triangle face, in the mirror, like always, a fist of face on wrist of neck, watching as I watched. A movement in the little throat, and I waited, Great Bird-Watcher in the Sky, Cosmological Ornithologist, to catch the song that's caught by hearing, to trap the prey that's trapped by seeing. It came finally, the word-notes hanging fragile and quivering in the dark air:

"I . . . I don't drink no beer." And he was gone again.

I had him. And having caught him, in the moment of catching lost him. This, then, was mine: to see the bird, to hear the song, to possess only the hearing and seeing, no more, no pinch of salt would help me. Yet still I hoped, and hoping brought me back to Orville's the next day, the fourth.

A woman. A woman at the bar, alone except for Orville, talking loud to him, like a logger. I came in in the middle of a sentence.

" . . . so he threw me out. After I had rode all the way from Seattle with him in that goddamn truck, and I treated him good all the way, and the son of a bitch threw me out. When he could of took me clear to Fresno. So now I got to hitchhike all that way."

She did not notice me until she heard my quarter hit the

bar. Then she turned. "Why hello, honey. Why don't you buy me a beer too?"

I looked at her, suddenly aware of perspectives that the darkness of the room had at first obscured. She was a giantess, huge, not fat, great muscular body bound tight in shiny black velvet pants and vest, hard thighs bursting, massive breasts heavy yet held high and full, and as she spoke she leaned toward me, flashing white teeth in lips like blood, then slid to the next stool nearer me, moving somehow graceful, a cormorant that is too big to fly yet can and does it with that heavy flowing grace when hunting little things. Close to my face now the mass of wild black hair, and I could smell its warm electric. One hard breast touched my arm. My hand trembled as I dropped another quarter on the bar.

Orville reached for a second beer. "All right. You can have this one. But if you drink any more you got to buy it yourself. I don't mind for a man to buy a lady a beer, but you can't come in here to bum."

"Christ," she said. "I bought one already, didn't I? What the hell is it to you who pays for me a beer?" She turned back to me. "Here I come all this way, and they all treat me like this. Clear from Ketchikan I come, and then this bastard throws me out of his goddamn truck, way out on the highway so I have to walk clear into town, and now *this* bastard don't want to sell me beer. What a goddamn hole."

"Ketchikan?" I said.

"You know, Alaska. All that way." She raised her bottle to drink, and as she did I felt her hand on my leg, rubbing, saw the hand there, thick-fingered, strong, nails long and polished whitesilver, hand taloned to tear open small soft bellies with, and I wished it had not touched me.

"What did you leave for?" (The hand I wanted gone still there.)

"Winter," she said. "Too goddamn cold up there. I'm going to Fresno till it gets warmer. I can't stand . . ." The fingers tightened suddenly on my thigh, the talons in my flesh, and she was staring at the mirror, seeing there the little face, flecks of gold that glistened already not for me and loggers ever again, but for her, for midair mating with the eagle swooping screaming openclawed upon him.

Freddy.

She whirled on her stool to face him. "Well Lord God," she said, her voice for once not loud, yet still it broke the silence like a shriek.

"You let him alone," Orville said from behind the bar. "He ain't botherin' you none."

"Hell's fire," she said, louder, "I ain't goin' to hurt him." Freddy stood against the wall, and I thought I saw a flutter of his heart, a tiny tremor in the mackinaw. "If you ain't the littlest son of a bitch I ever saw." She motioned to him. "Come over here."

He came to her, boots soundless on the wood floor, and her with claw distended, talons sinking light in mackinaw, gone, she picked up beer and them gone, guiding him to the far end of the bar, them too far from me, one-two-six stools off, her talking quiet to him, and all I heard was "You sure a little son of a bitch." And over tiny shoulder I saw the last of glitter, the end of twitch.

Then loggers. Standing strangely off, almost silent— "Hey, Arch, have a beer," but quiet, no hello Freddy, no *I cut down*—listening, her talking soft so none could hear. And finally pointed silver on brown bottle upturned, she standing massive bending for small square bag on floor, and they (claws making deep dents in the mackinaw) moved through the door, he looking not at us but her, to the sidewalk and gone.

Orville came from behind the bar and followed them, the room quiet with breath-holding, Orville through the door standing motionless on the sidewalk, looking after them. A long time passed that way. And then Orville came back, shrugging fat shoulders. "They went to the Timely Hotel. Went right in, by God."

"Went right in," Orville said not much later, the loggers gone, the room soft in dark silence. And I went home to my room, the walls all red from sketches pinned, the products of three nights' restless crayon, pulled them down and carefully ripped them into small neat squares. Because I knew then that no craft could make of him a work of art that one could touch: too delicate; the slightest breath would crush it. But in the night I awoke with sweat and trembling, all tangled in the clammy sheet, and made another sketch, this time not red but dead charcoal on white, a black thing winged and huge with cruel beak and claws that dripped black blood.

The next day there was no Freddy. But Orville said, "He's done been in today. And you know what he done, he bought hisself a case of beer—didn't even know what kind he wanted, so I gave him Heidelberg—and he carried it off, but it was like it weighed a ton, and I guess it did, to him. So I went out to the street and watched him, and he hauled it down there to the Timely Hotel. So I reckon she's still there."

"Well," I said, "I guess what he does is his own business."

"No it ain't," Orville said. "I could of stopped it. I could of threw her out before he came in yesterday. But hell, I didn't know." He looked down, his fat face sagged with sadness.

That night in the studio, the sketch before me, I made my own red glow, black iron that turned to solid fire in the soft roar of heat from the welding torch, and a thing took slow shape as I worked. When I could work no more, I stood and looked at its just-started form, and saw the bigness of it, as big as there was iron to make it, then saw not it but her, her body crushing his beneath it in the rumpled Timely bed, him not on top but under, his soft plucked belly scoured bloody by the coarse hair rubbing, the great breasts staring blind into the golden eyes, the claws scraping bright ribbons in the taut opalescent skin of his palmwide back. Black velvet flung to drape limp and shapeless across a chair, battered hat jaunty on the bedpost, mackinaw, pants, boots on the floor by the bed, and there the image ends, but what strange loves have those walls seen?

Then weeks of work, nights of watching iron dead and cold take life from heat and grow until at last I could perceive in it the vision, could almost hear the beating of the iron wings and the roaring rush of sky-thinned air in the spinning plunge from the clouded sun, cold talons tensed to seize the small warm body heedless hovering far below. And sometimes, as I twisted sweating steel to fashion those cruel claws, I felt them clutch and tear the flesh of my own back, and knew a little of what Freddy knew.

To Orville's only once in all that time. I fled the beaked black angel with its ponderous looming grace, fled through cold dry rain (dry because it had no life to water) to Orville's warmth and beer, and he said:

"You ain't been in lately."

"I had a lot of work to do."

"Freddy still comes in to get the case. Every day," he said.

"She . . . ?"

"Still there," Orville said. "I got the whole thing from the night clerk at the Timely. Now you ain't goin' to believe this."

"What?" I said.

"The bridal suite, by God. You wouldn't think they had one at the Timely, but they do, and them two took it. About a week after they first went up there, and been there ever since. It costs three-fifty a day, and when they went there is when he sold his pickup truck. At first he just stayed up there during the day, and then went home of an evening. But they say now he don't never leave town."

"The bridal suite?" I said.

"Yes by God," Orville said. "And there ain't nobody seen her since that first day she come in here. She don't never leave the room, just sends him out to run for hamburgers about six times a day. They say last week he took out a loan from the bank on his place, too. He couldn't of got much, though, nobody wants it. It ain't worth nothing to nobody but him. So I reckon it won't be long, now."

The door behind me rattled, and I turned to see for the first time the entrance of Freddy, who came no more by way of mirrors (had he ever?). Saw the clenched gray face, eyes sunk goldless in the gray, drained, their gold sucked out to pay for beer bought by the case, for hamburgers, for bridal suite.

"Case of Heidel . . . berg," he said, voice tiny, weak, its music suffocated by the struggle to say the words. His hand disappeared somewhere within the mackinaw, searching, emerged with crumpled dollars as Orville brought the beer. I saw the buckling of the little legs as he lifted the heavy case, heard him moan faintly, helpless watched him stagger as he moved through the door held open by a logger coming in. The logger filled the doorway as he watched Freddy and his burden go.

"Ain't a goddamn thing a man can do to help him," Orville said. "I want to tell him ever time he comes. But hell, I can't. I don't know what I'd say, even if I could tell him."

That night I embedded in the hot soft iron of a taloned palm a small red feather, a secret hidden there that none but I would ever know.

And went no more for weeks to Orville's, but worked and saw completion of the black birdangel, anchored now by a heavy concrete base, and wondered that my floor could hold it up. Wondered too how I could get it home to Kansas in the spring, devised fantastic plans for making shipment money, even though I knew that I was wasting dreams, that she would roost there till she pulled the building down upon herself, an eagle's aerie fallen to the town's dead dust. For I had neither door nor window big enough to free her from my loft, and she was trapped for good.

Yet when at night I lay on my mattress and watched her swooping motionless in the corner of my room, I was glad for the safety of that concrete anchor, because sometimes in my sleep I heard the heavy beating wings and felt myself carried up toward the fog-hazed moon, claws loosening in my flesh, plunging, whirling, my body jerking awake as it broke the highest branches of the tallest trees. Those times, I stayed awake to think of little birds, new-hatched, lying blue-bellied in puddles on spring sidewalks after storms.

· · ·

"She's gone. Been gone oh about two months, I guess it is. She left just like she come here, all of a sudden, and nobody seen her leave. Except the night man at the Timely, said she left way late at night, dressed the same as when she come, with them black pants and all. But he said she had on a red coat, looked like it was brand-new."

"Coat?" I said. "She didn't have a coat that first day."

"That's what I said, too. So I asked around, and I found out he bought it for her. Freddy, I mean. They claim he walked right in the Bon Ton Shop, they say he had a bag of hamburgers with him, and told them what he wanted, and what size, and they showed one to him and he paid cash for it and walked right out. Didn't even have them wrap it up. Just carried it off, with the hamburger bag stuck out to keep from gettin' grease on it."

"What happened to him when she left?"

"They say he stayed up there in that room, that bridal suite, for three whole days. All by hisself, and never come out to eat or nothing. So finally they got worried down at the Timely, and they went up and banged on the door, and after they had banged for a long while the door opened and he come out. Never said a word, just walked right past them and on down the stairs and stood at the desk till somebody come and told him how much he owed. And then he pulled out a handful of money, the night man said they had to count it for him, and they give him back two dollars of it, and he went on out."

"Was two dollars all that he had left?"

"I reckon. The bank took over his place some while back and sold it to the lumber company. They claim they're goin' to log off his trees and start up a new mill out there. I've bought me a piece of ground near where it's at, and I guess I'll build me a new place when they start up. But I reckon you want to know what's become of him."

"Yes."

"Well, if you stay here awhile today you'll find out. He goes around behind the stores to pick up bottles and newspapers they've throwed out. He brings the bottles here to sell to me. Don't nobody know where he sleeps, and they say he eats mostly just scraps out of the garbage, but whenever he gets enough bottle money saved up he goes down to the White Castle restaurant and buys hisself a hamburger. You wait around awhile, you'll see him, he'll be in."

But I didn't. I didn't wait to see a treeless Freddy, earth-bound for lack of branches. I went instead back to my room and through my window watched a sparrow in wet misery huddle on a telephone wire. Then slow darkness, and through the sparrow's feet curled tight about the wire hummed currents somewhere felt by Freddy's feet, his boots collecting raindrops at the bottom of the pole.

A streetlight soon came on, and my iron bird cast a great

black shadow on the wall, with my own shadow cowering under it. I reached out to touch her steel claw, clasped it tightly, saw my white fingers take those cold black talons, and felt a feathery tickle in my palm.

Such tickles are but the rub of love, and feeling it I saw that room again, this time not Freddy's but my own breath smothered in the hot flesh of her breasts, my own thighs pounded by those driving hips, and I could smell warm hair again, and sweat and love, all smells that Freddy knows. I had then become Freddy, and Freddy had become my own desire, had saved for her what I had kept for paler doves to pluck from me. I was to have no great black bird, except my iron one, whose cold steel claw my hand was making moist.

The sparrow on the wire waited in the rain for the heavy wings of some night-flying predator to swoop and carry him to clouded heights his own small wings could never reach. I saw the sparrow twitch with cold and fear and joy, and my feet ached to curl and feel the message Freddy sent him through the wire. I clutched the steel claw tighter. And longed for spring to come and free me from this place.

Endnote

For all its wretched excesses, I love this story. I wrote it in the winter of 1960, my second year at Oregon State College, as an antidote to all those freshman compositions I was grading.

OSC was at that time pretty strictly a vo-tech school, with an administration as hidebound and hammerheaded as a congress of warthogs; students who evinced an unwholesome interest in the humanities were sent packing after their sophomore year. Remarkably, however, among my English Department colleagues was Bernard Malamud, who had already won a National Book Award and universal critical accolades but was, inexplicably, still teaching three sections of freshman comp at OSC; the department had graciously rewarded his celebrity by allotting him a single section of creative writing, the school's only offering in that unpromising trade. We few lonely primates on the faculty (the rest were all lower life forms) had long been wondering what kept him in this academic backwater. One thing was certain, though: I'd never get my sandwich clamps on that creative-writing class as long as Bern was there. And Bern evidently wasn't going anywhere.

This inauspicious state of affairs prompted me to resume my assault on Mount Freelance, the first stage of which (to mix a metaphor like scrambling an egg) hatched "The Little-Known Bird of the Inner Eye." I couldn't believe I wrote it! Not only was it my first venture in full-bore, blow-a-gasket lyricism, not only was it about capital-A Art, but it even had a certified Troubled Young Freelance Artist in it—with whom, you may be sure, I identified pretty strongly.

My opening sally was to fire my new story off to *New World Writing,* no doubt imagining myself a latter-day Hollis Summers. They fired it right back, of course, but with it came an encouraging letter of rejection (and I wasn't even a subscriber!) from Arabel J. Porter, a famous literary editor of the day. I took heart and immediately relayed the story to *Contact,* where it landed on the desk of an editor named Bill Ryan, who, bless his grog-soaked Irish heart, loved it, and published it.

The publication in *Contact* of "The Little-Known Bird of the Inner Eye" (I boosted the title and much of the central imagery from the Morris Graves painting that is reproduced on the cover of this book) altered the course of my life in myriad ways: first of all, it caught the eye of Elizabeth McKee, a New York agent who represented Flannery O'Connor, William Styron, Evan Connell, . . . and, until her death thirty-six years later, me. She was a great lady, and I will miss her always.

In the summer of '61, "Little-Known Bird" got me admit-

ted to a powerhouse writers' conference at Wagner College on
Staten Island and a fiction workshop led by Saul Bellow. (The
leaders of the other two workshops were Robert Lowell and
Edward Albee.) Mr. Bellow and I didn't hit it off; he thought
I was a rube and a boob, I thought he was a snob and a swell.
Doubtless we were both correct. In any case it hardly mattered
because everyone else on the scene was so exciting; in the fiction workshop alone were Arno Karlen, who had published a
novel before he was even out of college, and Steve Dixon, who
was just beginning a career that would make him a master of
the modern American short story—and then too there was
this scholarly, reserved Mr. Peepers sort of guy from Texas
who, like me, had recently published his first story in *Contact.*
The story was "The Big Broadcast of 1938," and its author was
Donald Barthelme.

I got into the workshop on the dubious strength of "Little-
Known Bird," but what I submitted for Saul Bellow's grumpy
inspection were the first twenty pages of the new novella I was
working on. "From a Considerable Height" it was called, after a line in Céline's *Mort au Credit* that reads, in its entirety,
"I piss on it all from a considerable height"—which may reveal something about my state of mind at the time. (Twenty-
two long years later, the novella would become *The Natural
Man.*)

The director of the conference was Rust Hills, then—as
now—the fiction editor of *Esquire.* He liked my fledgling novella and asked to see it again when it was finished. I obliged
him, of course, and he almost succeeded in getting it accepted; the story made it all the way to the editor in chief,
Arnold Gingrich, who turned it down because he found the
language a bit too blue. But Rust steadfastly continued to
champion my work at *Esquire,* and in 1970, he even published
an excerpt from the Novella That Wouldn't Die. (It's mod-
estly entitled "The Greatest Writing Ever Wrote," and yeah,

it's right here in this very volume, a little further down the line.) When *The Natural Man* was finally published in 1983, Rust got off one of my all-time favorite wisecracks: "I love this book," he said. "I think I've always loved it."

In the next issue of *Contact* after my story appeared—augmented by that photograph of my brooding, existential young self, romantically shrouded in cigarette smoke—the magazine published a group of poems by a young Seattle poet named Richard Hugo, an employee of the Boeing Corporation whose photograph showed him in his uniform as catcher for the Boeing softball team. During the next dozen years or so, Hugo would be recognized as a major American poet, eventually becoming director of creative writing at the University of Montana in Missoula, where I taught for a couple of years in the mid-1970s. We soon became friends, and because I had written some autobiographical nonfiction, Dick asked me to read the autobiography he was working on. I jumped at the chance, of course, and was hugely entertained to discover, along about the middle of the third chapter of the manuscript, an admission that he had taken "perverse delight" in appearing in *Contact* in softball livery among all those "terribly affected" types with their faces "half hidden by smoke in the coffeehouse gloom"!

(Richard Hugo died in 1982. His splendid autobiography, *The Real West Marginal Way*, was published posthumously in 1986.)

Anyhow, for a while there, that chimerical little-known bird loomed as large as a turkey buzzard in the birdcage of my life. But maybe the most momentous thing the story did for me—or, depending on your point of view, the most pernicious—was that it gained me admission, briefly, to that select company of august rogues known collectively as Directors of Creative Writing. Here's how my elevation came to pass:

In the spring of 1961, just a few weeks after "Little-Known

Bird" came out in *Contact,* we found out why Bernard Mala-mud was still hanging around a stick-in-the-mud establish-ment like Oregon State, when he published a novel called *A New Life,* which proved to be a devastating send-up of . . . well, of ourselves. (I got into the book by virtue of having once taught a class with my fly unzipped.) So thorough was the whupping that Malamud administered to our beloved insti-tution—in particular to our beloved department chairman—that push had clearly come to shove and bridges had been burned. And I just happened to be the only other published fiction writer on the faculty. Hmmm.

Bern had a contingency plan, of course, and a pretty damned good one at that: on the morning of the official pub-lication day of *A New Life,* he took himself to the chair-man's office and announced that he had accepted what may have been, just then, the cushiest, most prestigious creative-writing sinecure in all of academe; he was leaving at the end of the term, he said, to become writer-in-residence at Benning-ton College.

Our clueless chairman, who knew only that he wanted to rid himself of this menace to his tranquillity and had no idea what an eminence his department was losing, was quite de-lighted at the news. I could tell that by the lilt in his voice when a few minutes later, he came down the hall, chirping, "Anybody wanna teach creative writing? Anybody wanna teach creative writing?"

"Yeah, Frank," I sang out happily, "I do!"

THE AUTHOR WAXES PHILOSOPHICAL FOR PROFESSOR HAVIGHURST'S FICTION CLASS, CA. SPRING 1953.

The Cynic

THE VOICE CAME FROM nowhere, loud and rasping and without meaning. "Cape City," it said. "Last stop. Connections for Chicago, Milwaukee, and points north."

Marty Rosen pulled himself up in his seat, vaguely aware of the dull ache in his cramped legs. His eyes were sleep-filled and burning, and he dug at them almost viciously with his knuckles, the realization coming slowly that he was on a bus in God-Knows-Where.

Marty stared blankly out the window. A few scattered neon lights blinked back at him, breaking the blackness of the night. "Drinks," one of them said. "Drinks, Drinks, Drinks." Jesus, Marty thought, this town must have gone out with the dodo bird. Imagine having to kill two hours in a dump like this! He wished to hell the company would furnish him a car. He must have been the only traveling salesman in the world who had to ride a bus.

Forcing his aching legs to support him, Marty stepped into the aisle. He pulled his battered suitcase from the rack above the window, and the small, gold-colored lettering on its side gleamed in the light from the street. "M. L. Rosen," it said. "Acme Plyboard Co., Cairo, Ill." Marty smiled grimly. All that glitters is not gold, he thought.

There were only three other passengers, and Marty fell in behind them as they shuffled off the bus and into the dingy little station. Once inside, the other three dropped wearily onto the straight wooden benches that lined the wall. Marty started for a bench, then changed his mind and turned toward the ticket window.

"Hey, Pop," he said to the old man who sat behind the iron grating. "How long I got to wait for that Chicago bus?"

"Just about two hours, mister," the old man answered. "She pulls out at 2:27."

"My bag be okay if I leave it here?"

"Sure. Put her on the bench over there."

Marty set the bag on the bench, took a few steps toward the door, and then stopped and looked questioningly around the lobby. "Men's room back there, mister," the old man said, thumbing Marty toward the rear of the room.

"Thanks, Pop," Marty said, relieved. Somehow or other, he always hated to ask strangers how to find the rest room.

The men's room was about as filthy as he had expected, Marty thought as he splashed the cold water in his face. The washbasin was spotted with the dirt of ten thousand gritty travelers, and Marty wouldn't have touched the thin bar of soap on a bet. He jerked a paper towel from the rack and dried off, studying the face that stared at him from the cracked, fly-specked mirror. Its eyes were puffed and red, and the dark skin of the cheeks was beginning to sag a little. The black wiry hair was thin in front and flecked with gray. Forty, the face said. Thirty-six, Marty argued, and then gave up, knowing the face would win anyway. He straightened his tie and went out.

Marty walked through the lobby and out to the empty street. Across from him, the neon sign flashed its message. "Drinks," it said monotonously. "Drinks, Drinks." He crossed the street and entered the bar.

A few tired-looking old men sat at the long, polished bar, gazing dreamily into their beer. Marty chose a stool at the end because the seat next to his was vacant and he didn't feel much like making conversation. The bartender, a dapper little man with a blond mustache, approached him. "Help you, sir?" he asked.

"Yeah," Marty answered. "Seven-and-Seven."

The bartender set a glass of Seven-Up on the bar. "Mix it?" he asked. Marty shook his head, and the bartender filled the shot glass from a brown bottle. "Forty-five cents," he said. Marty paid him and swallowed the whiskey quickly, feeling the warmth of it in his chest. I needed that one bad, he thought.

Hearing the door open behind him, he looked around. The man who entered the room was tall, very tall, and he had a clubfoot that dragged heavily as he walked. His face was narrow and fleshless, and his deep-set eyes were shadowed by the straight black hair that hung over his forehead. The man wore a ragged jacket and dirty khaki pants, and he carried a small bundle of clothing under one arm. He put the bundle on the floor next to Marty's seat and sat down on the vacant stool. "Beer," he told the bartender.

Marty stared at the man's reflection in the mirror behind the bar. What a weird-looking guy, he thought. He wondered if maybe the man was a Communist. The man took a long drink of the beer and then produced a bent cigarette from the pocket of his jacket. He turned to Marty. "Got a match, buddy?"

"Sure," Marty said, handing him a book of matches. He lit the cigarette and dropped the burnt match into the ashtray on the bar. Then he tore another match from the book. With a long, yellowed thumbnail he split the paper shaft of the match, pulling it apart until it formed a Y. He bent the tips of the split ends and stood the match on the bar. It looked like a tiny man with a bright red head. Marty watched him make another, and still another, of the little men, until finally there were a dozen of them standing on the bar. They reminded Marty of a row of tiny soldiers, brave and unflinching and ready to challenge every enemy.

"Excuse me," he asked the stranger, "but could you tell me what the hell you're doing?"

"Creating," the man replied, splitting the end of the thirteenth match. "I'm creating men."

Marty was a little surprised at the answer. "Yeah, I know," he said, "but for any particular reason? I mean, you don't strike me as the kind of guy who goes in big for party tricks."

The man placed the thirteenth soldier on the bar and turned to face Marty. "Of *course* it's for a reason," he said. "I'm creating them so they can be destroyed, the same reason *all* men are created."

Marty started to laugh, then thought better of it. The man seemed too confident, too sure of his logic. Instead, Marty offered his hand. "My name's Rosen," he said. "Martin Rosen. Traveling salesman. You know. People tell jokes about us. What's your line?"

The stranger didn't accept the outstretched hand. "Haven't got a line," he said. "Used to have. Used to write a newspaper column. Couple of books, too. But people were afraid to read what I wrote. Know why, Rosen? Because I wrote the truth, and they didn't like it. That's why. But that was a long time ago. Haven't got a line anymore." He lifted the cigarette to his lips and took a long drag from it, and the red ember moved slowly back the cigarette until it touched the flesh of his fingertips.

"Hey!" Marty almost shouted. "You're burning your hand!"

The man lowered his hand and gazed for a moment at the cigarette. Finally, he ground the butt into the ashtray on the bar. "If it doesn't bother me, Rosen, why should it bother you?" he said calmly, his thin lips twisted into what might have been a smile.

"No reason, I guess," Marty said uneasily. "Only—oh, well, to hell with it." He was no longer sure whether or not he had actually seen the smoldering tip of the cigarette touch the man's finger. Must have been his imagination. Or maybe the drink. Anyhow, not much point in worrying about it.

"A man has a right to destroy himself," the stranger was saying. "In fact, I suppose it's the *only* right he has."

"What kind of stuff do you—I mean, *did* you write?" Marty asked, hoping to change the subject. "I used to want to be a writer, when I was a kid."

"Doesn't make much difference to you *what* I wrote, Rosen," the man answered. "You wouldn't like it anyway. Because it tells the truth. Like a mirror. I'll bet you don't care much for mirrors, do you, Rosen?"

Marty, remembering the mirror in the bus station rest room, evaded the question. "Like I said, when I was a kid I always wanted to write. But Christ, I never even got to finish high school. Had to go to work."

"And now you're a salesman," the stranger said. "Tell me, Rosen, are you a good salesman?"

"No," Marty admitted without bitterness. "The truth is,

I'm a lousy salesman. I don't think I was cut out for it. I never was any good at telling funny stories."

"I thought not," the man mused, rubbing his unshaven chin with a bony finger.

Marty opened his mouth to speak, and then hesitated. He wasn't too sure he wanted to continue the conversation. Maybe it would be better to drop the whole thing. But it was impossible to ignore the stranger. The man's attraction was too strong, and Marty was powerless to resist it. He felt that there were a great many things he had to know, and he knew that the stranger could tell them to him.

"Look," Marty said suddenly. "Do you really believe what you said about men being created just so they can be destroyed?"

"How could I believe anything else?" the stranger said. "Take a look at humanity, Rosen. It's stupid, it's cruel, and it's ugly. What has it produced? Men like me, full of hate because there is nothing in the world worth loving. And men like you, Rosen, afraid to admit the hopelessness of the whole thing, afraid of the truth. It's *too late*, Rosen! There's no hope left! The only thing left is destruction. Can't you see that?"

"But you're wrong!" Marty said, his voice quivering with excitement. "You *have* to be! It *can't* be like that! I know lots of happy people, and I could be happy too, if I could just get out of life what it gets out of me."

"That's just the point, Rosen. You spend your whole life looking for something, without a chance of ever finding it because it isn't there. You're a fool, Rosen, because you seek happiness in your own mediocrity. What I mean is that there's more to happiness than just believing you're happy."

"But that's silly!" Marty said, anger rising in his throat. "If a man *thinks* he's happy, why, he *is* happy, that's all there is

to it! That's the trouble with guys like you! You don't do anything but criticize and tear everything apart! Have you ever
thought of trying to do something—something *construc-
tive*?"

The stranger laughed drily. "Waste of time. That is, it
would be a waste of time to construct anything *now*. The object is to destroy *everything,* tear it all down, and then start all
over again!" His eyes burned black holes in the milky cigarette smoke. "Would you like to hear what I would do if I were
God, Rosen?"

Marty had already forgotten his anger. Somehow, he had
no trouble at all picturing the stranger as God. "Sure," he said
eagerly. "Sure, go ahead."

"The first thing I'd do," said God, "would be to choose one
man and one woman, making sure that they had two characteristics. First, they would have to be intelligent. It doesn't
matter what they believe in, or what ideas they have, just so
long as they are intelligent. Second, they would have to be
beautiful, because beauty is very important when you build a
new world. And after I had selected the couple I wanted, I
would put them into a giant box, which would be lined entirely with mirrors, and it would be shaped like a prism, so
that everywhere they looked, they would see the image of
themselves. And I would put a door on the box, with a time-
combination lock on it, and I would set the lock to open in ten
years. And then I would build a tremendous fire, and I would
destroy every living thing outside the box, leaving nothing
alive—*nothing*. And the last thing I would do would be to
throw myself into the fire, because the only need for God is
the need for the power of destruction, and that need itself
would be destroyed in the fire. And the man and woman
would live in the box for ten years, always watching their own

images, always studying each other, and they would sooner or later see every flaw in themselves, and those flaws would be magnified, because they would see them no matter where they looked. A mirror can show one everything—stupidity, malice, greed, weakness, ugliness—*everything*. They would also come to love each other's beauty, both physical and intellectual, and these things too would become important to them. And at the end of ten years, they would be completely perfect, and when the door opened, they would go out and build a world entirely new, entirely beautiful, entirely good."

He stopped talking and stood up, pushing aside his empty glass. "It'll be like this," he said, and he scooped up the thirteen little soldiers and dumped them into the ashtray. He tore another match from the book, lit it, and cupped the flame in his palm. Then he dropped the matchbook into the ashtray, following it with the burning match. For a moment, it looked as though the flame might die, but finally another match flared up, and soon all the soldiers were caught up in the tiny inferno. The flames licked around the matchbook, and the bodies of the little soldiers writhed and curled up in their agony.

The man picked up his bundle. "That's all, Rosen," he said simply. "Good-bye." And he limped slowly toward the door.

Marty watched him go. Jesus! he thought. What an odd character! He shivered slightly as he turned back to the bar. The matches were black and dead, and a final wisp of smoke hung lazily in the air.

In the middle of the little pile of twisted bodies lay the matchbook, its edges scorched and crisp. Marty picked it out of the ashes and flipped open the cover. In it were two matches, perfect and untouched by the flames. Marty tore them out and carefully split their paper shafts with his thumbnail, as the stranger had done. He bent the split ends and stood them on the bar.

Marty sat for a long time, staring at the tiny figures. They reminded him of two travelers, lonely and almost lost in a vast mahogany desert, yet determined and unafraid.

Endnote

Dr. Havighurst was less than hugely impressed by this bold adventure in Deep Thinking. Nonetheless, I rewrote it (slightly), improved it (slightly), and changed the title to "The Prophet" for Dick Scowcroft's class at Stanford in the fall of 1955; later, I tried it on Mr. Cowley, Hollis Summers, and Bob Hazel. Unanimously, they hated it—even after I changed the title back to "The Cynic." But for me, there was something about those little match people—especially the "two travelers, lonely and almost lost in a vast mahogany desert"—that just wouldn't go away.

Also, this might be as good a time as any to mention that in the earliest stories collected here ("Little-Known Bird," "The Cynic," "Postcard," and the immortal "Fear and Hope and a Gutter") the attentive reader may detect a predilection for such "atmospherics" as flashing neon signs, scruffy, low-class dives, fly-specked mirrors, and characters whose eyes could be likened in various ways to black holes. I guess I should've curbed these descriptive tics with a retroactive blue pencil, but the fact is, I'm sort of fond of them.

I mean, you don't see many fly-specked mirrors in fiction nowadays. On the antique market, these would fetch a tidy sum.

MY FIRST HIT! "POSTCARD," A BY-PRODUCT OF A STUDENT TRIP TO EUROPE IN THE SUMMER OF 1953, WON FIRST PRIZE IN THE MIAMI UNIVERSITY CREATIVE-WRITING CONTEST AND WAS PUBLISHED IN THE STUDENT NEWSPAPER.

Postcard

THE MOIST HEAT of the little room hung over Vince like a blanket, and he opened his eyes reluctantly. The thin pillow was wet with sweat, and he could feel his T-shirt clinging to his chest. The room was almost dark, with only the flickering lights from the street finding their way through the open double doors that took up the whole wall opposite the bed.

"Holy Jesus!" Vince said to the empty room. "What time is it, anyhow?" He sat up on the bed and squinted at his watch in the darkness. 8:30! He should have been up two hours ago! He hadn't meant for that nap to last this long, and now it was too late to take a bath. There wasn't a drop of hot water in Naples by this time of night. He swore softly to himself at the idea of a hotel where you had to take a bath at a certain time. But hell, he thought, Naples has enough troubles of her own without worrying about whether or not he got his daily bath.

Vince slid his bare feet into the slippers on the floor by the bed. He stood up and reached for the string that hung from the ceiling. Above his head a naked bulb suddenly flooded the room with light. The brightness blinded him for a moment, and he sat down on the bed again and rubbed his eyes. When he opened them, the room seemed smaller, the dirty-yellow walls closer together. A soft hot breeze gently stirred the drapes that framed the double doors, and he felt it brush past him. A tiny trickle of sweat slid down his cheek. He nodded his head slightly and the sweat fell to the floor in a single, glistening drop. Finally, he got up and moved through the doors onto the narrow balcony.

Vince leaned over the wrought-iron railing; below him, in the Piazza Garibaldi, the crowds moved aimlessly along the sidewalks. Across the great square, pizzerias flashed neon appeals to a hungry throng, and an enormous mass of twisted glass tubing quivered, gelatin-like, as it pleaded "*Bevete Coca-Cola*" from above an office building. The sidewalks overflowed into the streets, and tiny automobiles with blasting horns pushed impatiently through the crowds. The air was pungent with sweat and exhaust fumes and garlic; a street musician's violin whined, and somewhere Vince could hear a baby crying. It seemed to him that in Naples there was always a baby crying. He turned back into his room.

He stood in front of the little washbasin, letting the cold water run over his wrists and hands. He hadn't really intended to go out that evening—the long trip to Capri during the day had been tiring, and he had to catch an early train to Rome the next morning. But it was too hot to stay in the room, and besides, it seemed foolish to spend his last night in Naples in the hotel.

As he finished dressing, Vince wondered why he had ever decided to make this trip. Christ, he thought, I shouldn't be in Europe! He felt guilty, knowing that the old man had wanted him to come into the business as soon as graduation was over. But what the hell. He had saved for the last four summers for the trip, and the store could wait another couple of months for him. The old man never wanted him to go to college either, for that matter. In fact, the old man thought the whole world turned around Moscow, Ohio, with the axis of it running right through Piersall's Grocery Store. As far as he was concerned, a man's education ended when he learned how to keep his thumb on the scale while he weighed a pound of hamburger.

Vince moved to the washbasin again. He looked into the fly-specked mirror on the wall. The image of his full face was twisted by the wavy imperfections of the mirror's surface. He moistened his hands and brushed back his blond crew cut with his palms. Then he turned out the light and groped for the doorknob. He stepped out into the long, dimly lighted hallway, closing the door behind him. He walked down the hall to the spiral staircase, gripped the rusty iron banister, and followed it down two flights to the ground floor, where it ended in the sudden brightness of the little lobby.

The lobby was deserted except for the man in the white suit who sat behind the high wooden desk at the front of the room. The man was studying a ledger, but when he heard Vince's footsteps he looked up quickly and smiled. Vince crossed the lobby and dropped the key to his room on the desk.

"Ah, signore," the clerk said, his white teeth flashing. "You are going out? You Americans, you like the nightlife, eh?" He laughed, and his heavy jowls shook. He reached into a drawer and handed Vince a small yellow card. "You would maybe be interested in thees, signore," he said.

"The tourist in Naples will enjoy the opportunity of attend a real Italian fiesta," the typewritten card informed Vince. "The Carnival of Saints will be hold this night, July 14, in the

Piazza Vittorio. There will be many souveneir selling, food-stuffs of all kind, amusements, and many sight seeing." At the bottom of the card, a printed line told him that "This information courtesy of the Hotel Syrena, the tourist's best bet in Naples."

"The translation ees okay?" the clerk asked. "I speak the English okay, but ees more deefeecult to write than to speak. Good for business to know the English."

"Yeah, sure," Vince answered, chuckling. "It's all right."

"You like thees fiesta," the clerk said. "In Napoli, ees good to go sometimes where people sing and dance and are not hungry. One does not see so much unhappiness at the fiesta. The *turisti* do not like to see the unhappiness. They do not understand."

Nobody likes unhappiness, Vince thought. And during his week in Naples he had seen enough of it. You could smell it in the air; it was in the faces of the old men who sold flowers on the streets, and you could hear it in the crying of the hungry babies.

"I guess maybe I *would* enjoy the fiesta," he said aloud. "Can I walk there, or should I take a taxi?"

"The taxi," the clerk answered. "Take the taxi. The streets near Vittorio are not safe to walk. Ees danger there. The poor ones, they hate Americans. Because you are rich and have plenty to eat."

"Thanks," Vince said, turning toward the door. "Thanks a lot."

The clerk waved his hand. "*Buona sera,* signore." Vince pushed open the plateglass door and stepped into the crowd. He worked his way to the curb and spotted a taxi parked not far from where he stood. The taxi looked like a squat little box, and reminded Vince of a scale model of the American cars of the early thirties. A man sat on the fender, waiting, his arms folded across his chest. When he saw Vince, he stood up and opened the door of the cab.

"Taxi, signore? You want taxi?"

Vince bent low and squeezed into the cab, and the driver closed the door behind him. The seat was too low, and he had to turn sideways to straighten his legs. The driver slid beneath the wheel.

"Where, signore?" he asked over his shoulder. "Where we go?"

"To Piazza Vittorio," Vince said. "Vee-toree-oh. Ca-peesh?"

"Sì, signore," the driver answered. "Beeg fiesta, eh?"

He started the engine and the little car quivered for a moment, then jerked away from the curb into the wide street. The driver wheeled the cab around a fountain that stood in the middle of the square, picked up speed, swerved to miss a vegetable peddler's pushcart, and plunged suddenly into one of the dark, narrow streets that radiated out from the piazza. The street was barely wide enough for two cars, and the cab had no headlights. The taxi bounced over the rough cobblestones, and Vince held his breath as he felt the black walls rush past.

At last, they emerged from the alley into another brightly lit street, and the driver slammed his foot on the brakes, almost throwing Vince to the floor. The cab eased into the heavy traffic, and Vince leaned back and breathed deeply. The street was crowded with cars and pushcarts and open trucks loaded with vegetables and people walking and children dodging in and out among the slowly moving vehicles. Vince's driver pushed patiently ahead. How in the hell could this guy be so patient now, Vince wondered, yet in such a goddamn hurry back in that alley?

Not far ahead Vince could see the rooftops silhouetted

against a pale red glow in the sky. The throngs in the street seemed to be moving toward the light. Vince leaned forward and tapped the driver on the shoulder.

"Fiesta?" he asked. "Is that the fiesta?"

"Sì, signore," the driver nodded.

"I'll get out here, then," Vince told him. "How much do I owe you? How many lire? Capeesh?"

"Tree hunna feefty lire, signore. *Capisce?* Tree hunna feefty."

Vince reached for his billfold and counted out four hundred-lire notes. He handed them to the driver and stepped out of the cab. "You keep the change," he told him through the window. The driver smiled his thanks, and Vince moved off into the crowd. He made his way through the maze of cars to the sidewalk, where the walking was a little easier. He knew that he probably should have listened to the hotel clerk's advice about walking in the streets near Vittorio, but he could make better time on foot than in the cab. Besides, nothing much could happen to him with all these people around.

An old woman stood near a pushcart loaded with flowers by the curb, and she shuffled in front of Vince as he approached. "Flowers?" she said, clutching at his lapel with a bony hand. She grinned at him, showing a single yellow tooth in the front of her mouth. Vince tried to smile back at her, but somehow it was impossible. He stuck his hand into his pocket and found two ten-lire notes. "No flowers," he told the old woman, handing her the crumpled bills. She held out a battered chrysanthemum to him, but he gently brushed it aside and moved on down the street.

He edged away from the carts that lined the curb, staying closer to the buildings. He passed a lighted doorway where a woman sat nursing a child. The pale breast hung long and flat and lifeless from the woman's chest, and as Vince passed, the child stopped its sucking to whimper softly. Dry, Vince thought. Every breast in Naples is dry.

A girl walked slowly in front of him, her thin hips sharply outlined in the tight skirt. Vince started around her, but she grabbed his arm. "Hey, Joe," she said, "you got smoke?" He handed her a cigarette. "You come go home with me, Joe," she invited. "I show you beeg time, cheap, only feefteen hunna lire." Her face was pallid beneath the heavy makeup, and the vivid smear of lipstick had failed to hide a raw-looking sore in the corner of her mouth. Vince turned away quickly, shaking his head. "No!" he said. "God, no!"

He was almost to the piazza now, and he could see the strings of bright red lights above the milling hordes. He heard the sharp, hard sound of exploding fireworks, and the air was full of music and laughter and the sweet smell of pastry, and Vince found himself suddenly in the midst of it all. He stopped in the street, and all around him there was movement and music, and he felt sickness rising in his stomach. He looked about for a place to sit down. Finally, written in yellow lights across the front of a building, he saw the word "*Ristorante*." He worked his way through the crowd, between stalls and booths that displayed fly-covered pastries and meats, toward the sign.

He found an empty table among those on the sidewalk in front of the restaurant and sat down wearily. It was the walk, he told himself. It's too hot to walk so much. He wiped the sweat from his face and caught the eye of a perspiring waiter. He ordered simply, "Vino, *per favore*. It doesn't matter what kind." The waiter quickly reappeared with a glass of blood-red wine, and after several fawning bows and smiles, he departed with a generous fifty-lire tip.

Vince sipped the warm wine gratefully. He felt better now,

and he began to look about him. At the next table sat two men, obviously American, talking loudly of their dislike for Europe. Beyond them was a group of women, probably schoolteachers from Muncie, Indiana, or somewhere, talking about Pompeii. The rest of the people seated at the little round tables were Italians, talking about God knows what.

A street band had just finished setting up its meager equipment near the restaurant, and Vince settled back to listen to their first number. Almost immediately he decided that although he had heard a lot of bad street bands during the past week, this was the worst one of all. The old man who played the accordion had barely the strength to squeeze an occasional moan from the thing, and the boy on the trumpet produced little more than a bleating monotone. The guitarist and the violinist could have been worse, he supposed, but they had no help from the others.

"Signore! Signore!" The words interrupted his thoughts, and he looked up. Beside him stood an old man, a hunchback. The massive dome of his back made his head appear as if it was set in the center of his chest. He carried a basket on his arm. "You maybe buy nice doll, signore?" he asked gently, and he reached into the basket and produced a little doll.

It was a pretty doll, dressed in the costume of an Italian peasant girl. It had shining black hair and rosy cheeks, and its dress was bright red, with white lace around the bottom. Vince thought of the little girl who lived in the apartment above the store back home—the plump, blonde-headed kid who always talked him into giving her bubble gum when he worked in the store. She would like a doll like this. "Only one thousand lire, signore," the cripple said eagerly. Vince nodded and handed him a bill. The peddler carefully wrapped a piece of newspaper around the doll and laid it on the table. Grinning, he moved on to another table.

Vince put the package in his pocket and turned back to the band. The trumpet player put the finishing blast on a segment of *Il Trovatore,* and the guitarist, a bloated-looking woman with a shining, greasy face, said something over the squawking public address system. She motioned behind her, and a little girl stepped forward.

The little girl's body was swollen by malnutrition. Her ragged dress was far too big, and her thin legs stuck out below it like the trunks of stunted saplings. Her dark stringy hair hung loosely about her face, and her eyes were like black holes burned into the fleshless pallor. She could not have been more than eight years old, but in her face Vince could see the cold wisdom of the prostitute and the futility that had been in the eyes of the woman who could no longer nurse her baby.

The accordion groaned, and the child began to sing. Her upturned face became expressionless, and her eyes rolled far back in their sockets. Her arms moved slowly with the music, and her hips began to sway. Her voice was throaty and low, and the song should have come from the lips of a torch singer. Vince couldn't understand the words, but it made no difference. The song was about death.

When the song was finished, there was no applause, no cheers. The Italians sat at their tables like unsmiling statues, and the American schoolteachers whispered nervously among themselves. The little girl moved from the microphone into the audience, her hands cupped in front of her. "Lire, signori, *per favore*," she pleaded. "See-gah-rette?" Those of the Italians who could afford it solemnly placed a few dog-eared ten-lire notes or occasionally a bedraggled cigarette into the outstretched hands, and some of the Americans offered her larger bills.

Vince watched her work her way slowly in the direction of his table. As she passed the bandstand, the guitarist grabbed her arm and took from her hand the wad of money and the cigarettes. Then she pushed the child back into the audience. Vince decided against giving her money, because it was obvious that the woman would not let her keep it, but he knew he must give something. He thought of the forgotten package in his pocket, and he brought forth the doll and unrolled the newspaper.

The little girl moved up to his table. "Lire, signore? See-gah-rette?" She was smiling, but the smile was seductive and hard, almost obscene. Vince pushed the doll toward her. She stared down at it, and he could see the smile change. Her eyes widened, and her expression became softer, more childlike; her eyes seemed to fill with wonder and delight as she reached for the doll. She touched the delicate lace with a grimy finger. Suddenly she jerked her hand away from the doll, and the smile disappeared. Her lips tightened into a straight line, and her face was again drawn and cold. She was no longer a child. "Lire, *per favore*," she insisted.

"For you," Vince said. "It's for you." And he held the doll out once more. Her lower lip curled away from her clenched teeth, and without warning, she struck out at the doll. It fell from Vince's hand and clattered on the cobblestones beneath the table. "Lire, lire, LIRE!" the little girl screamed, her face twisted with hatred. She turned and ran back to the bandstand.

Vince picked up the doll. There was a triangle of rough plaster where its nose had been. He sat for a long time staring at the scarred face. Finally, the doll clutched tightly in his hand, he stood up and walked away.

Endnote

The crossing from New York to Naples on the M.S. *Italia,* a rusty old converted World War II troopship, took

thirteen days. I was in steerage, way down in the innards of
this floating derelict; I bunked in a tiny, airless steel closet
with two other college guys and a Portuguese chicken-sexer.
(Don't laugh, now; he's still the only Portuguese chicken-
sexer I've ever met.) Aside from college kids, most of the passengers were Italians, going back to the Old Country for the
first time since before the war, so the mood aboard ship was
relentlessly festive—meaning thirteen days of free-flowing
chianti and strolling accordionists on deck playing "O Sole
Mio" at all hours of the day and night.

After Naples, traveling by train, we hit, in rapid succession, Rome, Florence, and Venice, then spent a week in Swit-
zerland in a wonderful old hotel in Vevey—the little Alpine
town where Frederic Henry and Catherine Barkley holed up
in *A Farewell to Arms*—followed by a week in Paris and a
week in London. It was a great trip. In the course of those
seven weeks I fell in love, learned to drink wine, ate my first
meringue glacée, saw the Folies Bergère, and discovered Henry
Miller; my life would never be the same.

With my Miami prize money for "Postcard"—a cool
twenty-five dollars—I bought a three-speed "hi-fi" at Wool-
worth's and two LPs (one of them Dave Brubeck's first album, which I treasure to this day), and I still got back enough
change to finance a couple of celebratory beers at Mac 'n'
Joe's, a favorite off-campus watering hole among us Freelance Writers.

ORIGINALLY PUBLISHED IN *ACE MAGAZINE* (JANUARY 1996), THIS
MEMOIR WAS REPRINTED UNDER A DIFFERENT TITLE IN *The Geography
of Hope: A Tribute to Wallace Stegner* (SIERRA CLUB BOOKS, 1996).

Captain Kentucky "Visits" the Left Coast: A Memoir of Wallace Stegner

THE DAY AFTER Wallace Stegner died, I was driving home from the Cincinnati airport (after seeing my wife off to Antwerp to look to her dying mother; these things have a way of coming in bunches), when I happened to tune in to an NPR commemorative replay of an interview with Stegner conducted a year or so before his death. In the interview, Mr. Stegner (I was never able to call him Wally, though he asked me to several times) speaks at length, and feelingly, about coming to terms with the memory of his difficult relationship with his long-dead father, which was the principal subject of his great novel *The Big Rock Candy Mountain,* the book that made him famous. The interview was very moving—like having him in the car with me for half an hour.

I first met Mr. Stegner in the fall of 1962, when I came to

Stanford on a Stegner Fellowship in Creative Writing just a couple of months after I'd lost my own father, with whom I too had had an uneasy relationship. Although Mr. Stegner was again on leave until the winter term, I often saw him on campus that fall. He was, at all odds, the handsomest, most urbane, most instantly certifiable *gentleman* I'd ever encountered—like one of those "Men of Distinction" gents in the old Calvert Reserve whiskey ads. I was awestruck. He would soon become a sort of surrogate father to me, first during the following winter and spring terms as my teacher in the fiction seminar, then as my boss when, after my year on the fellowship was over, he invited me to stay on as a visiting lecturer in the writing program. Naturally, like any dutiful son, I took it as my filial responsibility to espouse views and behave in ways that were anathema to him.

But did I say *visiting* lecturer? Hey, I hung on to that job like a barnacle; it took the English Department nine years to dislodge me from it.

It was an exhilarating time to be at Stanford. The antiwar movement and the civil rights movement and the Free University movement and the hippie movement and what we might call, in retrospect, the General, All-Purpose Up-Yours Movement were all flourishing, and I was ardently attached to each and every one. By the midsixties, I was industriously insinuating myself into every sit-in and teach-in and be-in and love-in that happened along. I was also going around the campus in a knee-length red velvet cape, accessorized with a mod-bob haircut and granny glasses and Peter Pan boots. "Captain Kentucky," I styled myself, while Daniel Boone turned over in his grave.

Now Mr. Stegner was as stoutly in favor of civil rights and as stoutly opposed to the war in Vietnam as I was, but he strongly disapproved of the movement's tactics, which he believed—correctly, I see now—were detrimental to the university and destructive of rational discourse. Nor was he all that thrilled by—to use the buzz phrase of the day—"alternative lifestyles," of which I was a gorgeously egregious specimen.

Yet throughout the sixties he not only kept this psychedelic eyesore on as his aide-de-camp in the writing program, he even let me share his office! He met my excesses and apostasies not with stern, authoritarian paternal disapproval but rather with unfailing—if somewhat bemused—kindness and unstinting generosity. In office conversation, he and I often disagreed about political and social issues, but—thanks largely to Mr. Stegner's good nature and forbearance—we never ever argued. Part of my job was to read and assess each year's fellowship applications, and he treated my evaluations of them with courtesy and respect. He took me to lunch at the Faculty Club and secured me invitations to what I like to call cocklety factail parties. Through him, I met William Styron and Frank O'Connor and Janet Lewis and Thom Gunn and Gary Snyder and Denise Levertov and Herb Gold and many other writers. When CBS television came to Stanford to film an hourlong special on the writing program, he chose me to read my work before the cameras. And when at the close of the decade the English Department began endeavoring in earnest to pry me and my anemic bibliography loose from its impenetrable hull, he steadfastly championed my already lost cause to the bitter end. I always had the feeling that he liked me *despite* his better judgment—which I take to be the highest kind of compliment.

That Wallace Stegner was a masterful writer and a great teacher, everybody knows. But for those of us who were blessed to know him personally, I'd venture to say it's his humanity, his dignity, and his generosity that we most sorely miss.

I wrote the original version of my story "Finch's Song" during my year on the fellowship, mostly under Mr. Stegner's watchful eye, and his gentle but astute critique of it all those years ago has been invaluable in helping me to understand what was wrong with the story and how to go about fixing it. I think the fact that it has at last been published is a tribute less to my perseverance than it is to the iron durability of Mr. Stegner's good advice. I only wish he could have been on hand to welcome this spanking-new thirty-three-year-old "grand-child" of his into the world.

Endnote

Since Mr. Stegner was on leave when I began my second stint at Stanford in the fall of 1962, Dick Scowcroft stood in for him in the workshop that term—and pulled another Tillie Olsen on me by reading, in the very first class, the opening three dynamite chapters of my fellow Fellow Robert Stone's great first novel *A Hall of Mirrors.* But this time I recovered, and Bob and I were soon—are still—fast friends.

So Dick was the first teacher upon whom I inflicted my preliminary feints at Bob Hazel's notion of a Good Idea— that old story (then fulsomely entitled "Consider the Lilies, How They Grow") about the school bus driver, which I'd already had on my mind for the past four or five years and which was to be my personal millstone for yet another thirty-five to come.

The story—about a twelve-pager, I figured when I began it—got off to a funereally slow start. My old three-adjective jones still had an iron grip on my sensibilities, as I began to realize somewhere around page thirty . . . of the prologue!

But Dick Scowcroft conned me into persevering with it by convincing me that I was a better writer than . . . well, than I'd been back in 1955, say. It's an old creative-writing teacher trick: lead the poor sap on until he's in so deep he has to write his way out—even if it takes him thirty-five years. And don't I love the sly dog for it! He kept me from giving up on what I now believe is the single best piece of writing I've ever done.

"GREATEST WRITING," WHICH APPEARED IN *Esquire* IN 1970, IS EXCERPTED FROM ONE OF THE NUMEROUS EARLY VERSIONS OF *The Natural Man*. BY 1983, WHEN THE NOVEL WAS FINALLY PUBLISHED, MONK HAD BECOME A LOT MORE AMIABLE, HARRY A BIT DRIER BEHIND THE EARS.

The Greatest Writing Ever Wrote

You are of the class, mammalia; order, primates; genus, homo; species, Kentucky.
James Fenimore Cooper, *The Prairie*

HERE'S PRETTY MUCH the way things went during the first weeks of August in my thirteenth year, after Monk LeMay, the meanest, ugliest six feet five inches and two hundred and twenty-five pounds of potential pivot man the victory-starved fans of the New Canaan County High Bulldogs (the Bullfrogs, as the disgusted crowd in Craycraft's Billiards commonly referred to them) had ever laid their covetous eyes on (*imagined*, even), moved from Newport ("that stinking Sodom of the South," our preacher, Brother Cecil Ransbottom, had once called it, proceeding to denounce its denizens as "those slickery slimy snakes in the Bluegrass") to Hamer's Lick ("population six and seven-eighths when they're all at home," the driver of the Cincinnati-Lexington Greyhound used to announce to his passengers over the impatient roar of the engine during his ten-second pause in front of the Eats Café):

Afternoons we—Gander Cunningham and Jimmy George Craycraft and my best friend, Woody Jefferson, and me, Harry McAtee (William Snakeshit the Noted Arthur as Monk named me when he found out I hoped to become a sportswriter if and when I grew up)—presented ourselves on the court behind the Hamer's Lick Elementary and Junior High School building, where this long-awaited champion of the Bullfrogs' long-lost cause pounded us into bruised submission (a misleading word, since it implies an intensity of resistance that in fact we never remotely approached) in a game whose rules he—Monk—evidently interpreted to countenance elbowing, kneeing in the groin, hip-throwing, straight-arming, shin-kicking, toe-tromping, belt-hanging, scratching, gouging, biting, goosing—oh yes; a singularly disconcerting defensive tactic, goosing—and, had he ever for a moment supposed it might propel him and Woody, his chosen teammate and the only decent player the opposition (the Shitbirds, Monk called our team—but then he called nearly everybody that at one time or another) might otherwise have had, a bit more swiftly along their satin-smooth road to—or rather, *through*, with scarcely a pause for a bow to our daily burgeoning audience of old men who but for Monk would never have forsaken their eternal euchre game at Craycraft's—an unbroken succession of triumphs, no doubt the enthusiastic deployment of clubs, broken bottles, knives, guns, lassos . . . in short, just about any side arm that came to hand during the heat of the fray. Basketball, believe it or not.

But whatever we suffered in the afternoons, it was those
sweet evenings in the courthouse yard that made our day,
those limpid hours of lolling in the grass getting our un-
formed little minds boggled by Monk's deliciously dirty jokes
and tantalizing tales of Newport nightlife. For according to
our standards he was a most marvelously gifted raconteur, a
real genuine card, Abbott and Costello and the Three
Stooges and the Bowery Boys and Amos 'n' Andy and every
eight-page Bible ever printed all rolled up in one great gamey
lump. He had at his command a supply of loose talk as rankly
bottomless as the devil's own cesspool, stories about what
went on behind Newport's bright lights ("Now for your Blue
Ribbon Special, see, she takes a piece of blue silk ribbon and
ties a knot in it about every two inches, see, and then
she . . ."), long, lickerish poems about Paul Revere ("Now
Paul was a mighty man, and strong, / With a pecker eighteen
inches long . . ."), and Columbus ("He pleaded with the
Spanish queen / To give him ships and cargo. / He said I'll
kiss your Spanish ass / If I don't bring back Chicago . . ."),
jokes about the lady sheriff from Tennessee ("the one that had
that great big posse . . .") and Bob Cox (Mrs. Cox, poking her
head into the barbershop: "Bob Cox in here?" Barber: "No,
ma'am, just shave and haircut"), dialect jokes ("Mandy, I
heered you husbin died of de diarrear. Is dat so?" "Naw*suh*,
Rastus, he never died of de diarrear, he died de gonerrear!
Mah husbin was a *spo't*, he wasn't no shitaiss!") and Confucius
jokes ("Confucius say, 'Man who lose key to girlfriend's apartment get no new key' ") and traveling-salesman jokes ("So the
farmer's wife brings him a douche bag, see, and he says I
reckon you didn't understand me, lady. I asked you could
I borry a monkey wrench. And she says, Well, that's what I
rinch *my* monkey with . . ."), jokes about sheep lovers and
ball-biting sharks and footprints on the dashboard upside

down, about mooseshit pie and the Old Log Inn, about nuns and midgets and queers and old maids, about Alben Barkley's antique organ and Mrs. Hadley's used centerpiece. There was, I think, a curious kind of genius just in the sheer breadth of his repertoire; these were more than mere jokes, they were fables, parables, they covered all knowledge, translated his goatish vision of the whole of human history into a language even fledgling shitbirds like us could understand. After his own fashion, I suppose, Monk was a teacher, our first real master in more ways than one.

Thinking back now on those old times, I can't help remembering something else old Brother Ransbottom, a man with his own gift for figurative language, once thundered from his pulpit: Sinning, he declared, was like nothing so much as drinking the contents of a cuspidor, for "hit's all in one piece, O my honeys! And once you've took up the spittoon and commenced to drink, you can't hardly quit till you've drunk her dry!"

If the warning registered any impression at all on my consciousness at the time, though, I wasted precious few moments contemplating it; my attention, like everyone else's, was on Monk LeMay. To our boundless admiration, he seemed to produce, as the need arose, a talent to suit any occasion whatsoever. That earlier reference to his prowess with a lasso, for instance, was no idle figure of speech; we discovered he could handle one of those the evening we played Foxes and Dogs, for when it came Monk's turn to be a Dog, instead of chasing the Foxes mindlessly about the courthouse yard until he ran them down, he simply went over to the county flagpole and relieved it of its rope, fashioned a lariat of it, and brought the Foxes down with that. He was good at it, too; any Fox who got within fifteen feet of him as good as had rope burns on his neck already.

And I learned how well he could throw a knife one night when we were sitting in the grass in front of the old World War II New Canaan County Servicemen's Honor Roll billboard, and I committed the grievous social blunder of leaning back against the warpy, scabrous plywood facing of the board and closing my eyes for a moment while I listened to the joke Monk was just then telling—it had to do with a little boy whose mother caught him stealing cookies and playing with himself, both in the same day. "So when the old man come home from work that afternoon," Monk was saying, "she told him how Junior had been carrying on, see, and how he'd have to do something about it. So he jumped up and run to the cabinet and got down the big iron skillet, and when she seen what he had she says, Oh lordy, you ain't going to hit him with that skillet, are you? And the old man says . . ."—when THWANGK-K-K-K something struck the billboard uncomfortably close to my head, and filled with trepidations I peeled back my eyelids and rolled my eyeballs in the direction of the sound, and there at the periphery of my vision, not three inches from my right ear, its slender silvery blade half buried in the plywood, twanged Gander Cunningham's nine-inch-long fish knife, which Monk had borrowed a few minutes before to pare his toenails with. The curved mother-of-pearl handle, I remember, was still quivering slightly, the blade still chattering in the wood; its tip pierced the exact center of the faded little red star that indicated that Corporal Somebody had got himself wounded in the Recent Unpleasantness.

"It ain't polite to shut your eyes when the Well-Built is talking, sport," Monk chided me mildly, at the same time leaning forward to pluck the knife off the board as easily as if it were a sweat bee on my earlobe. "So," he went on, turning his attention back to his toenails, "the old man says, Hit him?

Hell no, I ain't going to hit him, I'm going to fry that boy some eggs! He can't keep that up on cookies!"

Yet another of Monk's accomplishments was that he had somehow taught himself to break wind at will and in an apparently infinite variety of tones of voice. His nether larynx— the Toothless One, Monk had named it—could articulate, at its master's pleasure, squeaks and rumbles and burbles and booms, could sigh or mutter or moan or whistle, bleat or bark or buzz. He'd evidently trained it to comment on his behalf whenever it deemed its opinions worthy of a public airing; for instance, it was likely to deliver itself of an enviable raspberry at anyone else's jokes and squeal with delight at Monk's. And nearly every time it piped up Monk would cup his hand to his ear, feigning deafness, and importune, "Whisper again, O Toothless One!" And lo, as if to prove that its performance was no fluke, it would repeat its most recent utterance to the letter, reproducing every note to the veriest hemidemisemiquaver. The Toothless One's vocal range was really quite incredible; when it was in good voice it could run the scale from soprano to basso profundo. It was a real artiste, the Yma Sumac of fundaments, and its virtuosity established for all time that Monk LeMay was truly a man of many parts.

But it wasn't until the last Friday evening before Labor Day that Monk actually strode head on and twice as big as life into the mythology of Hamer's Lick (joining there the proud ranks of such immortals as James "Two-Nose" Harpe, who was sent to La Grange penitentiary for twenty years in 1941 for coining what was reputed to have been the most perfect counterfeit fifty-cent piece the government had ever been confronted with, and Hector "Doubleduty" Nickerson, currently the constable of Hamer's Lick, who had pitched twelve innings in relief for the Cincinnati Reds in 1927, and even old Reverend Filbert Hamer himself, that ancient reprobate who in 1781 ventured down the Ohio from Limestone to a salt lick in the godforsaken wilderness he promptly dubbed New Canaan, where he founded a mission-*cum*-grogshop from which he dispensed spirits both holy and unholy to passing redskins). Come to think of it, in fact, the heroic proportions of the role Monk was to play in our own histories were made manifest on the very same night that the knife-throwing incident took place; I remember because he'd gone back to trimming his toenails, bending intently to his task in the half-light of the gathering dusk, when somebody asked whether anybody had any notion what was showing at the New Paradise Theater on Saturday night.

"Yeah," Woody said, "*Guns Across the Mohawk.* Me and McAtee saw Egnew putting up the letters this evening on our way up here."

"Letters?" Monk said, glancing up from his toes for the first time in several minutes. "What do you mean, letters? What kind of letters?"

"Out in front of the show hall," I chimed in. Then, glad for a chance to redeem myself for my earlier impropriety, I explained that Newton Egnew, proprietor of the New Paradise Theater (where movies were shown only two nights a week, Saturdays and Sundays), had a bushel-basketful of foot-tall red celluloid letters and that Woody and I had stopped by for a few minutes to watch him post Saturday's title on the marquee. It was the only way to find out what was playing, I pointed out, because the New Paradise never showed previews; in fact, Mr. Egnew himself never knew what the distributor would be sending him until Saturday's film arrived in Friday's mail.

Monk, putting his shoes back on, looked thoughtful while I briefed him on the situation, and when I finished he tossed Gander's knife back to him—blade open—and fished a stub of pencil out of his jeans pocket, then began to cast about him for a piece of paper in the grass. Someone found him a candy-bar wrapper, and he smoothed it across his knee, licked the end of his pencil, laboriously wrote a few words, glanced up and inquired, "Was that 'Mohawk,' did you say?"

"Yeah," Woody told him. "It's got Johnny Mack Brown in it, I think."

"I don't give a rat's ass who's in it. You shitbirds shut up for a while and let me think, or I'll cut your goddamn ears off for you."

For the next fifteen or twenty minutes the only sound was the scritch-scratch of his pencil. My own ear still atingle from its recent peril, I scarcely breathed the whole time. Once Gander, overcome by curiosity, craned his neck to try to see what Monk was writing, but Monk fired such a forbidding look at him that he recoiled in silent terror. Everyone else sat deathly still and watched him scribble. His eyebrows, as he squinted at his paper in the waning light, were knit in a frown of concentration so intense that they rode his low forehead like some fierce black hairy spider, and his pencil moved almost ceaselessly. Yet it did not appear that he was actually *writing* anything. Rather, if one could judge by the restless motion of the pencil, he was putting down just one or two letters at a time, crossing something out here, adding a letter over there, now and then pausing to tap his teeth with the pencil or lick its point again, then changing the last letter he'd put down to something else . . . as if he were working out some kind of puzzle, perhaps some curious arithmetic problem (. . . *eight take away six and carry two* . . .) that involved letters instead of numbers. His face, wearing that grimly resolute look of scholarly endeavor, ought to have been ridiculous, like an ape wearing spectacles; even so, nobody cracked a smile. My own eyes were fixed hypnotically on the incessant stirrings of that unquiet pencil, and when after the longest possible time it came abruptly to a halt I twitched as if I'd been startled by a sudden sound.

"*There,* by god!" Monk exclaimed triumphantly, slapping his thigh and stuffing paper and pencil back into his pocket. "All *right,* then! Now do you shitbirds reckon anybody'd be hanging around the show hall tonight?" No, not on Friday, I told him; Mr. Egnew goes to choir practice on Friday nights. "Good!" he said. "Now then, has anybody got a stepladder they can get their hands on?" By now he was speaking in hushed, conspiratorial tones, so that when Woody allowed he could probably sneak his father's ladder out of the cellar as soon as it was dark enough, he too leaned forward and spoke in a half whisper, despite the fact that there was nobody anywhere near to hear it except Monk and Gander and Jimmy George and me. Stealth, I was discovering, is contagious.

Monk brushed aside our questions about what he was up to—"When I want you to know somethin', A-hole," he told Gander, "I'll buy you some goddamn clothes and send you off to school" —and, while we waited for full darkness to descend, killed the time with a few more jokes. He told the one about Oink Johnson, the one about the woodsman, the owl, and the knothole, the one about JoJo the Tight-Skinned Boy ("Each and every time he blinks his eye he jerks hisself off!"), and finished off with the Ballad of Pisspot Pete ("Out of the forest came Pisspot Pete / With snot on his whiskers and shit on his feet . . .").

"All right," Monk said at last, when it was dark enough to suit him, "Jefferson, you and shit-for-brains here"—that was me his thumb was indicating—"you and McElfresh get the ladder, and the rest of us'll meet you at the show hall in a few minutes. And if you get caught," he added ominously, "we don't know you."

"McAtee," I ventured. But nobody heard me.

Woody jammed his hands in his pockets, spun on his heel, and stalked off, with me following at a respectful distance. To tell the truth, despite the fact that we were supposed to be best friends, I understood perfectly well why he was grumpy; if I'd been him I'd certainly have preferred Monk's company to mine, just as he did.

When we turned onto Woody's street, we saw, several houses from the corner, his parents and his grandmother sitting on their front porch, small and still in the yellow light of the Bug-a-Boo bulb, so we cut through one neighbor's front yard and another neighbor's backyard, stole down to the cellar and up again with a ten-foot stepladder between us, Woody still leading, me bringing up the rear. By then Woody's folks had gone indoors, so we carried it straight up the driveway and on down the street. The night was moonless, already pitch black between the streetlights, and hardly anyone was about; everybody who wasn't at choir practice was either inside listening to Waite Hoyt's broadcast of the Reds game, or down at Craycraft's playing euchre, or in bed. At the narrow alley between Perry Snapp's barbershop and Hunsicker's grocery store, Woody turned in suddenly and sharply, swinging my end of the ladder out to the edge of the sidewalk. And just as I got straightened around and headed into the darkness after him, the screen door of the barbershop swung open and a head popped out.

"Whoa there, little McAtee! Where in the billy hell do you think you're going with that stepladder?"

Doubleduty Nickerson, the constable, with a towel around his neck and shaving soap up to his eyeballs.

I hesitated, unsure how to handle this development, and instantly felt a slight but insistent tug on the other end of the ladder. "Well, I . . ."

Doubleduty, scowling suspiciously at me above his foam-bearded jaws, stepped partway out the barbershop door. "You kids ain't up to no meanness, are you? Who's that you got with you?"

"Well," I said, "me an' . . ."

Suddenly, like a fisherman who'd unaccountably hooked into a whale, I was nearly jerked off my feet by a lusty pull on the ladder, and before I knew what was happening I was stumbling down the lightless tunnel of the alley, hanging on to the ladder as much to keep from falling as to hold up my end of it. I couldn't see a thing in the gloom ahead of me, but I knew there was a dogleg bend in the alley at the rear of the grocery store so that when I felt the front end of the ladder swinging to the right I'd have had a pretty fair idea of where we were even if I hadn't just then caught a good strong whiff of the rotten vegetables in Homer Hunsicker's spoiled-produce bin. "You squirts stay out of meanness, now!" I heard Doubleduty holler above the pounding of our footsteps on the cinders and the even louder pounding of my heart. And then my foot slipped on some bit of garbage that had spilled over from the bin, and by the time I'd righted myself I and my end of the ladder had already negotiated the dogleg, carrying me out of Doubleduty's line of sight behind the grocery store, and now I could see the streetlight at the lower opening of the alley, and I saw at last that it was no longer Woody Jefferson whom I was assisting in the transport of this ladder, not Woody who had hauled me by sheer main strength from one end of this alley to the other, not Woody but . . .

"I knowed you shitbirds couldn't do nothing right on your own. It's a damn good thing I thought to go up there and check you out, or you'd still be back there jawing with the law."

"Well, this goddamn McAtee," Woody panted, "he was fixing to squeal on me!"

Squeal? Me squeal on my best friend? Would I have done a thing like that? I had to admit it was a question I wasn't quite prepared to answer.

We were slowing now, and I saw Jimmy George and Gander slouched beneath the streetlight, waiting for us, and across the street was the New Paradise Theater, with its small rectangular marquee and the bold red letters proclaiming, just as Woody and I had declared they would,

GUNS ACROSS

THE MOHAWK

the words softly illumined in the urine-yellow glow of four naked Bug-a-Boos, one socketed at each corner of the white rectangle.

"Awright, Scrawn," Monk was saying to Gander as we drew up to him and Jimmy George, "you come with me and hold the ladder for me. The rest of you shitbirds stay here and keep watch to make sure nobody comes along."

"If anybody does," Gander whined, "they'll see us sure as hell."

"You got a point there, Scrag," Monk said, and almost as he spoke he bent and scooped up a fist-sized rock from the gutter and with a flick of his wrist sent it flying straight up at the streetlight, and half a second later our side of the street was plunged into instant, total darkness even before the shards of glass stopped tinkling to the blacktop. Now the only light anywhere near us was the marquee itself.

"If you're just going to put out the show-hall lights," I heard myself saying, "you don't need to bust them out with a rock. There's a switch up on top of the sign. Right over the G in GUNS. I saw Mr. Egnew switch it on this evening."

"Good thinking there, Snakeshit!" Monk exclaimed with an enthusiasm the genuineness of which I couldn't quite determine. "Don't old Snake have fine morales, boys? Ain't he good as gold?" He took up the ladder again. "Okay, Scrag, let's get busy. The rest of you keep your asses out of sight." Woody and Jimmy George and I obediently faded back into the alleyway to watch Monk and Gander glance furtively up and down the street, then tear out in a dead run for the theater building, the ladder as light in Monk's grasp as a majorette's baton. Within seconds they were beneath the marquee, spreadeagling the ladder's spindly legs, and now Monk was scrambling up, feeling along the top of the sign for the switch, and a moment later everything was dark.

"What do you all reckon he's fixing to do?" Jimmy George whispered.

By now my eyes were growing accustomed to the darkness so that I could just make out, against the facade of the building, Monk's shadowy figure perched apelike atop the ladder, huge and hulking, his hands busily moving the letters of the title about the face of the sign, and Gander, as reed thin as Monk was bulky, occasionally accepting a letter Monk handed him to hold, then handing it back a moment later when Monk motioned for it.

"Looks to me like he's changing—" I started to say. But Woody cut me off.

"Don't pay no attention to him, Craycraft," he said bitterly. "He's chickenshit to the bone."

I was just contemplating a response to the effect that Monk himself had just now testified to the excellent state of my morales, when I heard, from across the street, Monk and Gander's muffled snickering, saw Gander hand something up to Monk, saying through choked laughter, "Here's the last one!" Monk groped once more for the switch, and suddenly the marquee was awash with yellow light again, Monk's black bulk superimposed upon it, blocking out much of the two rows of letters:

CHE   RAW H   NOT

AS

"What's *that* say?" Jimmy George said. "It don't make no sense."

I opened my mouth to admit my own puzzlement—it was evidently my night for sputtering into sentences I couldn't finish—but before I got it said I saw that Monk held in his hand the M from MOHAWK, studying it momentarily, and as we watched he turned the letter upside down and fitted it, slightly askew, into the space just after CHE, and almost in the same motion flung up his arms like some great dark winged thing and leaped from the ladder, leaving emblazoned there upon the night the inspired imprecation:

CHEW RAW HOG SNOT

ASK US

Well, it utterly undid us. By the time Monk had gathered up the ladder and sprinted, with Gander at his heels, back to our side of the street, Woody and Jimmy George and I were doubled up with laughter, and a moment later all five of us— even Monk himself joined in—were reeling drunkenly about the alley's mouth, riotous, convulsed, fairly bouncing off the walls of that narrow passageway, pounding each other on the back in unspoken mutual congratulation for our happy complicity in the splendid outrage, tickled shitless that we'd been allowed to serve as accomplices to this Goth, this Vandal, as he scrawled his barbarous incivilities across the unblemished consciousness of Hamer's Lick. With a single stroke he'd defaced for all time our memories of the deadly dull days of our youth, and nothing could possibly have pleased us more. Because now at last we had something worth remembering; for the rest of our lives we'd be repeating what he'd written up there on the marquee, telling the story of that night over and over until the words entered our mythology, our history, our very language. He had made . . . dare I say it even now, almost a quarter of a century later? . . . he had made Literature.

What's more, judging from the next thing he said, he evidently knew he'd done it.

"Well, what do you think, Snakeshit?" he inquired when our jubilation had finally played itself out to fitful bursts of giggling, and we'd wiped the tears from our eyes and were standing at the mouth of the alley gazing in nearly mute admiration at his handiwork. "I mean, is that there a good piece of writing, or ain't it?"

No doubt about it; he had a way with words. "Shoot, yes!" I heartily exclaimed. "It sure is!"

"Is that all you got to say? I mean, goddamn, Snake, I used ever single letter! The way it looks to me, that took one hell of a good job of writing!"

I admit it, I was flattered. I'd never have supposed he'd hold my critical opinion in such high esteem. "Shoot *yes*!" I cried even more enthusiastically. "It's really *great*!"

"Why, you know, that's what I was thinking, too," he mused. "I been thinking it might just rate up there amongst the very finest. I mean, I tell you true, Snakeshit, it wouldn't surprise me a bit if it turned out this was just about one of the greatest little pieces of writing ever wrote. It might even be one of these masterpieces you hear about! How's about it, Snake? You'd go along with that, wouldn't you, goodbuddy?"

"Well, sure," I said, laughing uneasily, "shoot yes, I'd go along . . ."

"Why, Snake, I'm right proud to hear you say that! Because I'll bet you that when old man Egnew drives by here on his way home from choir practice and sees this here masterpiece on the front of his show hall, he's going to get to wondering who's the arthur of it. And I bet you another thing. I bet when he asks old Doubleduty Whatsisname, Doubleduty is going to remember who it was that he seen with the ladder, and he's going to tell Egnew that as far as he knows, Snakeshit McElfresh is his man."

Oh boy. My heart had long since plummeted like a stone into my churning stomach.

"And what's more, just to show you what kind of hairpin Monroe LeMay is, goodbuddy, I ain't going to tell *nobody* no different. Being as you aim to be a well-known writer and all, I'm going to let you take the credit for it, and I believe these other boys will do the same. How about it, boys, will you squeal on old Snake, or not?"

But by now the others were overcome by a new paroxysm of laughter so violent that it thoroughly mooted his question; they were crashing about in the darkness as if their delight were some terrible affliction, like the Saint Vitus' dance. As for me, I suppose the turbulence in my stomach showed up unmistakably on my face; to my mind's eye it manifests itself as a greenish pallor illuminating my whole countenance, a bilious glow quite bright enough that Monk could see it in the dark, for beneath the others' racket I heard him chuckling softly.

"Hey there, Snake," he said amiably, "you're looking kind of peaked, old son." Six inches from the end of my nose I saw his huge fist floating very slowly at me through the void; I shut my eyes and felt four knuckles the size of walnuts chuck me one by one and ever so gently on the chin. "You don't want to forget to keep smiling, Snake. I tell you true, buddy, I ain't been a writer myself but just a few minutes now, but one thing I've done learned is how your truly great arthur has got to keep smiling all the time. I mean, you know, that's how he keeps the public wondering what he's up to."

Struck blind by the blazing splendor of his genius, my mind empty of everything except illumination, I turned without another word and fled back up the alley, their laughter trailing me as I burrowed like a moon-blind mole into the loam of night.

Endnote

Rereading this story after so many years, I was amazed to see how much of it survives more or less intact in *The Natural Man:* the dirty-joke sequence, the Toothless One, and Noted Arthurs James Fenimore Cooper and William Snakeshit all made the cut. Even that old gross-out chestnut of mine about drinking out of the spittoon, which keeps turning up like a bad penny in just about everything I write, made its maiden public appearance in "Greatest Writing."

And there were other surprises: for instance, I had utterly forgotten that Monk McHorning was once named Monk LeMay—after Air Force General Curtis "Bomb-them-little-yellow-bellied-sapsuckers-back-to-the-Stone-Age" LeMay. Or that I had portrayed Harry Eastep né McAtee, who is, after all, my own alter ego, as such an insufferable little wuss. How could I have done that to myself?

The answer to that question partly resides, I think, in the fact that throughout all but the last few months of its twenty-one-year gestation, *The Natural Man* was a first-person narrative. I made an eleventh-hour shift to third person after many years of suspecting, intuitively, that the voice of the novel was somehow off the mark—that it was too confining, too claustrophobic. Rereading "Greatest Writing" now, I'm reminded of how right that intuition was.

All the same, there's no denying that I'm immensely—perhaps inordinately—fond of certain aspects of this story, especially the "chew raw hog snot" foolishness, even though I dropped it altogether from the novel. I spent *weeks* working out the "Guns Across the Mohawk" anagram; the movie's proper title is, of course, *Guns* Along *the Mohawk,* but I never managed to make anything sufficiently nasty of those letters, so I blithely invented my own movie and titled it according to my needs. Even so, I labored mightily to bring forth that anagram. And at last, like Monk LeMay-McHorning himself, I had just four letters left in my quiver, four stupid letters—E, C, H, M—that didn't even *hint* at a real word until, in the tiny confines of my mind, I idly turned that recalcitrant "M" upside down, and the lambent flame of intellect suddenly flared up to reveal—Voilà! The greatest writing ever wrote!

I like to think of the story as a sort of parable about the act of writing itself and about the nature of inspiration. Its publication in *Esquire* (thanks to my old friend Rust Hills) went a very long way toward validating all those years I'd already invested in working on—or at any rate in thinking about—my novella-*cum*-novel.

For a further gloss on the differences between early and final versions of *The Natural Man,* see "Empathy Follows Sympathy."

CHAPTERS TWO AND FOUR FROM ANOTHER ABANDONED EARLY DRAFT (CA. 1972) OF *The Natural Man*. NOTE THAT HARRY MCATEE HAS BECOME HARRY EASTEP, AND MONK LEMAY HAS BECOME MONK MCHORNING. THESE CHAPTERS WERE PUBLISHED IN *Limestone* (1989) AND REPRINTED IN *Kentucky Voices* (1997).

The Harry Eastep File

II. My *Vita*, If You Will

But first, before I go on about Monk McHorning, my *vita*, if you will:

NAME: Harrison Biddle Eastep, B.A., M.A. (and perhaps I should mention here that the latter designation refers to what, years ago when I was parting company with graduate school at Ohio State, my committee chairman sternly described as "definitely a *terminal* degree, you understand, Mr. Eastep"— meaning that the department would put a price on my otherwise worthless head if I ever attempted to pursue the Ph.D.).

AGE: 38 going on either 17 or 65, whichever comes first.

OCCUPATION: Assistant professor of humanities (another terminal designation, by the way) at Arbuckle State College

in Arbuckle, Oregon, where for the past eleven years I have
taught four large sections of a freshman course awesomely
entitled "The History of Western Civilization"—Necro-
mancy 101, I like to call it. My longevity at this wretched labor, I am told, is legendary within the profession; lesser peda-
gogues have gone raving off through the Groves of Academe
before they'd logged their first thousand hours of Western
Civ. Yet despite my lowly status in the humanities I am, if I
may say so, an uncommonly popular teacher. My sections are
always filled to the rafters, and even football players show up
early at registration to plead for places in "Doctor" Eastep's
class. Certain of my colleagues have snidely attributed my
popularity to the facts that the course is (a) required and (b) a
notorious Mickey; but I like to pretend I owe it to my piquant
lectures, my endearing penchant for such titillating icono-
clasms as "Socrates was a pervert," or "Catherine the Great
had slits tailored into her skirts for the convenience of her lovers," or "God is dead."

ADDRESS: An anonymous apartment on an anonymous street
in this thoroughly anonymous town.

MARITAL STATUS: None to speak of. Back in the early sixties,
when I was still in the final fading bloom of youth, I was married briefly to one of my former students. She was a bright,
wonderfully pretty girl, and to tell the truth I loved her much
more than I'd intended to. But the marriage didn't take,
largely because my chronically pessimistic assessment of the
current state of the human condition ran directly counter to
her desire for children. "You know what I think, Harry?" she
said tearfully as she was on her way out our door for the last
time, after two weeks of wedded bliss and four months of Ag-

onizing Reappraisal. "I think you're just *hiding* behind all that cheap cynicism. You're just *scared*, Harry!" *Cheap?* I wish I'd said. *If it's so fucking cheap, how come it's costing me so much?*

PERSONAL VICES: I'll admit to tee many martoonies—invariably—at cocklety factail parties. Anything else is ... personal.

VIRTUES: I keep myself clean.

· · ·

Well, enough of that. Sometimes it seems to me that all my life I've walked a narrow line between indolence and mild depression, like a cowardly tightrope walker who never strings his high wire more than two feet off the ground. My cynicism is the dullest act in the whole circus.

Yet it has its uses. How difficult it would be, for instance, to construct an accurate image of the Arbuckle State campus and student body without mockery and derision among one's tools—something like a carpenter who contracts to build, say, an outhouse and then discovers that the fine print obliges him to discard his hammer and saw and do the job with his bare hands. And come to think of it, I wouldn't be the least surprised to learn that those exact circumstances obtained when Arbuckle State was flung together: certainly whoever designed it was quite perverse enough to have written just such a provision into the builders' contracts. Fort Leonard Wood, Missouri, where, back in the late fifties, I spent two lost years mindlessly typing requisitions for laundry soap and toilet paper, is the only public facility I know of that can rival this one for pure ugliness. Our older buildings are crenellated red-brick horrors that look as if they might have been magically transported here across time and space direct from the industrial revolution; its newest ones (such as the five-story Food Technology building, which I swear to God the student newspaper proudly called "the biggest erection on the Arbuckle campus") all seem to be sheathed in sepia-tone reflecting glass and to have been carefully positioned to reproduce on all sides the image of their most hideous neighbors. The Humanities Department, where I toil, is housed in an impenetrable maze of interconnected one-story frame barracks, relics of the navy's wartime V-12 officer-training program. The diabolically clever campus planners, to mask their atrocities from the taxpayer's none-too-discerning eye, left several nice stands of native elms and maples about the grounds; in the spring these become leafy ambuscades for great raucous flocks of grosbeaks, who relieve themselves of their sodden ballast only when a member of the humanities faculty happens along the sidewalk below. One learns not to mind it much; in Oregon it's always raining something or other anyhow.

And the students. By and large they major in the monosyllabic disciplines: Cow, Crop, Stove, Teach; engineering majors are warily regarded as intellectuals, potential freethinkers. The faculty is instructed to advise any student evincing a morbid fascination with the humanities to transfer to another college after the sophomore year, before the condition becomes contagious. When I first came here in 1959, I was still idealist enough to suppose that I was obliged to try to teach a little something, so I included an essay question in my first examination; I asked my students to discuss briefly some of the influences of the Great Plague of London on the religious climate of the time. The first paper I read began, "In this modren world of ours today, our modren medical science . . ."

The second paper began, "Daniel Webster, in his dictionary, defines 'influence' as . . ." The third, "In his dictionary, Daniel Webster defines 'climate' as . . ." I dumped the whole batch of papers into the wastebasket then and there and began immediately to make out another test, multiple-choice questions only ("The Great Plague was spread by: a. dirty doorknobs, b. old paper money, c. rats, d. illicit sexual intercourse"); since then I've discovered that true-false tests ("Sir Walter Raleigh caught the Great Plague from an Indian maiden in America and brought it home to London with him, T or F?") are even less bothersome to mark, and nowadays I rely on them to the exclusion of all other forms.

The administration has officially designated humanities a "service department" and has also made it manifestly clear that the chief service it expects my colleagues and me to do our students is to make their brief sojourns in our classes as painless as possible without imperiling the school's accreditation rating. And I confess I no longer hold any real objection to that assignment. After all, our students, the poor weanlings, have quite enough on their tiny minds already, what with having to prepare themselves to man the battlements of the status quo for the rest of their natural lives; and anyhow, we in humanities are mere chaplains in the Army of the Protestant Ethic (APE for short), and as such it is our bounden duty not to sow the seeds of discontent amongst our troops but rather to see to their peace of mind, to protect the rear ranks against the infiltration of subversive influences. And should the enemy try germ warfare and the microbe of an Idea lodge itself in the vitals of one of our young warriors, we are expected to apply the soothing balm of Sweet Reasonableness, that spiritual Milk of Magnesia that eases all manner of distresses, great and small, in the mind's lower tract.

Which reminds me: we were speaking, weren't we, of Monk McHorning?

IV. Fear Itself

Nonetheless, for all my mewling and carping, here at Arbuckle I most decidedly am, and the tidy sum the state of Oregon stuffs into my pay envelope every month makes me not just another victim of this odious institution but its accomplice in its daily crimes against intelligence.

Once, though, before my infamy was quite so tightly sealed, I too had dreams, dear hearts; once, back in 1957 when Hector was a pup and I was fresh out of graduate school and had not yet begun to serve my apostasy, I had reason to believe—despite the strictures of my esteemed committee chairman (the old stick-in-the-mud had never liked me anyhow, not since I turned in a term paper entitled "Manifest Destiny and the Myth of *Penis Captivus:* A Freudian Interpretation of the Westward Movement" for his American history seminar)—that I too was soon to be admitted to the august company of reputable scholars. Let me elucidate:

During the spring of '57, when I was polishing off my M.A. thesis (*Cosmic Optimism and the Theory of Historical Periodicity in Nineteenth-Century American Thought,* a seventy-three-page, pound-and-a-half monument to pedantry fashioned entirely of bullshit and gall) and desultorily memorizing dates in preparation for my finals (they made the exams mercifully easy for those unhappy few who'd already been diagnosed as terminal cases) while I tried to come up with some new way to evade the military draft now that my student days were almost over, I met, kept company with, and shortly became rather tentatively engaged to a fellow graduate student—call her Jane—a math major, the only daughter of a professor of accounting in the Ohio State School of Business, who as it happened was also the celebrated author of that great nationwide best-seller *Fundamentals of Cost Accounting,* which had been *the* standard college textbook on the subject through eleven editions in twenty years and had thereby rendered its creator a very well-fixed gentleman indeed—a fact that had not escaped my own discerning eye during my ardent courtship of his daughter.

Now Jane was a rather reserved, studious sort who had neither sought nor been besieged by courtiers thus far in her young life (I think she was really quite surprised to discover herself somehow engaged to me, so distracted was she by her own graduate studies that spring), which circumstance doubtless inspired the Celebrated Author to a more tolerant response than might otherwise have been expected when his bookish daughter began to entertain the suit of a callow swain whose prospects, as best the worthy parent could determine, were approximately as limited as his intelligence and industry. Moreover, it also happened that the Celebrated Author was an alumnus of a small but quite respectable private liberal arts college in Lexington, Kentucky, named (let's say) Underwood College and that he had just recently made an extremely generous contribution toward the endowment of a new School of Business Administration the Underwood trustees had long been coveting. So of course it naturally occurred to him that perhaps he might, by means of a couple of calls to certain persons of his acquaintance in high places down at the old alma mater, be of some small assistance in Cupid's delicate work and at the same time ensure that the aforementioned young lout would at least be gainfully employed. (*"Grease,* Harrison my boy!" he declared to me as he hung up the phone that evening in his study. "It's *grease* that makes the wheels turn in the higher education bidness!") Thus it came to pass that in Lexington, Kentucky, at a certain o'clock on a certain day late that June, I appeared, brand-new briefcase at my side, at the door of the office of one Professor Ernest J. Furlong, chairman of the History Department at Underwood College, for the purpose of being interviewed by said Dr. Furlong with an eye—a *favorable* eye, my prospective father-in-law assured me—to future employment in (this is the best part) the 100 percent guaranteed draft-proof higher education bidness.

I suppose I'd just as well say here and now that—with the possible exception of the time I tried to swallow an enormous hunk of leathery barbecue and very nearly succumbed to a café coronary in a place called Fred's Pit, just outside the main gate of Fort Leonard Wood, Missouri—that wretched interview remains the absolute worst experience of my life.

Not to suggest, let me hasten to add, that the good Dr. Furlong was in any way inhospitable or otherwise uncooperative; on the contrary, that courtly (if somewhat bemused) old gent was most cordial and professed himself quite delighted to meet the brilliant young Ohio State graduate of whom the Dean and, yes indeed, even the President himself had spoken so warmly at the faculty luncheon the other day. . . . No, this little old wheel had clearly been well greased, and fatuous counterfeit though I most assuredly was, I don't doubt that if I'd kept my head I could've somehow weaseled my way through the interview and onto Dr. Furlong's distinguished faculty. But I couldn't handle it. My very handshake was clammy and infirm, and even as my interrogator made preliminary small talk I could feel my ill-gotten confidence slipping away from me. My mouth was suddenly so dry it tasted as if my teeth had rusted, my face was aflame, my voice rattled with irresoluteness; try as I might, I could not bring my uncontrollably shifty eyes to meet Dr. Furlong's amiable gaze, and three times during our first five minutes of conversation, alas, I called him "Dr. Furline." When he politely inquired whether I might enlighten him as to my perception of the theory of historical periodicity as expounded in my no doubt masterful treatment of the subject in my thesis, I heard myself saying, "Well, uh, like, see, history goes around in, you know, *cycles,* see . . ." By now my tongue was flopping about like a beached fish inside my mouth, and I was in the grip of a nameless and terrible panic that had effectively obliterated the entire span of human history from my mind; I couldn't have told Dr. Furlong so much as the date of the Battle of Hastings, much less who fought it or who won. At last, in desperation, I tried to pull my Freudian interpretation of the westward movement on him, but when I noticed that every time I said "penis captivus" he began absently but frantically to pluck what I can only describe as invisible butterflies from the lapel of his seersucker jacket, I knew the jig was irrevocably up. And our interview was no more than twenty minutes old (I was just pointing out to him that expansionary capitalism was obviously the natural issue of an anal-retentive national pathology) when, instead of a butterfly, he plucked up his watch from the pocket of his red tartan weskit and glanced at it and said, Ahem, quite, quite, but he must say that he personally had very grave doubts, very grave doubts indeed, Mr. Eastep, as to whether this *wallowing,* if I'd forgive him that characterization of it, this modern *wallowing* in the very lowest reaches of human psychology (or, heh-heh, as he preferred to call it, *sick*ology) was the proper work of the serious historian; but that in any case he'd just remembered a pressing appointment that unfortunately necessitated that we terminate our little chat at this time; he did hope I secured suitable employment soon, perhaps at some nice junior high school somewhere . . .

I've said the fear that gripped me as I entered Dr. Furlong's office had no name, but at Craycraft's Billiards, where I loitered away the days of my youth back home in Needmore, they'd have recognized my symptoms instantly: I was suffering an acute attack of buck fever—a condition afflicting, for instance, certain nine-ball players (my miserable self among them) in whom excessive eagerness is compounded by an overpowering sense of personal inadequacy to the task at hand, rendering an otherwise perfectly competent pool player constitutionally incapable of sinking the nine ball— which of course is the only ball that counts. My ex-wife ("You're just *scared,* Harry!") was also familiar with my condition, I regret to say. It was my old nemesis, the Only Thing We Really Have to Fear, the dread Fear Itself.

Anyhow, from then on things moved fast: before I was out of his outer office Dr. Furlong was on the phone to the Dean, and before I was off the Underwood campus the Dean was on the phone to the President, and before I was out of Lexington the President was on the phone to the Celebrated Author, warning that loyal and generous Son of Underwood that his beloved daughter was about to take a sex deviate to her bridal bed. An *unemployed* deviate. I called Jane that evening from the Greyhound station in Cincinnati, where I had a layover, and she rather dispassionately advised me that her father (who had often revealed himself to be a slavering Europhobe in the conversations I'd had with him about the World Situation) had suddenly decided that a tour of the Continent was just what Jane needed to round out her education. She'd be leaving in a day or so, she said, and until then of course she'd be *awfully* busy; but we'd *definitely* get together to talk things over when she got back in the fall . . . (Later on that summer, when I went back to Columbus to clean out my carrel at the library, I ran into one of her sorority sisters, who took undis-

guised delight in telling me she'd heard that in Europe, Jane
had sprung forth from under her bushel like Venus on the
Half-Shell and was leaving a trail of broken hearts all across
the Continent.) As for me, I wandered from the bus station
up Vine Street to the Gaiety Burlesque Theater, where I sat
through three complete shows and was rewarded for my perseverance by three single fleeting glimpses of Rose La Rose's
nipples, six nipples all in all. Deep in the night, I boarded another Greyhound, this one bound not for Columbus but for
Dayton, where my mother lived then (as she does still); the
bus was pulling out of the terminal when I remembered, not
without a certain morose satisfaction, that I'd left my briefcase—with my thesis in it—under my seat at the Gaiety,
where it was no doubt keeping company with the foulest kind
of trash.

I spent the rest of that summer languishing in my mother's
apartment in Dayton, to her growing annoyance. Near the
end of August I went to my local board and submitted to a
process called, mysteriously enough, "volunteering for the
draft"; and in September I departed for those two dismal
years at Fort Leonard Wood, Missouri, thence to Arbuckle,
Oregon. And as I said before, here I am.

Endnote

During one of *The Natural Man*'s many early mani-
festations, I toyed briefly with the idea of inserting into the
narrative alternate chapters, numbered and titled, dealing
with the life of the adult Harry Eastep, who has grown up to
become a disenchanted and embittered young academic.
Later, when it became apparent that the insertions were
undercutting the gentler tone I was striving to establish
(again, see "Empathy Follows Sympathy") in the rest of the
novel, I abandoned the strategy.

Still, I enjoyed writing these chapters at the time, and I think the work enlarged my understanding of Harry's character. And in its way, the effort is finally paying off: I've been planning a sort of left-handed sequel to *The Natural Man,* in the form of a contemporary courtroom drama titled *The Return of the Son of Needmore,* in which Harry Eastep, by now a respected, widely published West Coast historian, returns to his Kentucky hometown and settles down to live out his retirement years. (Eventually, he is called for jury duty and serves as foreman in a murder trial.) Much of the novel, though, will recapitulate Harry's academic career, and these two little chapters will provide the mother lode for that—the "backstory," in screenwriter-speak.

The opening line of *The Return of the Son of Needmore* will echo the last line of *The Natural Man:* "The show goes on, because it must."

I WROTE THIS LITTLE ESSAY FOR *The Writer* MAGAZINE (FEBRUARY 1984), SHORTLY AFTER *The Natural Man* APPEARED.

Empathy
Follows Sympathy

M̲Y NOVEL, *The Natural Man,* entered the world under a different title and in the form of a novella in 1961. Mercifully, it was never published.

In that manifestation, my narrative chiefly concerned—as it does still—two adolescent boys in the small town of Needmore, Kentucky, in the late 1940s. One of the boys, now named Monk McHorning, is a hulking, swaggering young orphan who has been adopted, for his athletic prowess, by the local high school basketball coach. The other, Harry Eastep, serves as Monk's acolyte and foil and pawn and is the point-of-view character. Minor characters include the victory-hungry coach, a dyspeptic gambler, Harry's hefty employer at the town's movie theater, and the theater owner's even heftier daughter, after whom both Monk and Harry lust. In all those respects and in many others as well, the final version is much the same as the original.

Yet the novella was a gloomy, joyless business, fraught with heavy-duty symbols, dense "poetic" prose, Freudian innuendo, and existential despair, while reviewers have seen fit to describe the novel as "light-footed and exceptionally funny" (*Newsweek*), "a joy from start to finish" (*People*), and "graceful, earthy, and very funny . . . a delightful entertainment" (*Harper's*). The point being that a story that was once as depressing as a toothache has metamorphosed into one most readers seem to find refreshing and amusing.

What happened, of course, is that over the years, as I launched periodic assaults on my recalcitrant material, my attitude toward it was undergoing a gradual but ultimately radical change. The nakedly autobiographical novella I had conceived as a searing indictment of southern small-town values and mores became, almost in spite of me, a sort of celebration of them. (Perhaps I should own here that in 1961, when I wrote the first draft, I was safe in Oregon, about as far in the continental United States as it is possible to get from my own Kentucky hometown.) The novella had had a villain—Monk—and two victims—Harry and the theater owner—but no heroes; its themes were rejection and alienation. In the novel, the former villain and his victims alike emerge as heroes, and the themes are friendship and reconciliation. Characters who had once borne my enmity or disdain now have my affection and respect. Values I once condemned have somehow become . . . *my* values.

Obviously, I was effecting my own reconciliation with Kentucky during those years. Although I continued to live in the West, I felt myself more and more powerfully drawn toward Kentucky. My visits there lengthened, and I anticipated them with ever increasing enthusiasm. I made a conscious—perhaps self-conscious—effort to maintain my Kentucky accent. As a protohippie in California in the 1960s, I styled myself "Captain Kentucky," while Daniel Boone turned over in his grave.

Then, in 1972, I came back to teach for a year at the University of Kentucky in Lexington, where I had once gone to graduate school. During that year, I renewed an old acquaintance with a popular (some would say notorious) Lexington nightclub performer named Little Enis, "the World's Greatest Left-Handed Upside-down Guitar Player," and wrote a long, reflective profile of him for *Playboy* magazine.

Now Enis was a terrific musician, but his reputation around Lexington also had a great deal to do with the fact that he was one rude, crude, lewd little dude. He would say anything, absolutely *anything,* and the stories of his bacchanalian appetites and marathon priapic exploits would curl a satyr's mustachios. Barely five and a half feet tall and weighing in at around two twenty-five, with an underslung jaw and a decided insufficiency of teeth, he was, to the naked eye, something less than prepossessing. Sexist and racist epithets were as natural to his conversation as aroma is to a billy goat. I don't suppose he'd ever read a book in his life.

Yet I adored him. "I yam what I yam," says Popeye the Sailor—and that was Enis; he was, emphatically, what he was. Hanging around with Enis, I used to say, was like keeping company with one's own id. The affectionate evocation of him that I wrote for *Playboy* was, and it remains, a personal all-time favorite of mine. When he died in the mid 1970s, I mourned his passing as if a part of myself had gone with him.

In 1976 I came back to small-town Kentucky, this time to stay. Once here, I began again to try to come to terms with my old nemesis, the former novella, now long since grown into a novel, though still not a very good one.

Someone has observed that all good writing flirts with sentimentality. It was a risk that I felt myself ready, now, to run. I wanted at last to write *lovingly* of Kentucky, of the hometown I'd maligned all those years ago, even of Monk McHorning, once the personification of so much that I'd deplored. A tall order, that one. How, without sugarcoating the characterization to the point that the old Monk McHorning was no longer recognizable, was I to render this profoundly unattractive figure in an appealing light?

For the answer, I looked to my late friend Little Enis: the way to render Monk was simply to *let him be himself,* to lighten up on him, to leave off judging him—through the medium of Harry Eastep, my spokesman in the novel—and begin instead to appreciate him for what he was. Character, I reminded myself, is not fixed and rigid but fluid; it seeks a level all its own. The solution lay not in altering Monk's character as such but in repositioning Harry in the narrative so that he could function not merely as Monk's disgruntled lackey but as his friend and confidant. Once sympathy was established, empathy could follow. "A door is always open," Flannery O'Connor has written, "to possibility and the unexpected in the human soul." But it wasn't Monk who had to find the door; that was up to Harry, and to me.

The Monk McHorning who emerged in the final draft inherits many personal characteristics from Little Enis. Indeed, if Enis had been six feet five instead of five feet six and had played basketball instead of left-handed upside-down guitar, he'd have been, as a boy, just like Monk. I'd like to think *The Natural Man* is a tribute to both of them, as well as to Kentucky, and to the small town where I grew up. *He was a son of Needmore now,* Harry Eastep tells himself near the novel's end, *and that would never change.* I think it's the best line in the book.

Endnote

When "Empathy Follows Sympathy" was published, my agent, the late Elizabeth McKee, was quite sure that the people who put out all those how-to books for would-be writers would soon be falling all over themselves in a mad scramble for the reprint rights. But Elizabeth was wrong for once, and the stampede never happened—so I've included the essay here, just to give the how-to types one more chance to snap it up.

I guess I should apologize for having recycled (in the Wallace Stegner memoir) that line about Daniel Boone turning over in his grave—but I'm so attached to it that I don't think I will.

I wrote "Great Moments" especially for this book. It appeared in *Louisville* magazine, February 1998.

Great Moments in Sports

> O the clear moment, when from the mouth
> A word flies, current immediately
> Among friends; or when a loving gift astounds
> As the identical wish nearest the heart;
> Or when a stone, volleyed in sudden danger,
> Strikes the rabid beast full on the snout!
>
> Robert Graves, "Fragment of a Lost Poem"

Like everybody else, I've told my favorite sports stories so many times I almost believe them myself—even the ones I probably made up. For instance:

When I was twelve years old (stop me if you've heard this), Happy Chandler gave me an autographed baseball. I once rode on an elevator with Jim Thorpe. I know a guy who knows a guy whose father once stood next to Lou Gehrig at a urinal in Yankee Stadium. I saw Ewell "the Whip" Blackwell pitch a no-hitter for the Cincinnati Reds in 1947, and Tom Seaver duplicate the feat in the next Reds game I attended—

thirty-one years later. Gay Brewer Jr., the golfer, once bird-dogged my girlfriend. My friend Gurney Norman claims to have tossed a Ping-Pong ball into a Dixie cup from twenty feet away. (I believe him, of course—but hey, what are friends for?) Waite Hoyt once let my uncle buy him a drink. In college, I was employed as a "tutor" by my university's athletic department, in which capacity I took, by correspondence, an entire sophomore English literature survey course for a first-string All-American tackle.

("Now don't get me no A," my protégé cautioned, the night before I was to take the final for him. "Get me about a C+, that'd be about right." It was a line that stayed with me until I put it to good use twenty-five years later in *The Natural Man.*)

Well, I could go on, but modesty forfends; my record in Vicarious Athletics speaks for itself.

But there were a few times when I actually got into the fray myself, in quest of that elusive Perfect Moment. Like the time I ran fourteen balls in a game of straight pool (and had a straight-in shot at the fifteenth—and scratched). Or the time I won a dollar and thirty-five cents in half an hour pitching pennies on the courthouse steps (and lost it all back in the next twenty minutes).

Or the time twelve guys on our high school basketball team came down with the flu, and I was abruptly—not to say precipitously—elevated from second-string jayvee to the furthermost end of the varsity bench, and suddenly found myself, deep in the third quarter, not only in the game but endeavoring to guard the great Cliff Hagan, then of Owensboro High, later of the University of Kentucky Wildcats and the Saint Louis Hawks. On the first play he broke for the basket and went twinkle-toeing up my chest like he was Fred Astaire and I was the Stairway to the Stars. Hagan—Mr. Hagan—accumulated eleven points during my two-minute tenure, mostly on shots launched from some vantage point afforded him by my reclining anatomy. If there were a statistic called "percentage of defensive assists," I'd have set some kind of record.

Still, every mutt has his Moment, and mine was coming up.

By the spring of 1950, when I was a junior at Maysville High and my glory days on the hardwood were but a distant memory ("Mac," our estimable Coach Jones had said, drawing me aside one day after practice, "Mac, you're a good, hardworking boy, but son, your hands are small, and I just don't believe you've got the equipment to make this team"), I had long since limited my athletic exertions to the rigorous pursuit of female companionship.

In other words, I was spending a disproportionate amount of time mooning about the house and grounds of a certain Mr. and Mrs. T. C. Stonebreaker, who had four beautiful daughters still at home. Alas, I was but one of many, a restive, milling herd of rampant teenaged billy goats strutting our dubious stuff before the less-than-awestruck Mam'zelles Stonebreaker. On Saturday afternoons (when school left us at large and also when Mr. Stonebreaker, who tended to get grumpy during these invasions, usually beat a strategic withdrawal to his euchre game at the Moose Lodge), the testosterone level in Stonebreaker Hall could have peeled the wallpaper.

For these occasions, we trotted out all our highly developed social skills—which is to say we maligned and demeaned and bullied and belittled one another mercilessly, in the hope of raising our own stature in the eyes of the four fascinators; we cut up and showed off like drunken sailors and talked as dirty as we dared for the edification of that beguiling audience.

Such was the scenario on that memorable Saturday afternoon in the spring of 1950, which was to be the day of my very own Great Moment:

. . .

Mr. S. is at his euchre, Mrs. S. is out shopping, and the house fairly teems with postpubescent boys of every size and description, from eighth graders vying for the attentions of Gracie, the youngest Stonebreaker, to a couple of pipe-puffing college freshmen home for the weekend expressly to pay court to Mary Margaret, the eldest, who graduated from high school last year and now has an office job at the cotton mill. Once again, the objects of our affection have reduced us all—even the college guys—to the developmental level of the eighth graders, who themselves are behaving like fifth graders. Naturally, there have already transpired numerous episodes of pantsing, not to mention various hotfoots, noogies, and wedgies, and the atmosphere is redolent of bathroom humor so sophisticated that it has left the sisters Stonebreaker fairly gasping with (let us hope) admiration.

I'm there too, of course, but for once I've held myself aloof from these base shenanigans, having somehow cornered Bernice, who is to my mind the fairest Stonebreaker of them all, over by the piano, where I and my Lucky Strike are demonstrating my prowess at French inhaling, blowing smoke rings, and—like Tony Curtis on the cover of the paperback of *The Amboy Dukes* ("A Novel of Wayward Youth in Brooklyn! Now a Thrilling Motion Picture!")—making suave conversation while the Lucky is parked roguishly in the corner of my mouth. I have also lately cultivated, in the wake of my departure from the uniformly crew-cut Bulldog squad, a prodigious Wildroot-lubricated pompadour, complete with a lank Tony Curtis forelock that dangles ornamentally over my right eye; and I'm sporting my brand-new oh-so-cool two-tone jacket with the collar turned up—just like Tony's!

("How come you've got your collar turned up that way, Eddie?" Bernice has just interrupted my suave conversation to inquire. "It's not a bit cold in here!")

And now into this tranquil domestic circle swagger the last two guys in all of Christendom whom the rest of us—the males, I mean—want to see, namely the dread Speedy Little Guards (so-called in the local press), a brace of Bobbys—let's call them Bobby One and Bobby Two—indispensable Bulldog mainstays, One a razzle-dazzle ball handler, Two a nonpareil set-shot artist, both of them brash, bandy-legged, and, in the unanimous opinion of the Stonebreaker girls, devastatingly cute.

Bernice quickly escapes the narrow confines of our tête-à-tête and joins her sisters, who are gathered 'round the Bobbys to admire their new Bulldog letter sweaters, acquired just last night at the annual awards banquet. (How come they're wearing sweaters? I hear myself grumbling inwardly. It's not a bit cold in here!) Then we all troop dutifully outside to see Bobby Two's new short—actually his mother's new short, a dumpy, frumpy 1950 Nash Rambler, the apocryphal upside-down bathtub. Still, the Nash is profoundly snazzier than the scuffed penny loafers that at present constitute my own principal means of locomotion, and I am positively viridescent with envy. And this condition is further aggravated by my growing certainty that if Bobby Two has his way, he and Bernice will be snuggling up in that goddamn Rambler at the RiverView Drive-in Theater tonight.

Once we're all back inside the house, the two Bobbys, along with Marcella, the second-eldest sister, and (sigh) Bernice, promptly disappear into the kitchen, from whence soon begin to issue various muffled giggles, sniggers, chortles, titters, and similar sounds of suppressed merriment. Meanwhile, the eighth graders are entertaining Gracie with a tiny-tuba ensemble of rude armpit noises, and the pipe puffers regale Mary Margaret with BMOC tales (featuring, of course, themselves), leaving the rest of us Lotharios to loll about the living room shooting pocket pool while we feign indifference to the jolly proceedings behind the kitchen door.

After ten or fifteen minutes the merrymakers emerge, the girls still all a-giggle behind their hands, the Bobbys all a-smirk. Each Bobby is carrying, inexplicably, an egg.

"Okay," Bobby One announces, stepping to the center of the room, "let's see which one can bust his egg on the othern's head!" With that, he and Bobby Two begin comically bouncing around the room on their toes like sparring spermweights until, after a brief and thoroughly unpersuasive flurry of pseudofisticuffs, Bobby One, egg in hand, smacks Bobby Two on the noggin and—how could I have been so surprised by this?—*mirabile dictu,* the egg's not loaded, there's nothing in it. The empty shell shatters harmlessly on Bobby Two's crew-cut pate.

Of course the Bobbys—being Bobbys—act like this is the greatest joke since the chicken crossed the road. There wasn't nothing to it, they aver, clapping each other on the back in the throes of their hilarity; we just punched little pinholes in them eggs and blew the insides out.

And right there is where I make the dumbest move of my young life.

"Let's see that other one," I hear myself saying, unaccountably, to Bobby Two. "Lemme take a look at it." To this day, I don't know what in the world I was thinking of.

"You wanna see the egg?" says Bobby One. "Hey Bob-o, McClammerham wants to see the egg!"

Bobby Two is grinning, and there is a gleam in his eye that should have given me pause. Could that be a corresponding gleam in the eye of Bernice, who is standing just behind him? Why do I feel like I'm in a play, and everybody knows the script but me?

"Sure, Hammerclam," says Bobby Two, putting his hands behind his back. "Which hand?"

Christ, I'm thinking, it's only an eggshell. But hey, I got my forelock, got my Lucky hangin' on my lip, I'm cool. So I play along.

"Uh, the left?"

"Nope," he says, showing me his left hand, in which there is, of course, nothing at all. Meanwhile his right hand—in which there is, of course, not an eggshell but an egg, in all its fullness—is describing a high, sweeping arc from behind his back to the top of my head, where it arrives with a disgusting splat, much to the immediate detriment of my pompadour.

"Sorry," says Bobby Two, wiping his palm on my Tony Curtis lapel, "wrong hand."

So there I stand in the Stonebreaker living room with a coiffeur nicely dressed out in egg yolk, a viscous thread of egg white trailing, snotlike, from my forelock to my Lucky Strike, and all about me a tumult of eighth graders rolling on the floor, college boys roaring, Stonebreaker girls hugging themselves in their mirth, Bobbys pounding each other on the back to the point of bodily injury. My dignity, I fear, has been seriously compromised. Time to regroup.

To which purpose I slink off to the kitchen, where I stick my sodden head under the faucet in the sink and shampoo my hair as best I can with dishwashing liquid, dry it with Mrs. Stonebreaker's dishtowel, and sponge off my jacket with her dishrag. Then I comb my hair; the egg-yolk residue is beginning to set up, which actually helps a little in the reconstruction of my pompadour. Finally, I go to the refrigerator and help myself to two more of Mrs. Stonebreaker's eggs. Thus armed, I return to the scene of Clamhammer's Humiliation.

In the living room, things have sorted themselves out predictably in accordance with the New Social Order: the armpit ensemble has resumed serenading Gracie, and the college stuffed shirts, solemn as owls, are once again puffing industriously away on their calabashes, throwing up a smoke screen around Mary Margaret as dense—and certainly as aromatic —as an enchantment. But now Bobby One is cozying up to Marcella on the sofa, and Bernice, that Jezebel, has joined Bobby Two over by the piano—in *our* corner!

Such is the sordid scene that Clamhammer the Redeemer bursts upon, with blood in his eye and vengeance on his mind.

"Awright, you sorry bastids," I thunder—yes! I actually *thundered*!—brandishing an egg at first one Bobby, then the other, "now I would hate to have to throw this right here in Mrs. Stonebreaker's living room, but I've got one of these apiece for you two sonsabitches, and if you're not outta here by the time I count to three, you're definitely gonna get egged! *One!*"

The Bobbys exchange stricken glances, and I know that I am terrible in my wrath.

"*Two!*"

Now Bobby One half-rises from the sofa, while the craven Bobby Two endeavors to shield himself behind Bernice.

"*Three!*" I cry, and with that the Bobbys break simultaneously for the doorway into the front hall, and I am in hot pursuit, my throwing arm cocked at the ready. But not for nothing do their admirers call them the Speedy Little Guards, and by the time I make the hall, they are scrambling out the front door. And the truth is that despite my threat,

I am not quite willing to throw an egg within these sacred premises, owing to the certainty that Mrs. Stonebreaker would forthwith banish me from the temple forever and ever, world without end.

So I hold my fire, and in another instant I'm on the front stoop and the Bobbys are already legging it across the street toward where the Rambler awaits them. I reach the curb just as Bobby Two arrives at the Rambler's driver-side door, and I have a clear shot at him, a perfect target inasmuch as even if I miss, I'll still hit his mommy's car. Then, just as I'm going into my windup, what suddenly looms up between us but a city bus, lumbering along as huge and poky as a steamship. And when the bus is out of the way at last, I see that Bobby Two is at the Rambler's wheel, revving up, and his door is closed. Bobby One is just opening the passenger-side door; I can see his head above the roof of the car, so I uncork a desperation throw at it—not a bad throw, actually, except that he sees it coming and ducks into the car as the egg sails over his head and splatters abortively against a telephone pole. Then Bobby Two pops the clutch, and the Rambler peels out more spiritedly than I would have dreamed it could, while I stand there on the curb shaking my fist after them, cursing them for the unprincipled knaves they certainly are, cursing myself for not having at least managed to egg the car—all in all, a masterful study in futility.

But wait, what's this I see! Down at the far end of the block, the Rambler is hanging a U-ey! Can it be that they're actually going to come back past me? Yes, they are; the Rambler has wallowed through its turn and is headed back in my direction. Maybe they don't realize that I still have an egg in my arsenal. Or maybe Bobby Two is figuring *Wot the hell, we'll just take the car down to Bobby One's big brother's Texaco station and hose it off, no big deal.*

Nonetheless, there'll be some small satisfaction even in so negligible an aggravation—and this time, I am vowing grimly as I palm my egg, I won't miss.

As the Rambler draws nearer, I see that—as if to add insult to injury by demonstrating their indifference to any vengeance I might wreak—they aren't even hurrying. Then the car rolls slowly past me; Bobby One has his thumbs in his ears and is making donkey faces at me behind the passenger-side window. I draw a bead on his ugly mug and cut loose a vicious Ewell "the Whip" Blackwell sidearm bullet that I know even as it leaves my hand is a wild pitch and that it will miss the strike zone by a mile.

Now there are those who will maintain that an egg is, after all, only an egg, a stupid, insensate, ovoid article of no cognitive power whatsoever unless and until it somehow gets a chicken in it—a beast itself not conspicuous for its intelligence, by the way. But that does not describe *this* egg. For this is *my* egg, friends, as surely as if I'd laid it myself, and this egg is smarter, even, than its proud parent; it has a mind of its own and knows *exactly* where it wants to go. And this egg of mine has *eyes,* dear hearts, and as it spins off my fingertips it sees what I have not seen, which is that although Bobby One has his window snugly closed, his wind-wing—that little triangular vent that all cars used to have, back in the days when carmakers were smarter than, say, chickens—his wind-wing is . . . wide open!

And this little egg of mine finds that tiny opening with all its eyes, and it flies as true as Cupid's arrow straight through the vent and smacks the Rambler's windshield and explodes in a bright golden sunburst all over the interior of Bobby Two's mommy's brand-new short, all over those accursed Bobbys and their goddamn letter sweaters! Thus have I struck the rabid beast full on the snout!

Luck? You dare call it luck? Was it luck that directed Gurney's Ping-Pong ball into that Dixie cup? No indeed. Luck, I think, is synonymous with money; it's strictly a business proposition, wherein good luck produces a payoff, bad luck a payout. Nor, of course, was it skill; neither I nor Gurney could duplicate our feats in a thousand thousand years. No, this was *destiny,* pure and simple; we had, each of us, a blind date with Immortality. Did Cliff Hagan ever toss a Ping-Pong ball into a Dixie cup at twenty feet? Did Ewell the Whip ever fling an egg through the wind-wing of a moving car?

And while I'm asking questions, I'll ask these: Were the Stonebreaker girls all watching from the stoop when my egg burst like a de Kooning masterpiece inside the Rambler? Did they scream and squeal like bobby-soxers when this miracle of art and magic and athletic prowess transpired right before their very eyes? Did Bernice and I go to the movies that night—the sit-down movies, not the drive-in—and did I, when I took her home afterward, kiss her on the lips on that very stoop?

No, sports fans, I'm afraid not, I'm afraid not. But . . . O the clear moment!

Endnote

When my excellent friend and coconspirator Tom Marksbury and I first began thinking about assembling this book, we decided right away that it should include a substantial measure of new writing. We planned to include some pretty recent work, of course ("Bob's Lost Years," "Captain Kentucky 'Visits' the Left Coast," and "Furthurmore," were all written in the nineties), and the endnotes would be so new that—well, they weren't even written yet. What was required, though, was some fresh, independent writing that would lend a little credence to our notion that this is really a book about a writer finding his voice.

For a long time I've toyed with the idea that someday I'd

produce a sort of knock-off of *Famous People I Have Known* called *Great Moments in Sports* which, in my imagination, would begin with an account of my starring role in the miraculous eggsploit you have just borne witness to. Here, suddenly, was a Moment fairly begging to be seized.

So now I have yet another book to finish. And the show goes on, because it must.

NEAL CASSADY, FAMED AS THE FRIEND AND RUNNING MATE OF BOTH
JACK KEROUAC AND KEN KESEY, DIED IN MEXICO IN 1968. THIS
MEMOIR APPEARED IN *Place* MAGAZINE (WINTER 1973).

Visions of Neal: A Dirge

THE FIRST TIME I saw Neal Cassady was in the
fall of 1962, a couple of months after my first wife, Kit, and our
little daughter, Kris, moved down from Oregon. It was in our
cottage in Menlo Park, just a few blocks from Perry Lane,
where Ken Kesey was already trifling with Forces Mortal
Men Were Never Meant to Tamper With. I was in the
creative-writing program at Stanford then, and a bunch of us
neophyte literati and our long-suffering friends and depen-
dents were in the habit of getting together every few weeks to
read our deathless prose aloud.

We had conscripted a pretty good crowd that evening—
Ken was there with the first few manuscript chapters of *Sometimes a Great Notion,* and Larry McMurtry (whose first novel
was soontobethemajormotionpicture*Hud*), and Bob Stone,
my Stanford classmate who was working on a great novel
called *A Hall of Mirrors,* and a minimultitude of lesser lights,
maybe twenty-five of us in all, hunkered haunch to haunch
on the floor of a room in which half a dozen constituted a

mob, and we were just settling down for a nice long evening of
ego-tripping when suddenly the front door burst open and in
blew this amazingly handsome working class hero–looking
stud, with flashing blue Burt Lancaster eyes and a Kirk
Douglas jaw and a Paul Newman build, stepping with comically elaborate carefulness over people's heads like Slewfoot
Sam in the mushmelon patch, talking up an absolute storm—
*". . . just passin' through, folks, don't mind me, my shed-yool just
happened to coincide with Mr. Kesey's, here, just by coincidence you
understand, always had the greatest respect for, yes, and all that re-
dundancy as well, not to mention the works of, ah, Alfred Lord
Tennyson, you see, and the worst of the poems of Schiller, huntin'
and peckin' away there as they did, so I'll just say how-d'ya-do to
my friend Mr. Kesey and then we'll be on our way, have to get
there in plenty of time, you understand . . ."*—coming on like
some crazy conflation of Lord George Buckley and Professor
Irwin Corey, and trailing him into the room like pale shadows were a muttering, wildly gesticulating young blond stalwart (this, I discovered later, would be Bradley Hodgman,
an erstwhile Stanford tennis star who had lately become
Neal's most dedicated acolyte), and a cadaverously emaciated,
toothless dude wearing a floor-length black overcoat (I never
did find out who that one was), and a pretty but somewhat
disoriented woman (Neal's longtime old lady, Anne) and her
child, a ragtag little fellow wearing jockey shorts outside
his pants, and having studied my Kerouac as diligently as ere
a would-Beat who ever paid fifty cents for a thimbleful of
cappuccino in the Coexistence Bagel Shop, I knew right
away that the leader of this small invasion, that Lancaster-
Douglas-Newman-Buckley-Corey stud, was—*had* to be—
Neal Cassady! Because after all, who *else* could it be? But
scarcely had that cosmic information fixed itself in my bemused consciousness—Dean Moriarity! In the flesh! Right

here in my very living room! Instant immortality! Great moments in American literature!—than Neal and his scrungy little convoy were already at the door again, Neal still rapping demonically away—". . . *in fact, in* fact, *a hundred years ago it was 'Lord Tennyson, here we go!' and 'Lord Tennyson, don't y'know!' But Alfred, he had another thing in mind, he had in mind Romero, ah, Alfred Romero, ah, Alfa-Romeo, ah, Caesar Romero, yes, and Fangio too, I tell you that boy could drive, I mean he was only human but he lapped them time after time, you see . . .*"—and almost before I knew for sure they'd been there they were gone, all of them out the door and gone, except . . . my God, the kid! There he stood in his galligaskins amongst all those sober, gaping upturned faces, looking as forlornly lost in this enormous sudden silence as another child might be discovering himself abandoned in the middle of a busy thoroughfare. And of course it was Faye Kesey, Mother Superior, who first recognized his plight and scooped him up and ran outside to catch them just as they were pulling out of the parking lot and handed the little guy back to his mama, who was so enraptured with Neal's ceaseless soliloquy that she hadn't quite gotten around to missing him.

To this day we don't know what they came for.

After that I saw Neal lots of times, glancingly—he had a knack for popping up at parties—but the next time I got caught up in the pyrotechnics of his endless dramatic monologue came one night a few months after both the Keseys and the McClanahans had moved to La Honda, the woodsy little community twenty-five miles or so west of Palo Alto. Kit and I had invited my boss's son, our friend Page Stegner, to dinner that evening, and it being something of an occasion, Kit had done us up a special spread, New York cuts and all the fixin's, and just as we were sitting down to pitch into it a gang of rowdies came roaring up the driveway in one of those cacopho-

nous old bangers Cassady was always driving—a 1956 Olds
88, say, hitting on about five—and moments later the house
was full of Pranksters, half a dozen or so of them all stoned to
distraction on Colonel Owsley's private stock, come to raid
my bookcase for my copy of M. C. Escher's sike-o-deelic
drawings, which was the favorite trip enhancer of the day.
And during the ten minutes they were there Neal sat down
with us at the table and scarfed Page's entire *dinner*—soup,
artichoke, steak, baked potato, glass of wine—then went to
the kitchen and came back with a cup of coffee and a choco-
late mousse and polished them off as well and never *once*
stopped talking, and I swear to Kerouac it was the same
soliloquy!

"*. . . so now Fangio, doin' a hunnert and twenty, lowers his
goggles for the first time, y'know, but there's a problem somewhere,
anxiety out there somewhere, starting with, ah, Wordsworth, you
see, and working backwards in the traditional fashion, straight
through Pliny the Elder and* beyond, *possibly, because clean-and-
jerk was definitely not their best lick, you understand, no, the
snatch was just right for those middleweight boys, especially when
you consider the discourse that accompanied Shelby's run at Day-
tona, or was it Pebble Beach . . .*"

Incredible! But had he actually picked up the thread right
where he had dropped it all those months ago? Or had I by
simple coincidence tuned in on him the second time just
when his monologue chanced to convolute my way again?

Then there was the night at Kesey's La Honda house,
where the Pranksters were gathered around the big round
dining room table attempting to conduct some sort of
thought-transference experiment requiring intense group
concentration, when suddenly Neal was in the room:

"*. . . yessir, they were goin' two mile an hour,* backward, *with
the exhaust valves wide open, and the petcocks too that you've*

sometimes seen, except of course Jayne Mansfield, heh-heh, and in
July and August, just drivin' through, why, who knows *what that*
cost us? But when you take a radiator, and just consider it, ah, aes-
thetically, you understand . . ."

Well, by this time, of course, there was plenty of concentration going on, all right, but precious little was directed toward the ESP doings. "Listen, Neal," Kesey interjected, just a
bit wearily, "we've got a sort of a thing goin' on here, so if
you'd just . . ."

". . . still, goin' full bore down the chute in a 1954 Studebaker
Commander, why, you just naturally get your velocity *mixed up*
with your veracity, *you see, yet only four days before his death,*
Ralph Waldo Emerson made the same point, to, ah, the effect that,
as Fangio himself put it after that disastrous *finish at Nur-*
burgring in '57 . . ."

By now Neal was moving about the room in a kind of sup-
ple, twitching soft-shoe shuffle to the tempo of his own voice,
shaking his shoulders in little seizures of Dextasy, tossing a
jingling ring of car keys into the air and catching it one-
handed behind his back and tossing it again, gliding and
turning beneath the spinning key ring like a hip update of
Saint Vitus, a sinuously spastic Fred Astaire who shoots
speed with a phonograph needle. And the ever-faithful Bradley too was on his feet and moving now, muttering in low
counterpoint to Neal's riff, his hands as busy as a loquacious
deaf-mute's.

"Yeah, right," Kesey sighed, drumming his fingers impatiently on the table, "but listen, Neal . . ."

". . . a well-known fact that the platonic structure, combined,
you understand, with remote retrieval as practiced by Eeeee-
lizabeth Barrett Browning and also Eeeee-lizabeth, ah, Taylor,
you see . . ."

"True, true," Kesey said, "that's my opinion too, and always has been, but you realize of course that you haven't taken into account the very significant study of, uh . . ." Clearly, Ken had recognized the futility of trying to talk Neal out of talking and was now endeavoring simply to outtalk him. A hopeless enterprise.

". . . *now what* were *those intellectual agnostic sentiments of the period, I ask you, except of course insofar as where you draw the line, that is, but in any case I believe it was at, let me see, yes, Sebring, when Ferrari* . . ."

". . . mumble mumble mumble . . . ," Bradley agreed.

"Uh, yeah, some would say so," Ken ventured, "but, uh, now you take your intellectual agnostics, I mean accordin' to my information, they would . . ."

"MUMBLE MUMBLE MUMBLE!" Bradley objected.

"Well, that band was playin', why, you could hear it out back! So there we were, coastin' through Houston, or roastin' in Austin if you will, but Proustian-wise, all the authorities agree that . . ."

And now for the first time I began to get some small inkling of the mysterious kinetics of Neal's mind, the internal dynamics of his rap. I was finally beginning to understand that his monologue wasn't at all fractured and fragmented and chaotic as I'd always supposed but rather just incredibly fluid, that his demented rantings were in fact a kind of atonal scat singing, that he dealt not in mere subjects but in themes, leitmotifs, that he was not just prattling, vaporing, he was making *music*! Of course! And this scene that was going on right now, with Kesey and Cassady up there honkin' away at one another while Bradley backed them up on bass—that was like one of those "Battle of the Saxes" numbers in Norman Ganz's old "Jazz at the Philharmonic" road shows, where guys like Flip Phillips and Illinois Jacquet strove to blow each other off the stage.

Kesey never really had a chance; for once in his life he'd

overmatched himself, and to his credit he realized it quickly and acknowledged it, after his own fashion, gracefully— which is to say that as soon as he saw that he was out of his league, he grinned and nodded to Ken Babbs and George Walker and the three of them jumped up and grabbed Neal and picked him up and carried him feetfirst straight out the door and deposited him gently in the yard, Neal declaiming eloquently through it all—"... *nonetheless, the way she wore that dress was a* disgrace, *friends, but of course there's no accounting for tastes, after all, it's a well-known fact that the heart, like the steam engine, has four chambers, you see ..."*—Bradley mumbling after them, loyal even into exile.

It was for Kesey an act of genuine—if backhanded—humility; he wasn't ejecting Neal, he was paying homage to him, bearing him in triumph from the field of epic struggle. And no one there understood that any better than Neal himself, who turned right around and followed George and Babbs and Kesey back into the house, where he was greeted by a rousing little cheer from his admiring audience, which in his honor immediately abandoned the ESP exercise in favor of a joint-rolling contest.

The last time I saw Neal was in 1967 at Kesey's coming-out party, the night they let Ken out of jail. I can't testify to much of what went down at that gala affair—there was, as you might suppose, a bountiful spread laid out before the celebrants, grass and hash and acid and laughing gas and about a bucketful of bourbon, so my recollection is understandably murky—but one moment of it I do recall with almost painful clarity:

It was getting on toward three o'clock in the morning (they hadn't turned Ken loose till a minute after midnight), and I was languishing on a low, pasha-style couch with one of those huge government-surplus weather balloons half full of laughing gas in my lap, all laid back there clinging to the underside of that great soft black sphere, rooting after the balloon's nozzle like a panel out of some R. Crumb wet dream involving Mr. Snoid and Angelfood McSpade, when from somewhere out beyond the rubbery black horizon I heard Neal talking—*"Yes indeed, some do, whereas, the poets tell us, some definitely do not, no indeed, not even Stirling Moss, you see . . ."*—but when the pinwheeling of my eyeballs had slowed enough for me to look about me, I saw not Neal but . . . the devil! No kidding! Old Nick himself standing right there before me, naked except for a long, flowing scarlet cape and blood-red knee-high booties and red boxer-style loincloth and a sinister black mask and a dark, Mephistophelian mustache, breathing jets of evil bluish fumes from both nostrils and talking a mile a minute with his foot-long forked tongue—

". . . not even Stirling Moss, *great as he was in the old Maserati days, would have attempted such a fusion of the existential and the transcendental, or, if you will, the universal and the transmission, because ever since the time of Mamie van* Doren *there has been . . ."*

Well, it was Neal, of course, Neal who'd snuck into the bedroom where the guests' coats were stashed and stripped down to his red socks and boxer shorts and shades and donned my own long red velvet cape, slicked down the only mustache I've ever known him to grow, jammed Ken's brother Chuck's hash pipe into his mouth—the pipe was a hollowed-out, two-pronged length of deer antler—fired it up, and somehow metastasized himself out into the living room, where he reappeared in a puff of blue smoke just in time to catch me and Angelfood in fragrant dee-likt-oh on the couch. Shameless old miscegenist that I am, as soon as I realized that it was only Neal and not Old Bloody Bones himself who'd witnessed my degenerate dalliance, I sank back into the pillows and greedily buried my face in that billowing dark bosom, and by the time I came up for air again, Neal had put his clothes back on and split. The next I heard of him, a few weeks later, he was in Mexico; and the next after that, he was dead.

. . .

A few years after Neal's death, a student at Johns Hopkins named W. Klausmeir wrote Ken a great letter in which he speculated that Neal had been reincarnated as a virus that was already being tracked back across the border on the soles of wetbacks' huaraches. Could be. Because one evening in 1971, long after Neal had dropped his body, I sat in the kitchen of my house in Palo Alto and heard him say—well, all right then, the voice was George Walker's, but the lyrics were vintage Cassady:

". . . If this 1940 Cadillac 8 banger (not Bangor, that's another Maine; not the one I fear is busted by this King of the Road, if that has any bearing) (maybe I cracked the Cam too, woo!) can't be fixed I'll . . . Let me tell you about this machine, a real dream . . . best truck I ever fucked up. A 1947 ¾ ton, with overload springs, International . . . got a 1962 6 speed GMC gear box—never use compound Low so really a 5 speed—a 1957 Metro van rear end, 2 fuel tanks holding about 26½ gallons . . . 2 brand-new 8 ply Nylon 750 × 16 (cost $90) on the rear and . . ."

George was reading aloud from *The First Third,* which is Neal's autobiography "and other writings," posthumously published just that week by City Lights; Ken had happened upon a copy of it that afternoon in a bookstore, flipped it open, and found himself reading a letter Neal had written to him from someplace called Wakeman, Ohio, in 1965 during one of Cassady's careening cross-country odysseys, a letter Kesey never received. (He still has no idea, he says, how the letter found its way into the book; presumably, Neal never got around to mailing it.) So of course he bought the book, and when he and George dropped in to visit me that evening, they brought it with them, and now George—who'd spent a lot of time on the road with Neal and had been particularly close to him—was reading it aloud to us, Kesey receiving the letter six years late, via ear mail, as it were.

Since then I've read the rest of the book, and I suppose I'm obliged to say it never quite lives up to the Kerouac quote on the jacket comparing Neal to Joyce, Céline, "Dusty" (Dostoevski), Proust, Dreiser, Wolfe, Melville, Hemingway, and "Scott Fitz." Because writing is essentially a sedentary, static art, and Cassady was never, *never* still. So it's no surprise that the book is really an assemblage of fragments rather than a sustained performance or that much of the writing is a little on the clumsy side. Neal was no lowly scribbler; he was a classic American hero, an intrepid pilgrim reconnoitering the face of the land like Huckleberry Finn before him, with a literary lineage that stretches all the way back to Odysseus. Writing, as a general rule, isn't heroes' business, actually; writing is what the Homers and Twains and Kerouacs are for. How often can Superman take time out from his hero work to fool around on Clark Kent's typewriter?

But that letter to Kesey . . . I could happily have sat there in the kitchen till the cows came home, listening to Neal (through George, his medium) carry on:

". . . we set out to look for someone to trade a motorless truck for practically anything that runs—& after all day looking (including as near misses a 1949 black Chev, a 1953 green one with smooth tires & a 1938 ton & ½ flatbed Dodge truck) we've come up with a 1955 Studebaker yellow station wagon with 49,000 miles, but no spare wheel or tire, radio, heater & such a badly leaking muffler that not only must all windows be left down, but one must take aspirins hourly for the headaches produced; also right smarting is the eye irritation. Anyhow, it runs, altho burning so much oil the hiway behind is festooned with smoke & fumes . . ."

Carrying on. That was the business of Neal's life; no matter what, he carried on. And if we're still getting letters from him from Wakeman, Ohio, then that's where he must *be*, right? Out there in Wakeman, Ohio, carryin' on . . . and on . . .

Endnote

"Visions of Neal" began life as a review of *The First Third* (City Lights, 1972), but it swiftly (and, considering the subject, inevitably) degenerated into a personality piece instead.

I can claim no credit, by the way, for either remembering or inventing the samples of Neal's multiloquence that are threaded throughout this memoir. They are in fact loose renderings of Neal's own voice as it occurs on one of the many tapes the Pranksters made of him when he was the wheelman of Ken's fabled bus, Furthur.

I had already tried the recurring-voice device in my piece about the Grateful Dead (published in truncated form in *Playboy,* March 1972, and coming up shortly in this volume) and I was preparing to use it again in the essay I had just begun, about my Lexington rockabilly pal Little Enis, the All-American Left-Handed Upside-down Guitar Player (which was also published in *Playboy,* and became the centerpiece of *Famous People I Have Known*). So I welcomed the opportunity to experiment with the stratagem one more time in the Neal memoir before I took the big plunge into Enisography.

Although I've done a little cosmetic rejiggering of the prose here, I've left my overlong, overloaded sentences and paragraphs largely intact, because in those days I was operating on the theory that writing ought to *be* what it's *about,* and the density of the prose seemed to me to demand of the reader the same kind of attention that Neal's conversational style demanded of his listener. (Speaking of long sentences.)

FRED WAS MY COHORT DURING THE OLD FREE UNIVERSITY DAYS OF THE SIXTIES. I WROTE THIS LETTER TO BE READ ALOUD AT A MEMORIAL GATHERING OF HIS CALIFORNIA FRIENDS, AFTER HIS SUICIDE IN 1985. FOR MORE ABOUT THE NOW MORIBUND FREE UNIVERSITY MOVEMENT, SEE THE ENDNOTE.

Fredpitaph:
Remembering Fred Nelson

Port Royal, Kentucky
March 10, 1986

Dear Friends o' Freddy:

Okay, here's my Fred Nelson: This great bony long-legged long-armed gangly angular tangle of ganglia, all knees and elbows and long trembling fingers and coffee nerves and cigarettes, Ivy League from his button-down collar to his cordovan loafers yet irrepressibly, irredeemably hip, perched on the edge of his chair like some huge improbable red-crested crane, talking a mile a minute, gesticulating extravagantly in that jumpy, jittery, herky-jerky way of his that made you think he might fly all to pieces at any moment, self-destruct in a paroxysm of anxiety . . . yet at the same time somehow giving you to understand that he was not merely reliable but absolutely steadfast, that if he told you he'd be there on time with the work finished you knew he'd not only be there on time with the work finished but also that he'd do a hell of a job for you . . . A perfect study in contradictions, old Fred was: awkward and ridiculous and graceful and beautiful, immensely gifted yet gnawed to a frazzle by self-doubt, undeniably comic yet ineffably sad, embittered yet desperately loving . . .

Fred was, I guess, the unhappiest person I've ever known, yet he had a wonderful capacity for a good time and would pursue one to the ends of the earth if he thought it had possibilities. A couple of years ago, for instance, at a time when he was stone broke and out of work, he flew all the way to Connecticut on a whim and a prayer to attend my daughter's wedding—where, in his desperation to be of use, he made an utter but delightful nuisance of himself and contributed indispensably (though not, perhaps, exactly in the way he had intended) to the joy of the occasion.

The best time I ever had with Fred was back in 1970 or '71, when he and I went to New York to try to persuade some hapless publisher to produce an anthology of writing from the *Free You,* the Midpeninsula Free University magazine of which I was an editor and Fred was the guiding genius. We made the trip purely on spec, of course, paying for our tickets out of our own pockets, and Fred groused all the way up to the S.F. airport about how nobody in the Free University appreciated what we were doing for the institution, the sacrifice we were making, etc., etc.

We'd booked seats on the midnight red-eye to New York. I was wearing a shirt that had removable collar stays, and I'd replaced them with two joints. As soon as we were airborne we headed for the rest rooms to toke up, and on Fred's way back he happened to notice that the stewardess (excuse me,

flight attendant) had parked her cocktail cart, unflightat-
tended, in the galley while she copped a few z's in a nearby
empty seat. In the blink of an eye every pocket of Fred's her-
ringbone tweed blazer was loaded to the gunnels with those
cute little bottles of scotch and bourbon and gin, and by the
time the plane was over Reno we could've supplied its motive
power all by ourselves, never mind the engines.

We partied all night long, staggered ashore at JFK still
drunk as owls, careened down about a thousand miles of corridor into the terminal—where I discovered that I'd lost my
return ticket. Back down that endless corridor to the plane,
which we searched from stem to stern, to no avail. Back to the
terminal. Back to the plane, a little more sober now, for another search. Back to the terminal, where, just as I was about
to throw myself on the mercy of the Traveler's Aid Society as
an itinerant indigent, I felt some foreign object in my high-
heeled, pointy-toed frootboot. Sure enough, there was my
ticket, along with a tiny Old Grandad empty. Fred's mirth at
my expense almost got both of us busted right there in the terminal, New York cops being unaccustomed to jolly people at
seven o'clock in the morning.

Remarkably, we prevailed with the publisher too, and by
the time we were ready to fly back to California a few nights
later, we had our book deal locked up so tight that we decided
to celebrate by reserving seats on the helicopter down to Palo
Alto from the S.F. airport, so we called ahead to get someone
to meet us. And I'll not soon forget Fred's amazement and delight when we stepped off the copter in Pally and were greeted
by maybe forty or fifty Free U freaks in party finery, cheering
and waving signs that said stuff like "Welcome Home, Fred
'n' Ed!" and "Good Goin', Editor & Freditor!"

It was one of those rare times when Fred—visibly, judging
from the look of joy on his face as he stepped down from the

helicopter—had to admit to himself that people loved him, even if he didn't love himself. And I know that now we all wish we'd made sure there were more such moments in his life. But listen, you all: Fred knows it too, at last.

> xoxo,
> Ed

Endnote

The original idea behind the Free University movement was simple enough: great "real" universities being, essentially, mere elitist repositories of great minds, their faculties ought to "give something back" to the local communities they inhabited by going off-campus and offering free, ungraded, noncredit courses in their academic specialties to the poor, the disenfranchised, the working class, and the chronically alienated. The movement got its start somewhere back east—possibly at Columbia—but it quickly spread to most major American universities. And nowhere did it flourish more exuberantly than at Stanford in the late sixties.

The Midpeninsula Free University of Palo Alto (i.e., Stanford) began with the noble purpose outlined above, but in keeping with the populist, left-libertarian instincts of its founders and adherents, it soon evolved into a much more wide-open, anything-goes proposition. A $10 membership bought one not only the opportunity to sign up for any course(s) listed in the catalog but also the right to *offer* any course he or she felt competent to teach. The catalog listed courses in every discipline from Astral Projection to Explorations in Psychedelics; there were touchy-feely massage seminars and group-grope marathons, parapsychology workshops and encounter groups, *I Ching* study groups and Tarot-reading groups. The distinguished faculty included pacifists and Black Panthers, flower children and old Wobblies, Stanford professors and auto mechanics. In its peak years, the Midpeninsula Free U claimed more than a thousand members; it operated a restaurant, a head shop, and a free store; and most important of all, as far as I was concerned, it published this wildly eccentric magazine, the *Free You.*

When Fred Nelson, Jon Buckley (rumored to be a nephew of William F.), Gurney Norman, and I were editors of the *Free You,* our sole editorial precept was that never, under any circumstances whatsoever, would we reject *anything.* The magazine would be an open forum, available to all—"the only publication I know of," as Fred once put it, "where the readers are encouraged to climb in and become writers." Our editorial responsibility, as we understood it and undertook to exercise it, was just to make sure that every issue would include some stuff worth reading. To that end, we badgered our writer friends and acquaintances mercilessly for contributions and even, when we absolutely had to, wrote it ourselves.

Suddenly, then, I had a podium and a large, attentive, friendly audience; all that was left to me was to crank out a stem-winder every few weeks. It happened also to be the era during which Tom Wolfe and the so-called New Journalists were making such a stir, and I was eager to try my hand at these new forms. I learned (or taught myself) to write nonfiction in the pages of the *Free You;* two of the pieces I published there were reprinted several times in other publications, and both eventually became key chapters in *Famous People I Have Known.* During the early seventies, when my fiction seemed to be going nowhere, I sustained my career by writing, after the manner I'd cultivated in the *Free You,* what I called "personal journalism," mostly for *Playboy* and *Esquire.*

The anthology of *Free You* writing and art that Fred and I were flogging in New York included work by Robert Stone, Richard Brautigan, Ken Kesey, L. J. Davis, Thom Gunn,

Wendell Berry, Judith Rascoe, Speer Morgan, and my old friend Vic Lovell (who'd gone into the psychotherapy racket but hadn't managed to cure himself of the writing bug), not to mention the illustrious editors and many writers who— as writers—were never heard from again. It was published by Doubleday Anchor in 1973, under the title *One Lord, One Faith, One Cornbread.* Around three hundred copies were sold, at $2.95 per; the rest met an ignominious fate in the jaws of the shredder.

Mint-condition copies are now worth, according to last report, $150.

This review appeared in *Rolling Stone* (December 1971).

Richard Brautigan's *Revenge of the Lawn: Stories, 1962–1970*

Reviewed by Gurney Norman and Ed McClanahan

Gurney: The other day when the review copy of Richard Brautigan's new volume of stories came in the mail, Ed and I got into a discussion about whether or not Brautigan's stories belong to the literary genre formally known as "the short story." I said I thought they probably didn't, that they seemed to me too short to be short stories. (Of the sixty-two stories in the book, only half a dozen or so are over twenty-five hundred words long, and many are under five hundred.) Ed's reply to that was something like: Bullshit; Brautigan's stories are prime short stories, absolutely within the tradition of the modern epiphany as perfected in this century by writers like Joyce and Hemingway. Our separate halves of the hour of rap that followed seemed equally brilliant, though perhaps undermined a bit by the fact that neither of us had read the stories at the time. Since then we've both read them, and we both love them. But the question remains: are they "short stories" like your English teacher told you about short stories, or are they something else, something newer, perhaps something even better?

ED: As one of those very English teachers, I confess I fail to see what *length* has to do with it. Because although it's true that some of Richard's stories are indeed pretty short ("The Scarlatti Tilt," for instance, is thirty-seven words long, including the title), it's also true that in Hemingway's *The Fifth Column and the First Forty-nine Stories* there are at least half a dozen pieces that aren't appreciably longer. And you don't catch us English teachers going around saying *he* didn't write short stories.

GURNEY: As a matter of fact, though, length does have something to do with it. It's not everything, of course. It's not even the most important thing. But it is a factor. Length implies room for something to develop in. Character, action, ideas. I agree that it's possible to achieve development in thirty-seven words. But it's not usual. And even if it were usual, that's not what we're talking about. What we're talking about is whether or not Brautigan achieves development in the shortest of the pieces here. So let's look at one. Here's "Lint," fifty-two words long:

Lint
by Richard Brautigan

I'm haunted a little this evening by feelings that have no
vocabulary and events that should be explained in
dimensions of lint rather than words.

I've been examining half-scraps of my childhood. They are pieces of distant life that have no form or meaning. They are things that just happened like lint.

The thing I have in mind is that the term "short story" is a particular name of a particular literary form, like "haiku" or "sonnet." The dictionary says a haiku is "a Japanese verse form in three lines of five, seven, and five syllables, respectively." A sonnet is "a poem of fourteen decasyllabic lines." The short story is nowhere near as fixed and rigid as those two forms of poetry. Indeed, critics and writers have been disagreeing about the elements of the short story since the genre was invented. But there's a lot of agreement about the short story, too. There is agreement that it is a genre distinct in form from the ancient narrative modes like the tale, fable, parable, and so on. There is agreement that it began in the midnineteenth century with Poe in America and Gogol in Russia, and has evolved through masters like Chekhov, Turgenev, Frank O'Connor, Katherine Mansfield, and more recent Americans like Eudora Welty and Bernard Malamud, and dozens of others, of course. I realize all this sounds pretty English-Department. Is it relevant to Brautigan at all?

ED: Meanin' no disrespect, sir, but hell no, it ain't relevant. A "short story" is plainly and simply whatever a short-story writer *says* it is, because however convenient such descriptive labels may be for critics and academicians, the artist has no choice but to insist that insofar as they have any application at all to *his* work they must remain eternally, infinitely elastic. Otherwise, they're meaningless—worse, they're in the way. So when Richard Brautigan calls "Lint" a short story, he's not violating the term, he's merely *enlarging* it, just as he enlarged the meaning of the word *novel* when he said *Trout Fishing in*

America was one. Besides, the very fact that there is no "development" is precisely what "Lint" is all *about*. I mean the story's a perfect metaphor for itself, it's a Whole System, it excludes the very *possibility* of development!

And anyhow, why is it that so far we've mentioned only the two shortest, most constricted stories in the volume? If we don't watch it we're going to give our reader the badly mistaken notion that Brautigan is a miniaturist, that he'd just as well be putting in his time inscribing the Lord's Prayer on the heads of pins. How about a story like, say, "Forgiven," which is sure to take its place in the history of American literature as another "Big Two-Hearted River" in . . . uh . . . miniature?

GURNEY: Okay, it's your question, you answer it.

ED: Well, the thematic similarities between "Forgiven" and "Big Two-Hearted River" are as real as they are apparent: both are about solitary young men trout-fishing in streams in which they recognize some dark, mysterious power that fills them with a nameless dread when they feel it tugging at them. (Not uncharacteristically, Brautigan's sensitive, finely tuned hero flees the ominous place in panic, whereas Hemingway's Nick Adams permits himself only the merest hint of a mental shudder before he manfully turns his back on his forebodings and stalks away.) But the point is that in terms of both visual expansiveness and psychological complexity, "Forgiven" really does compare favorably to "Big Two-Hearted River." Just listen:

> *Below the second bridge, which looked like a white wooden angel, the Long Tom River flowed into very strange ways. It was dark and haunting and went something like this: Every hundred yards or so there was a large open swamp-like pool and then the river*

flowed out of the pool into a fast shallow run covered over closely
with trees like a shadowy knitted tunnel until it reached the next
swampy pool and very seldom did I let the Long Tom River call
me down into there.

Now it seems to me that the apparent simplicity of that passage is very deceptive, because for all its breathless brevity the language is emotionally powerful, the imagery rich and resonant. As a matter of fact, I think the density of the language throughout this volume provides the best defense to date against the argument that Brautigan's work is too often slight, fey, even cute. He is still Richard Brautigan, of course, and there are still moments when his natural impulse to be playful gets the upper hand and trivializes an idea. ("The Gathering of a Californian," for instance, is rendered almost indecipherable by such overly cunning similes as "like a metal-eating flower" and "like the Taj Mahal in the shape of a parking meter.") But by and large the language in this book has a density and power unequaled anywhere in his work, not even in *Trout Fishing in America,* and there is scarcely a page without at least one image—such as the "large unmade bed that looked as if it had been a partner to some of the saddest love-making this side of the Cross," or the Point Reyes Peninsula landscape "which of course unfolded like layers of abstraction and intimacy constantly being circled by hawks," or the senile old lapdog that "had been dying for so long that it had lost the way to death"—that if you yield to it, will break your heart.

GURNEY: I think your phrase "yield to it" is important, because Brautigan is not a hard-sell kind of writer. It's not his style to overload the senses. He very softly invites you into his fictional world. But once inside, indeed, your heart may well be broken, because within these apparently delicate pieces are people up against the ultimate issues of love, loneliness, and death.

"Coffee" is a story about loneliness. A man goes to visit a former girlfriend. She is not glad to see him. When he asks for a cup of coffee, she sets out a cup and a jar of instant coffee, puts water on to boil, then disappears into another room until he leaves. Then that night the man visits another ex-girlfriend. "What do you want?" she asks. "I want a cup of coffee." The second girl tells him where the instant is, then she too goes into the bedroom and closes the door behind her.

> *I looked down the hall into the kitchen. I didn't feel like going into the kitchen and having another cup of coffee by myself. I didn't feel like going to anybody else's house and asking them for a cup of coffee.*

The story is only four pages long, but this lonesome guy's world is so fully rendered that the reader is inevitably sucked into it and made to feel pretty damn lonely himself. The story is powerful because it's about experience that everyone can claim as his own. Everybody gets lonely from time to time. And practically everybody drinks coffee. Readers can't help but be affected subliminally by its repetition throughout the story (twenty-one times in four pages). After about the tenth time the reader is damn near salivating, longing for the warmth of the cup in his hands, the hot liquid on his tongue, the vitalizing influence of coffee in his system. He wants coffee like the protagonist wants coffee, which is to say, he wants love and warmth like the protagonist wants it, from *some*body on such a cold and lonely night as this.

ED: Exactly; it's the old shock-of-recognition trick, it's what pathos is all about, actually—epiphany too, for that matter—those painful, joyous moments when in the artist's experience, we recognize our own.

And that sense of recognition is just as vital to good comic writing—of which there's an abundance in this book—as it is to pathos. Consider the story "Complicated Banking Problems," for example: breathes there a man who, dropping by his bank to cash a small check, hasn't found himself standing impatiently in line behind his own version of Brautigan's little old lady in a long black coat (from which emanates a peculiar odor, "the first sign of a complicated banking problem") who insists on depositing in her savings account "the shadow of a refrigerator filled with sour milk and year-old carrots"?

Then too, of course, there is the other kind of comic writing, the rollicking, imaginative variety that depends on surprise and exaggeration, the sort of crazy, down-home burlesque that Faulkner and Flannery O'Connor—and Brautigan, it turns out—are so good at. Any reader who can make his way through the scene in "Revenge of the Lawn," Brautigan's title story, in which a gaggle of barnyard geese, having stoned themselves into a drunken stupor on sour mash in a moonshiner's basement, pass out and are taken for dead and plucked by the moonshiner's wife, only to awaken "in despair" with "devastating hangovers" and gather "in a forlorn and wobbly gang" in the front yard until the moonshiner drives up and, discovering the defrocked geese standing there beneath his pear tree "staring on like some helpless, primitive American advertisement for aspirin," smashes his automobile into the house and . . . well, anybody who can read *that* without cracking up wins my vote for the Grump of the Year award hands down.

GURNEY: I'm glad you cited Faulkner and Flannery O'Connor. I think you can go farther into Brautigan off of them than you can off of someone like Hemingway, who is a little too one-tracked in his attitudes and concerns to delight me forever. Hemingway doesn't laugh much, but you'd never say that about Faulkner, Flannery O'Connor, or Brautigan. Not that they are "happy" writers, by any means. Their fiction can be as heavy and as grotesque as life itself, but what's refreshing, as you say, is that they have a supreme comic sense as well as a tragic vision. They're double-edged, sharp on both sides.

The fascinating thing about Brautigan is that he's more than double-edged. He's got more edges, more places to grab hold, than anyone else I can think of now writing. He's a poet and a novelist and a short-story writer. And then he's something else besides. He's a curious kind of inventor, which takes me back to what I said earlier: that, to me, the short pieces like "Lint" and "The Scarlatti Tilt" do not fit the genre of the "short story" as I understand it, while "Coffee" and, say, "The World War I Los Angeles Airplane" (which encompasses an entire lifetime in five pages) and several others most certainly do. Brautigan is one of those rare writers who can operate *within* traditional form and *outside* it. Most writers place themselves in one camp or another, seeking either to master an inherited set of rules or else to discover new ones. A story like "Coffee" is a story out of settled literary places. But when he writes that curious "Lint," I think Brautigan is out on the frontier of something. He goes out, and then he comes back in again. He plays in the interface, at that special meeting place of underground and overground, of the familiar and the avant-garde. The tension between those opposing directions is one of the main sources of the energy behind the stories in this volume, stories about common things told in very uncommon ways.

I think it's in there somewhere that Brautigan's enormous popular success is explained. He's popular because he is a man peculiarly of his time and place. He's a very contemporary guy. He's a California writer, and his perception is "stoned." He gets *behind* the little episodes of these stories, gets into the emotion behind the action, in a way that more intellectual writers seem incapable of, or at least not very interested in. Feelings flow freely in Brautigan's fiction, sweet feelings as well as bitter ones, and that makes it a rare commodity in a country as violent and repressed as the United States. As a California writer he stands as a kind of gift from the West Coast to the rest of the nation, which, judging from the enormous circulation of his books, is a gift the country willingly accepts.

And *Revenge of the Lawn* is the latest of Brautigan's lovely gifts to us all.

ED: Well, I'm sure as hell not about to quarrel with you on that. But I wonder if you'd care to arm-wrestle for permanent possession of the review copy?

Endnote

I first heard of Richard Brautigan's work in 1967 when I came across a fragment of graffiti in, of all places, the faculty men's room of the Stanford English Department, which read enigmatically, "TROUT FISHING IN AMERICA *IS* THE GREAT AMERICAN NOVEL!" And sure enough, at least for the time being, it was! When I finally came across the book a few days later—and not in the outdoor sports section, either—I immediately fell for it ass-over-teacups, this cryptic, idiosyncratic, strangely poignant little haiku of a novel—perhaps I should say "novel," since I'd never read anything remotely like it in any genre—with its improbable title and its Zen sensibilities and sly, subtle humor. Nor were the men's room scholar and I alone in our enthusiasm, for within weeks, *Trout Fishing* was a national sensation, and Brautigan was a famous man.

During the next few years his fame was much enhanced by

his publisher's (or his publicist's, or his own) brilliant ploy of gracing the front cover of each new book with a photograph of its distinctively goofy-looking author—almost absurdly tall and lanky, with an immense Andy Gump mustache, granny glasses, and an outlandish hat—always accompanied by his current girlfriend, who was herself usually something of an eye-catcher. He changed girlfriends with every new edition—thereby making of his book jackets a sort of ongoing mini–soap opera, a prefiguration, perhaps, of today's Taster's Choice TV commercials.

(Curiously, when *Revenge of the Lawn* came out, they dropped Richard altogether from the picture in favor of a photo of his new girlfriend—a petite, pretty young woman with big, dark eyes and a winsome smile—all by herself. Nonetheless, the style of the cover was by then so familiar that one instantly recognized the book as the latest Brautigan, almost as though Richard were a ghostly presence haunting the photograph, as faint—and as indelible—as a premonition.)

At any rate, no one would ever dream of putting Gurney Norman and me in a soap opera, but we'd already been (as we still are) particular friends for many years, from our Bob Hazel days at UK; we'd both landed in California in the early sixties, thanks to mutual Stegner fellowships at Stanford, and both of us had somehow managed to hang on and become resident rustics in paradise. Eventually, we took neighboring twenty-five-dollar-a-month offices on the second floor of a derelict old Palo Alto office building known as the Poppycock, after the rock-'n'-roll-'n'-fish-'n'-chips joint downstairs. In 1970, we'd collaborated on a piece for *Esquire* about the new publishing phenomenon *The Whole Earth Catalog.* So when the opportunity to do it again presented itself—in the form of a review of *Revenge of the Lawn,* probably the only collaborative review between, say, Addison and Steele and Siskel and Ebert—we didn't have to think twice before we jumped at the chance.

I'd met Richard several times by then, at readings and parties, and I'd come to like him very much. He could be fey to the point of utter silliness (as when he insisted on reading "poems" by kindergartners to an audience of Stanford English majors) or as petulant as the veriest prima donna (as when he walked out of his own reading because a carpenter was rattling around backstage). But he was also sweet and charming and funny, and he enjoyed his newfound celebrity enormously and was rumored to delight above all things in lavishly entertaining his friends with the fruits of his success.

So when Richard liked our review enough to invite Gurney and me to lunch in San Francisco, biscuit mongers that we are, we could hardly wait. The day we were to go happened also to be the day our friend Ken Kesey was to fly in from Oregon for a two-day eminence-in-residence gig at Stanford. Ken planned to stay at my house in Palo Alto, and Gurney and I had agreed to pick him up at the airport late that afternoon; we'd have lunch with Richard, we figured, then hang around the city for a couple of hours, and meet Ken's 4:30 plane on our way home.

We neglected, however, to reckon with Richard's own agenda for the occasion, in accordance with which, when we arrived at his house in San Francisco at noon, our amiable host greeted his two jug-o'-Gallo Kentucky colonels with a spanking-new fifth of Maker's Mark bourbon at the ready. The cocktail hour, it seemed, was punching in a little previous that day.

It took Richard and me a good hour and a half of diminishingly coherent literary conversation to polish off the fifth. (Gurney was driving and, responsible citizen that he is, he wouldn't help us much.) Then the three of us hit the streets in a state of high bonhomie and somehow wended our way, under Richard's rather abstruse direction, to a big, fancy Japanese restaurant, where we tucked into a muchness of inscrutable Oriental comestibles while as the afternoon careened along, Richard and I steeped our faculties in martinis, sake, Pouilly-Fuissé—Richard *loved* Pouilly-Fuissé—topped off with a beaker or three of Courvoisier, and generally had ourselves a raraparooza of a fine old time.

Everybody knows that tempus fugits when you're having whatever gets you off, so four o'clock shouldn't have come as quite so much of a surprise—but suddenly Gurney and I are saying, Uh, lissen, Richard, we hate to eat and run, but we gotta get to the airport, see, to pick up Kesey, so we'd better . . . And Richard sez, Kesey? Hey, I'll go with you! And we sez, Sure, fine, but, um, what then? And Richard sez, Why, we'll come back to the city and . . . and go out to dinner!

So that's what we did. We left the Japanese restaurant and hightailed it down the Bayshore Freeway in Gurney's VW bus and scooped up Ken at the airport and hightailed it back up to San Francisco and went out to dinner at a *Chinese* restaurant.

But did I mention that no sooner was Ken in the bus than we were wreathed in the sickly sweet blue smaze of the dread devil weed? Or that upon our return to San Francisco we did make a quick pit stop at a liquor store for yet another celebratory fifth of Maker's Mark? Or that this naturally required us to drop by Richard's house again in order to drink it?

While we were there, Richard called the aforementioned current girlfriend—i.e., the *Revenge* girlfriend—and invited her to join our happy number. She turned out to be a young San Francisco schoolteacher named Sherry—altogether as winsome as she'd been on the cover of the book—who'd come west from, of all places, Louisville, Kentucky! This development occasioned many a toast to southern womanhood, to such an extent that this bottle of Maker's also shortly disappeared to the very last drop. Once again, the incorruptible Gurney had declined to help us much, so Ken and Richard and I resigned ourselves to carrying the load.

After that, it got a little drunk out. Richard called ahead to the Chinese restaurant and reserved a huge booth and ordered up a feast called, cross my heart, The Feast, which to my befuckled and befoggled recollection consisted largely of several great big fishes staring stonily up at me from bright red platters, and yet another deluge of what I was by then referring to as Pooly-Foosy or, alternatively, Fooly-Poosy.

Afterward, we somehow made our way to Enrico's, a North Beach sidewalk café where the main attraction (aside from the Irish coffee, of which we soon put away an insupportable quantity) is in spotting cheesy local celebrities among the passersby. "There goes Mel Belli!" the patrons would cry. "There goes Carol Doda! There go the Mitchell Brothers!" Along about the third or fourth Irish coffee, Richard decided—let's assume unjustly—that Ken was hitting on Sherry, and took umbrage, and fell into a pout. I, meanwhile, was seeing celebrities who weren't even there: "There goes Ambrose Bierce! There goes Bishop Pike!"

Gurney, that Philistine, had long since gone off for a meditative stroll around North Beach. His meanderings eventually brought him back past Enrico's, whereupon Richard Brautigan and Ken Kesey—despite their differences—leapt to their feet in unison and cried in a single voice, "There goes Gurney Norman!" Gurney swears he didn't plan it that way, but I don't intend to believe him until he agrees to forget that I rode all the way home to Palo Alto that night with my head in his lap, while Ken snored mightily in the backseat.

Gurney awakened us from our slumbers by some stratagem like hollering "Fire! Fire!" as he pulled into my driveway,
and then politely reminded us not to let the car door hit us in
the ass as we got out. Ken and I, roaring like a pair of Vikings
on shore leave, staggered into the house and caroused our way
as far as the kitchen, where we somehow got our several legs
entangled and went crashing to the floor, four hundred and
fifty pounds of authorial omniscience rattling that big old
redwood barn right to the rafters and alerting my entire
household to the stately and dignified return of the lord of the
manor and his distinguished guest.

Twelve hours later, when I came to, there was much—very
much—of the preceding day that had escaped my memory,
but one thing remained luminously clear: from the first Oriental inscrutables to the last Irish coffee, from the first drop of
Maker's Mark to the last drop of Poozley-Foozley, Richard
had paid for *everything*.

I saw Richard two or three times over the next few years,
the last in Livingston, Montana, in 1975 when I was teaching
at the University of Montana in Missoula. I was in Livingston for an overnight visit with my writer friend Bill "Gatz"
Hjortsberg and his wife, Marian, who were part of the community of writers, artists, and Hollywood expatriates that
had assembled there around the novelist and film director
Tom McGuane. Richard's success had by that time bought
him hideaways both in Bolinas, on the California coast north
of San Francisco, and in Livingston, where he had a place just
down the road from the Hjortsbergs' little spread.

So okay, I admit that Gatz and Richard and I did go out
drinking that night, but there's no particular reason to subject
my hungover reader to still more boozy hijinks. I will mention, though, that the next morning I had coffee with Richard
in his writing room in the loft of a stable on his ranch, and he

showed me an enormous handgun and pointed out the bullet holes he'd blasted in the walls and ceiling. At the time, I got a good chuckle out of this latest Brautigan eccentricity, but that moment would become, in later years, a disquieting and painful memory.

In 1976 I moved back home to Kentucky permanently. I pretty much lost touch with Richard after that, although I did occasionally hear about him over the years, via West Coast and Montana friends. By the early eighties, the word was that he wasn't doing so hot; his career hadn't been going well, and neither had his love life. His attempt at a screenplay hadn't worked out, sales of his books were in decline, and there'd been an unfortunate marriage followed by the inevitable expensive divorce.

In 1984, when I was living in the tiny northern Kentucky community of Port Royal, I got a phone call one day from, of all people, Sherry. Amazingly, she and her new husband had just moved into a house about a mile down the road from me. After we recovered from our astonishment at the mysterious workings of a destiny that would bring the two of us, who had crossed paths just once on a crazy night fourteen years before, back together on a microscopic dot on the planet twenty-five hundred miles from where we'd met, I finally got around to asking what she'd heard from Richard lately.

Well, she said, I hate to tell you this, but the day before yesterday I got a call from an old friend of Richard's, and he told me that Richard . . . died.

C'mon! I said. Richard's dead? What happened?

Well, said Sherry, they found him in his house in Bolinas. They say he shot himself.

A REVIEW FOR *Place* MAGAZINE (SUMMER 1973) OF KRASSNER'S FIRST COLLECTION, *How a Satirical Editor Became a Yippie Conspirator in Ten Easy Years* (PUTNAM, 1971).

Zen Bastard to the Rescue:
A Tip of the McClanahat
to Paul Krassner

THE MAN WHO, as the curtain closed on the opening-night performance of the antiwar play *Macbird,* leapt to his feet and shouted, "Fuck you, Walter Kerr!" The man who, in a black suit and a clerical collar, soul-kissed a nun (actually celebrated hooker Margo St. James) in the lobby of the San Francisco International Airport, while dozens of dumbstruck travelers stood a-gaping. The man of whom the late American Nazi party *Kommandant* George Lincoln Rockwell once said, "You got balls of steel. For a Jew, you shoulda been a Nazi."

Paul Krassner: the best satirical journalist in America.

The terms ordinarily applied to satirists—"irreverent," "iconoclastic," even "scurrilous"—are as inadequate as a description of Krassner as "felon" is to describe Charles Manson or "religious" to describe Jesus Christ. Next to the social, cultural, and political satire he has been publishing for the past dozen years in his magazine *The Realist*—the best of which is collected here—such popular wits as Mort Sahl and Russell Baker seem as bland as mush, milk toast turning soggy in the curdling milk of sacred cows.

Krassner is a latter-day Twain, a priapic Mencken; in his own time his only peer was his dear departed friend Lenny Bruce—whose obituary Krassner wrote and published a full two years before Bruce's death so that (as he told Bruce at the time) "when you *really* die, my reaction will be pure, I won't have to think, on some level of consciousness, 'Oh, shit, now I'll have to write an obituary.'"

The Realist—of which Krassner is founder, publisher, editor, chief correspondent, and (according to the current issue's masthead) "Zen Bastard"—made its debut in 1958, at the height of the first post-McCarthy wave of anti-Communist hysteria ("I've come to ask you to stop harping about H-bomb tests," says John Foster Dulles to Bertrand Russell in an imaginary dialogue in one of those early issues. "You're only aiding the Communist cause."), and it has been resolutely, fearlessly chronicling the Twentieth-Century Nightmare ever since.

In the early sixties, Krassner published crusading super-atheist Madalyn Murray O'Hair's attacks on the repressive authoritarianism of the Catholic establishment, himself conjecturing that "so-called 'flying saucers' are actually diaphragms dropped by nuns on their way to Heaven." In 1962, when Adolf Eichmann was languishing in an Israeli jail cell awaiting execution, Krassner published the "rumor" that Eichmann had written a song entitled "If I Knew You Were Coming, I'd Have Baked a Kike," and marveled in print at "how all the Caryl Chessman fans finked out on Adolf Eichmann." He was on hand again in 1964, when Leary and Al-

pert were offering consciousness-expansion seminars at Mill-
brook ("I'm a terrible failure when it comes to meditation. All
I do is sit there and say to myself, 'Well, here I am, meditating
. . . yup . . . that's the way it goes . . .'"). And he was with the
Yippies in Chicago in 1968, wondering "how many years can
[we] go on listening to General Westmoreland say that we
have to continue the bombing as long as they keep using those
antiaircraft guns?" and fantasizing an apocalyptic TV spec-
tacular ("Joe Pyne engages in a wooden-leg duel with Al
Capp . . . The Flying Nun goes down on Johnny Carson . . .
Nelson Rockefeller cheekily applies the new TV pancake
makeup Bishop Sheen to Richard Nixon's jowls . . . The Fed-
eral Marshalls' Atonal Chorale and Percussion Ensemble, ac-
companying themselves on their children's skulls with nightsticks, sing the ever-beautiful 'Where Have All the Flowers
Gone?'"), and at last concluding, wearily but intrepidly,
"Fuck them, O Lord, they know *exactly* what they do!"

But *The Realist*'s most audacious caper was the 1967 publication of a piece entitled "The Parts That Were Left Out of
the Kennedy Book," in which Krassner describes, brilliantly
re-creating William Manchester's turgid, homogenized
prose style, Jacqueline Kennedy's discovery of Lyndon Johnson standing over the president's coffin performing an act
someone other than myself has described as "neckrophilia"
upon the wound in her slain husband's throat.

"It was," Krassner wrote later by way of explaining why
he'd perpetrated the hoax, "the mutual simultaneous culmination of Jackie's and Lyndon's consciousnesses."

The response to the piece was exactly what Krassner, taking Swift's *A Modest Proposal* as his catechism, had known all
along it would be, which is to say that it ranged from cautious
acceptance ("One can never be quite certain," wrote one
critic, "how much of the revealing journalism is Krassner's

imagination, and how much is plain fact . . .") to querulous disputation ("The body of JFK was supposedly in a casket," a doctor in London opined; "therefore, short of lifting out the corpse, an act of inverted para-fellatio would be physically impossible") to outraged *denial* ("The incident, of course, never took place," sputtered UPI columnist Merriman Smith). Thereby proving once again that (as one of Krassner's readers pointed out) when William Blake said, "Everything possible to be believed is an image of the truth," he sure knew what he was talking about.

In any case, it's Krassner, as usual, who gets the last word on the matter: to an interviewer who asked if he "really condoned necrophilia," he replied, "Yes, but only between consenting adults." And besides, he added later, "for all we know, it might have been an act of love."

In the main, though, Krassner is so acutely alert to the already existent madness that rules all our lives that he has little need to inspire more of it. "Was it my fault," he pleads, his shrewdness masked in wide-eyed innocence, "that when Pope Paul visited this country, the band at Kennedy Airport played 'Hello, Dolly'?"

Thus it was that back in 1966, when *Time* magazine "discovered" a faintly malodorous American literary phenomenon it called "black humor" and identified Krassner as a leading practitioner of that unholy art, he explained, again a little wearily, that "black humor is in bad taste by definition because it's about the way life *is,* and life happens to be in bad taste."

Endnote

I met Paul in 1971, when he came to California to co-edit, with Kesey, *The Last Supplement to the Whole Earth Catalog*. I liked him instantly; anybody would. An elfin, bright-eyed little guy with a mop of dark, curly hair, a knowing grin, and a wicked sense of humor ("Rumpleforeskin," he sometimes dubbed himself), he is without exception the funniest, most entertaining person I've ever been around. By turns wiseacre and wise man, cherub and imp of Satan, Norman Mailer's former son-in-law and Larry Flynt's former stand-in as publisher of *Hustler*, he may also be the nearest thing to a saint the American Left can claim.

But (this is a commercial) don't take my word for it; see for yourself. Paul, in his dotage, has taken to doing stand-up comedy, and a couple of kick-ass funny CDs of his act are afloat in the world, as well as three chock-full-o'-chuckles collections of his writing. And to the amazement of none who really know him, he's still publishing *The Realist* and resolutely intends to do so throughout the raggedy-ass remnants of the millennium—thirteen final issues, he says, and you can get 'em all (either one at a time as they come out, or all in a wad after the fact) by sending twenty-five bucks to: *The Realist,* Box 1230, Venice, CA 90294. It's a steal.

The main body of this piece appeared, in somewhat different form, in *Playboy* (March 1972). The "Brief Exegesis" of the lyrics of "New Speedway Boogie" appeared separately in *The Last Supplement to the Whole Earth Catalog* (March 1971).

Grateful Dead
I Have Known

If you've got it all together,
what's that all around it?
Inscribed on my bathroom wall by Ken Kesey,
who attributes it to Brother Dave Gardner

A BRIGHT SUNDAY afternoon in August 1971, just one week after Bill Graham closed the doors of the Fillmore West forever and ever, and I'm sitting in the living room of Jerry Garcia's new house on the headlands above a coastal village an hour north of San Francisco (a very nice house, by the way, not luxurious or anything, but altogether nice enough to reflect the Grateful Dead's rising fortunes during the past couple of years); and if I were to glance over my shoulder, I could see beyond the picture window all the way down the tilting rim of the continent to the shimmering Pacific. Only right this minute, I'm not into scenery at *all;* right this minute I'm deeply engaged in being paranoid about my tape recorder, just sort of *stroking* the treacherous little bastard before I entrust to its tape-eating maw the wit and wisdom of Jerry Garcia, lead guitarist and chief philosophical theoretician of what some claim is the greatest rock-'n'-roll band in the world—Captain Trips, they call him.

Jerry, meanwhile, is doing exactly what he always does— playing it as it lays, which right now means sitting there beside me in his rocking chair, gazing benignly out the window, beaming within the dark nimbus of his hair and beard like a stoned-out John the Baptist, waiting.

"What I'd like to do," I'm prattling, rather desperately trying to fill with the sound of my own voice the void my incompetence has created, "I'd like to feel free to take as many liberties with this interview as I've been taking with the rest of the material, to, uh, interpolate and rearrange things here and there when it seems . . . But maybe you . . . ?"

"Sure," Jerry says cheerily, waving aside my question. "You're gonna lie a little, you mean. Sure, you can say I said anything you feel like. I don't give a shit."

"Good deal! Because what I'm planning to do, see, is to take this interview and sort of write myself out of it, my own voice, I mean, so that what's left will be just *your* voice, disembodied, just rapping out loud. Like, for instance, did you happen to read John Sack's interviews with Lieutenant Calley? Do you remember how Sack himself isn't really a *presence* there, how it comes down as if it were just Calley alone, telling his own story? That sort of thing. And then I'll just take your voice and weave it through the piece, probably in italics or something, just lacing it in and out wherever it seems . . ."

Jerry grins and says, *"Sure, feel free, whatever. Only the erroneous assumption in that, see, is that a guy like Calley might ever*

volunteer any information at all. Or me, for that matter. I mean,
nobody ever hears about some of the shit that comes out in inter-
views unless somebody asks me, you know what I mean? In fact,
it's like the basis of the reality from which you write, because you
wouldn't write this thing if you'd never talked to any of us, would
you? I mean, you know what I mean? If you weren't interacting in
there, the story would never have occurred. So it's like you can in-
clude yourself or not, but either way, it's all you. . . ."

· · ·

OK, then—*me,* by God:

So there I am in September 1970, early morning, and I'm
hurrying home to California to write about the Grateful
Dead after a three-week hiatus back East, barreling along in
my big Dodge camper all alone through the everlasting vasty
reaches of central Iowa, on a back road forty miles in some direction or another from Cedar Rapids, and it's raining like a
cow pissing on a flat rock, a cold, driving rain that chills me
even with the camper's heater ramming hot air up both pants
legs; and beside me on the hump of the engine's housing are
spread my Official Accuracy Reporter's Notebooks filled with
overwrought, three-week-old scribblings (garcia missing 2
joints midl. finger rt. hand!—phil lesh leanness *lincolnesk!*—
sam cutler rd. mgr. look like capt. hook!!—bob weir billy the
kid!!—john mcintyre bus. mgr. *elegant,* look like yng. *rich*
widmark!!!!), and several yellowing copies of *Rolling Stone*
featuring articles about the Dead, and my little portable stereo tape recorder and five cassettes of the Dead's albums,
and—here comes the weird part—on my head I'm wearing,
Buck Rogers–like, an enormous pair of superpowerful stereo
headphones plugged into the recorder, and the volume is
turned up full blast, and the Dead's "Turn it *on*! Turn it *on*!"
is crashing into my eardrums, and I'm bouncing ecstatically

in my seat and hammering the heels of my hands on the steering wheel to Bill the Drummer's surging nineteen-to-the-dozen rhythms, while the guitars scream as loud as locomotive whistles; and now an image swirls to mind and shapes itself: the interior of my skull has somehow become the interior of the Fillmore West, San Francisco's onetime Carousel Ballroom, this cavernous old relic of a pleasure palace amid whose tawdry grandeur our forebears forbore Guy Lombardo and Shep Fields and His Rippling Rhythms that we might live to dig the Dead, my throat and tongue the Fillmore's threadbare maroon-carpeted lobbies and stairwells and my teeth its curlicuing rococo plaster balustrades and my brainpan the grand ballroom itself, my medulla oblongata its vaulted ceiling festooned with heavily sagging billows of silvery-gray asbestos damask, and there are three thousand dope-crazed Dead fans crouched haunch to haunch in the darkness on the immense dance floor of my mind, while at the far end of the great chamber, onstage, dwarfed beneath the high, curved, bleached-white band shell that is the inner surface of my forehead, the Grateful Dead are getting it on, a demon-driven suicide squad of assassins under the harsh command of the archbrigand Pigpen ("*Turn* it on! Jes a leetle bit hi-eee-yer!"), a murderous little band of renegades, savages, tartars in cowboy mufti, angels of death armed not with three super-charged guitars and a set of traps but with three choppers and a mortar, mercilessly laying waste to the shrieking, writhing mass of defenseless supplicants spread beneath them, and against the backs of my eyeballs the giant light-show screen behind the bandstand is ablaze like the night sky above a battlefield with the garish lightning of their fusillade; it is more than just a massacre, it is a by-God *apocalypse* hurtling along right here inside the fragile eggshell of my skull at seventy

miles an hour through the Iowa monsoon, the incredible cacophony of it thrumming in my blood and beating wildly
against the backs of my eyes, mounting and mounting and
mounting until it peaks out at about eleven million mega-
decibels, and Pig screams, *"Yeeeeeeeeeee-o-o-o-o-o-o-o-o-o-o-o-
owwwwwwwwwwwwww!"* and barks, "And *leave* it on!" and
within the headphones there descends an abrupt and wondrous stillness, a silence made infinitely deeper and more
profound by the absence not merely of the Dead's righteous
racket but of *all* sound, the headphones baffling out even the
engine's roar along with the slap-slap-slap of the wipers and
the steady suck of tires on the flooded roadbed, as if the whole
wet world were inexplicably and without warning stricken
mute, and as the wipers streak the veil of water on the windshield, I see, standing stalwart by the lonely Iowa roadside
like heaven's own herald, an enormous billboard, sky blue,
with great, thick, square white letters proclaiming, for no
good reason at all,

TIME ENDS

ETERNITY WHERE

and even as the windblown water sheets the glass again, blur-
ring, then fracturing the image beyond all intelligence, I hear
Jerry Garcia begin the next song on the tape, his voice rising
sweet and clear and plangent into the silence:

> You know Death don't
> Have no mercy
> In this land. . . .

• • •

*"I mean, everybody who's makin' a big thing about the closing of
the Fillmore, that's a crock of shit, actually. Because, you know,*

what'd they do before there was a Fillmore? I mean, there's always been a musician scene, musicians have always traveled around, and you could always hear music. And that's gonna happen no matter what. In most places, see, there isn't any Fillmore. And that doesn't affect anybody except, you know, the Fillmore freaks. I think the end of the Fillmore is just the beginning of different space."

.   .   .

"The first time I saw Jerry Garcia," my young friend Harry (who is said to be a genius in molecular physics, his major at Stanford, but nonetheless retains a certain charming innocence in matters of the spirit) was telling me the other day, "was in the Straight Theater up in the Haight in '67. I'd never even *heard* the Grateful Dead except on the radio; I was just beginning to find out about the head scene in those days. But I just loved their music. And when they came on that night— I remembered the light show was all these yellow, swirling things going all the way up to the ceiling; it was like *sunshine*—I went up to the front by the stage and stood there lookin' up at Jerry, and I was thinkin' how I'd just never *seen* anyone like this before, this far-out, mellow dude just playin' that rock 'n' roll, the notes so clear and uncluttered, a beautiful, sparkling thing, you know? And so I looked up at Garcia, and I just couldn't *help* but smile, it was just that . . . the *calm* on his face, it was like a Buddha, you know, like you can see where the Buddha is *at*, Nirvana, you know . . . and Jerry saw me lookin' at him, saw me smiling, and *he* smiled at *me*! And that just blew my mind! It was so *different*; this dude was just so *different*. I mean, before that I could *never* have smiled at a rock musician; they were all guys who were just showing off. 'I'm the big stud,' you know. It was all just a big *pose* kind of trip with them, showing off for their chicks and the audience, being tough guys. But *this* dude—I mean, you could relate to him *directly,* with just your *eyes* that way. . . ."

•   •   •

It's a late-July Saturday night backstage at the Fillmore West, and out front the Grateful Dead are blasting away on the third and final set of the evening, but I alone of all the three thousand mind-blown music lovers in the hall can't hear them, not at this particular moment anyhow, because my head has just now bottomed out of one of those bottomless nitrous oxide tailspins and is only just beginning its swifter-than-the-speed-of-sound ascent, whizzing upward toward a reality I'd just as lief not hurry to confront, thanks all the same, this tiny overheated broom closet of a dressing room with six or seven freaks (foremost among them Zonk the Gasman and his faithful chrome-plated sidekick the Tank, that immortal pair to whose mutual beneficence the rest of us owe this glorious occasion) laid out on the floor in one or another stage of laughing-gas hog-wildness, grunting and groveling and slobbering and scuffling for the hose like so many French pigs rooting after the Ultimate Truffle (one spaced-out little groupie has had about twelve separate and distinct sets of convulsions in the past half hour, so many that her seizures have become part of the decor of the high; we anticipate them now, and when it's her turn to toke on the hose, we observe her as coolly as if her drooling rictus and spasmodic shudderings have been provided by the management for our amusement between our own tokes), and up there in the real world, where this particular gas flash is about to surface, I'll be obliged to open my eyes again and deal with the dismal fact that the Dead's final set is well under way and I have yet to really listen to a note they've played all evening, not to mention the equally onerous fact that my tape recorder and my brand-new Official Accuracy Reporter's Notebooks are lost somewhere amid the melee at my feet (I've somehow succeeded, by the way, in commandeering the only chair in the room, an overstuffed old number that's just right for doing nitrous oxide in, since it's so thoroughly rump-sprung I can't possibly fall out of it), and sooner or later I'm going to have to dig them out—the ignominious tools of this ignoble trade, I mean—and Get Down to Bidness, fall by the nearest phone booth and slip into my Front-Page Farrell suit so that when the Dead have wrapped up this set, I'll be all primed and cocked to zap them with the ole five Ws, the way Miss Parsons taught us in high school journalism (Who-What-Where-When-Why-and-sometimes-How-are-you, Grateful Dead?), when suddenly my head pops through the surface of my consciousness like the bobber on a fishing line that has just been gnawed in two by the Big One That Got Away, and the sound of the Dead catches up to me all in one great roaring rush, the voice of Jerry Garcia amplified to boiler-factory rumbustiousness yet still somehow as sweet and gentle as the purest babbling branch water, chiding me:

> Please don't dominate the rap, Jack,
> If you got nothin' new to say. . . .

Oh, well, I tell myself happily, settling back into the welcoming embrace of my armchair, probably Jerry's got the right idea there; probably I'd better just have me one or two more tastes on them there noxious gases, just to clear my head, and then I can go out there nice and fresh, all primed and cocked to . . .

. . .

SCENE: *The Dead's business office in San Rafael, where* BOB HUNTER, *the Dead's lyricist, has just been telling everybody about a friend recently returned from a trip to Cuba. Enter* RAMROD, *one of the band's equipment handlers.*

HUNTER: Hey, you know who so-and-so talked to? Fidel Castro!

RAMROD: Yeah? Far out! How'd he get his number?

• • •

Now, the first time *I* ever saw Jerry Garcia was in midwinter 1965, in Ken Kesey's house up in La Honda. I'm lounging around Kesey's living room, see, and this extraordinarily curious-looking party comes shuffling through. In point of fact, he's the very first true freak I've ever laid eyes on, this somewhat rotund young man with a hairdo like a dust mop dipped in coal tar, and after he's gone, Kesey says, "That was Jerry Garcia; he's got a rock-'n'-roll band that's gonna play with us this Saturday night at the San Jose Acid Test. Their name is the Warlocks, but they're gonna change it to the Grateful Dead."

At the time, to tell the truth, I wasn't exactly galvanized with excitement by this bit of news; after all, only a few Saturday nights before that, I'd attended what I've since come to regard as the Olde *Original* Acid Test, a curiously disjointed but otherwise perfectly ordinary party at Kesey's house featuring nothing more startling than an abundance of dope and a drunken Berkeley poet who kept loudly reciting Dylan Thomas and, at midnight (hours after I'd gone home, adept as ever at missing the main event), the ritual sacrifice and subsequent immolation of a chicken.

But what I didn't know then was that four hundred people

would turn up for the San Jose Acid Test, which begat the Palo Alto Acid Test, which begat the Fillmore Acid Test, which begat the Trips Festival, which begat Bill Graham, who (to hear *him* tell it, anyhow) begat Life As We Know It. Still, like I said, I couldn't possibly have known that at the . . .

· · ·

Michael Lydon (in *Rolling Stone*) on Jerry Garcia: "Some call Jerry a guru, but that doesn't mean much; he is just one of those extraordinary human beings who looks you right in the eyes, smiles encouragement and waits for you to become yourself. However complex, he is entirely open and unenigmatic. He can be vain, self-assertive and even pompous, but he doesn't fool around with false apology. More than anything else he is cheery—mordant and ironic at times, but undauntedly optimistic. He's been through thinking life is but a joke, but it's still a game to be played with relish and passionately enjoyed. Probably really ugly as a kid—lumpy, fat-faced and frizzy-haired—he is now beautiful, his trimmed hair and beard a dense black aureole around his beaming eyes. His body has an even grace, his face a restless eagerness, and a gentleness, not to be confused with 'niceness,' is his manner. His intelligence is quick and precise and he can be devastatingly articulate, his dancing hands playing perfect accompaniment to his words."

· · ·

"The thing about us, I guess, is that we're not really layin' anything on anybody. I mean if you're tellin' people directly how to 'be right,' how to act, how to do, if you're talkin' to people on that level, then the kind of feedback you get is gonna be more of, like, 'You promised me this, man; now, where is it?' It's the I–demand–to–

speak-to-John-Lennon-personally syndrome. Like, one time this guy came into our office, this fucked-up guy, just walked right up and started staring at me in this intense way, man, and he was so heavy, it was as if he was about to say something really important, you know, really urgent; he looked like he was on the verge of exploding or something, and finally he says, 'Listen, when are you guys gonna get it on, man? Because you know Scientology's got a good head start!' But it's just the price you pay for standin' up in public; you get stuff comin' back at you, and if you're a little fucked up yourself, you get fucked-up feedback, that's all."

· · ·

**A Brief Exegesis of
Certain Sociophilosophical Themes
in Robert Hunter's Lyrics to
"New Speedway Boogie"
by Edward P. McClanahan, B.A., M.A.**

The Grateful Dead were deeply involved in planning the Rolling Stone's disastrous Altamont concert—they were the ones, according to most sources, who suggested that the Hell's Angels be employed to police the area around the stage—and Robert Hunter's lyrics to "New Speedway Boogie" may properly be regarded as their "official" public statement about the meaning of the grisly events of that unhappy day.

First, then, the lyrics, as sung by Jerry Garcia on the album *Workingman's Dead:*

Please don't dominate the rap, Jack,
If you got nothin' new to say.
If you please, don't back up the track;
This train's got to run today.

I spent a little time on the mountain,
Spent a little time on the hill.
Like some say, better run away;
Others say better stand still.

Now I don't know, but I been told,
It's hard to run with the weight of gold.
Other hand, I've heard it said,
It's just as hard with the weight of lead.

Who can deny, who can deny
It's not just a change in style.
One step's done, and another begun,
And I wonder how many miles.

I spent a little time on the mountain,
Spent a little time on the hill.
Things went down we don't understand,
But I think in time we will.

Now I don't know, but I was told,
In the heat of the sun, a man died of cold.
Keep on comin' or stand and wait,
With the sun so dark and the hour so late....

You can't overlook the lack, Jack,
Of any other highway to ride.
It's got no signs or dividin' lines,
And very few rules to guide.

I spent a little time on the mountain,
Spent a little time on the hill.
I saw things gettin' out of hand;
I guess they always will.

Now I don't know, but I been told,
If the horse don't pull, you got to carry the load.
I don't know whose back's that strong;
Maybe find out before too long.

One way or another,
One way or another,
One way or another,
This darkness got to give.

The song is, on the one hand, an expression of apprehensiveness and confusion and, on the other, an exhortation to a new order of wisdom, a higher and truer vision. However, unlike the authors of most of the journalistic postmortems on the Altamont debacle (especially those handwringers and breast-beaters who insist on "dominating the rap" even though they "got nothin' new to say"), Hunter is not of the Altamont-as-Armageddon persuasion, and he does not agree that the quest after salvation—the voyage that began in the Haight-Ashbury and carried us all the way to Woodstock—has dead-ended at last in the molten yellow hills of California just twenty miles east of where it started, impaled on the point of a Hell's Angel's rusty blade, skewered there like one of those suicidal Siamese frogs that travel great distances only to fling themselves upon the spikes of some rare thornbush. Rather, the poet suggests, the journey has only just begun, and the way is long and arduous and fraught with peril; Altamont is but one dark moment in . . .

• • •

Another summer Sunday afternoon and I'm driving up to Marin County to see a softball game between—get this—the Grateful Dead and the Jefferson Airplane, and just before I get on the Golden Gate Bridge, I pick up this most remarkably scroungy, stringy-haired, snaggletoothed hippie hitchhiker—"Wheat Germ," he called himself, I swear he did—who says he is bound for Sausalito, and in the slow Sunday bridge traffic I fire up a doobie and rather grandly offer him a hit, all the while coming on (I admit it, I'm freakdom's own Major Hoople) absolutely shamelessly about the Great Mo-

ment in Sports that the editors of a certain Nationally
Known Publication have prevailed upon me to cover for them
this afternoon, and Wheat Germ coolly takes his toke and
lays a fat smoke ring against the windshield and then goes for
the inside pocket of his ragtag old Goodwill Bargain Basement tweed hacking jacket and outs with ... gasp! ... a
badge? a *gun*? No, just a saddle-soap tin, the kind that's about
twice as big around as a Kiwi can, which he extends to me the
way one might proffer a tin of lozenges, and I see that it's full
of these little purple tablets, *thousands* of them, tiny lavender
pastilles that slither around inside the can like collar buttons
when Wheat Germ shakes them gently, saying, through a
sudden spray of spittle so dense that as his excitement rises, I
can sometimes almost make out a rainbow in it, "Serve yourself, dad. Go on, take some. Shit, yeah, all you want. Me and
my brother Yogurt's got a factory up in Sausalito puts out
seven hunnert of these tabs an hour. It's good acid, man. I
mean, I've moved over six million dollars' worth of dope in
the last three years and nobody's got burnt yet!"

Yogurt? Six million?

"Shit yeah, over that. And that don't even *count* the ship-
load of hash the Interpol narcs shot out from under us down
at Yucatán last month! Them Interpol pigs, man, they're all a
bunch of Commies or somethin'. Fifteen hunnert keys, man,
straight to the bottom of the Pacific!" (The Pacific? Uh, say
there, Wheat Germ, Yucatán is ...) "Shit, yeah, I mean they
tar-*petered* the mother, man! But I don't give a shit. I got me a
crew down there right now, divin' for it. I mean, I'll get the
bastid back, fucking-A dig it, dad. I deal for all the *big*
people, see, the really *heavy* dudes. I mean, Janis and me was
just like *that,* dig, and whenever I need anything done, I just
... I mean, I got people all over the fuckin' country workin'

for me, man, in my organization. The syndicate, me and Yogurt call it, hee-hee-hee. Listen, man, are you *sure* you can't use a hit of this acid? Because I was just thinkin', you know, I wouldn't too much mind doin' a little dealin' to them guys, the Dead and the Airplane." He pauses long enough to glance down at the array of Official Accuracy Reporter's Notebooks spread between us on the engine housing, and adds, "Reporter, huh? I can dig it. What are you, dad, a sportswriter or somethin'?"

• • •

"I don't have too much trouble with that kinda stuff, dealers and guys like that. Because I think there's a thing to it, like bein' able to say, 'No, man, I don't feel like goin' on that kinda trip today.' And when you learn how to do it, you just don't find yourself in those situations very often. And it's not necessarily to be putting somebody down or even to be turning down some kind of energy exchange or whatever; it's just learning to assume that everybody can understand everything and just tryin' to communicate with that principle always in mind. So I don't have too much trouble with those guys, actually. . . ."

• • •

Anyhow, I didn't go to the San Jose Acid Test. But a few Saturday nights later I did make it over to a ratty old nightclub called Ben's Big Beat, in the mudflats beside the Bayshore Freeway, for the Palo Alto Acid Test; and the what's-their-names, the Grateful Dead, they were there, too, Jerry Garcia plucking strange sonic atonalities out of his Magic Twanger, backed up by a pair of cherubic-looking boys named Phil Lesh, on bass guitar, and Bobby Weir, on rhythm guitar, and a drummer—Bill Kreutzmann—who looked so young and

innocent and fresh-faced that one's first impulse was to wonder how he got his mama to let him stay out so late, and
mainly, this incredibly gross person who played electric organ
and harmonica and sang occasional blues vocals—Pigpen,
someone said his name was—beyond a doubt the most marvelously ill-favored figure to grace a public platform since
King Kong came down with stage fright and copped out on
the Bruce Cabot show. He was bearded and burly and barrel-
chested, jowly and scowly and growly, and he had long,
Medusa-like hair so greasy it might have been groomed with
Valvoline, and his angry countenance glowered out through
it like a wolf at bay in a hummock of some strange, rank fo-
liage. He wore, as I recall, a motorcyclist's cap, crimped and
crumpled Hell's Angel style, and heavy iron-black boots, and
the gap between the top of his oily Levi's and the bottom of
his tattletale-gray T-shirt exposed a half-moon of distended
beer belly as pale and befurred as a wedge of moldy Jack
cheese. Sitting up there at that little spindly-legged organ, he
looked enormous, bigger than life, like a gorilla at a harpsi-
chord. But the ugly mother sure could *play*! To one as dull of
ear as I, who'd always pretty much assumed that the only fit
place for organ music outside of church was the roller rink,
those ham-fisted whorehouse chords he was hammering out
seemed in and of themselves to constitute the most satisfying
sort of blasphemy. And sing? The way this coarse-voiced ogre
snarled his unintelligible yet unfathomably indecent talkin'-
blues phrases would make a serial killer's skin crawl; fathers of
teenage daughters must have shuddered in their sleep as far
away as Burlingame that night. Verily, he was wondrous
gross, was this Pigpen, yet such was the subtle alchemy of his
art that the more he profaned love and beauty, the more his
grossness rendered him lovable and beautiful. "Far *out*!" the
teenyboppers and their boyfriends in Ben's Big Beat kept ex-

claiming while Pig worked. "Isn't he far fuckin' *out*!" It was an expression I'd not run into before, but even at first hearing, it seemed destined, if only for its commodious inexactness, to be with us for a good long while. In any case, it accommodated Pigpen very nicely; he was indeed one far-out gentleman, no doubt about it, none at all.

. . .

Summertime, midmorning, and I'm sitting in the living room of what was then Jerry Garcia and Bob Hunter's house, under the redwoods up a canyon in Larkspur, fifteen or twenty miles north of San Francisco, sitting there in an old easy chair reworking my notes on last night's three sets at the Fillmore ("An Evening with the Grateful Dead," the show is titled, and Jerry played all three sets, straight through from 8:30 until nearly 2:00 A.M., two sets with the Dead and one with their country-cousin stablemates, the New Riders of the Purple Sage, and will do the same tonight and again tomorrow night; yet while he's playing, he looks as if he could happily go on forever). While I'm sitting there, Jerry, yawning and stretching and scratching like a freshly dehibernated bear, is puttering around the stereo in search of a record by a vocalist he's so far identified only as "my favorite girl singer," and Jerry's lady, Mountain Girl (a great, gorgeous creature, an Amazon's Amazon, a Valkyrie with raven tresses, the sort of awesome Venus-of-Willendorf beauty who inspires me to pure press-agent flackery, the "160-pounds-of-eye-poppin'-pulchritude" school of prose) . . . ahem . . . and as I was saying, Mountain Girl is banging around in the kitchen fixing breakfast for me and Jerry and Hunter (who is right now standing in the doorway blinking myopically behind his enormous, sleep-frazzled Pecos Pete mustache), and Hunter's lady, Christy, is out back playing with Jerry and Mountain's two kids, and Jerry, dark eyes suddenly aglint behind his dandelion-yellow-tinted glasses, hollers, "Eureka!" or "Aha!" or whatever and plunges his hand wrist-deep into a disordered stack of albums and comes up with . . . no, no, not Joplin, not Grace Slick, not Joni Mitchell or Joan Baez or Laura Nyro, not even Tina Turner or Big Mama Thornton, but . . . Dolly *Parton*?

Who'da thought it? Who'd ever have supposed that the favorite girl singer of the spiritual leader of the Heaviest Rock-'n'-Roll Band in the Known World would turn out to be *my* favorite girl singer . . . Dolly Parton, the fairest wildflower that ever bloomed in Tennessee, the best female country vocalist since the prime of Kitty Wells? Far—how you say?—*flung*! Far fuckin' flung!

Jerry's at the turntable now, flipping switches and adjusting dials, blowing invisible dust off the record with French-maid fastidiousness, delicately plucking up the tone arm, catching it the way one might pick up a small but outraged serpent, with two fingers just at the base of the skull, gingerly almost to the point of reverence, and a moment later the room is filled with the exquisitely melancholic strains of Dolly Parton's mourning-dove-with-a-broken-wing voice, keening:

> In this mental insti-too-shun,
> Looking out through these arn bars . . .

It's her beautiful "Daddy, Come and Get Me," about a girl whose husband has had her committed ("to get me out of his way"), and when Dolly comes to the lines "It's not my mind that's broken / It's my heart," Jerry Garcia, standing limned in soft morning sunlight before the arched front window, turns to me and—remember now, this is *the* Jerry Garcia,

Captain Trips himself, the same Jerry Garcia who only twelve hours earlier utterly blew out three thousand of the most jaded, dope-devastated heads ever assembled even at the Fillmore (Dead fans are notorious in that regard)—*that* Jerry Garcia turns to me and clasps his hands to his breast and rolls his eyes after the goofy, gaga fashion of a lovesick swain and utters an ecstatic little moan and swoons into the nearest chair . . . and for the next half hour, while our breakfast turns cold in the kitchen, he and Hunter and I sit there in the living room tokin' on a taste of Captain Trips's morning pipe and groovin' on Sweet Dolly's bucolic threnodies about lost loves and dying lovers and stillborn babes, and by the time her last words ("O Robert! O Robert!") fade into silence, I swear to God there's not a dry eye in the room. . . .

. . .

It is, I suppose, my unhappy destiny to be eternally numbered among the Last of the First; 'twas ever thus, even in 1966. For, by the time I arrived, stoned to the eyeballs, at the Longshoremen's Hall in San Francisco for the final night of the Trips Festival, it had somehow got to be one or two or three o'clock in the morning, and the Dead were packing up their gear and nearly everybody had gone home. Some late-lingering hanger-on was fiddling with a slide projector, running through old slides that one of Kesey's Pranksters had shot in the La Honda woods, and even as I walked into the vast, almost empty hall, there flashed on a giant screen above the bandstand, purely by cosmic coincidence—the *synch*, Tom Wolfe named it—a gargantuan medium close-up of . . . right . . . of *me*, slapped up there behind the stage like some kind of weird wallpaper, head and shoulders in monumental proportions, my eyes masked behind a twelve-foot span of impenetrably black wraparound shades and my nostrils as big as manholes and my tightly pursed mouth, a furrow the length of the grave of a good-sized dog, fixed in what I must have intended to resemble a pensive attitude but that now seemed fraught with nameless apprehensions (to tell the truth, for all the time I put in hanging around the edges of the La Honda scene, I never did quite manage to shake off that vague stranger-in-a-strange-land uneasiness that is the special affliction of us day-trippers); and dwarfed by my looming monolithic visage, the Grateful Dead and their equipment crews slouched about at their assorted chores, a shadowy platoon of climbers grouping to scale a one-man, two-dimensional Mount Rushmore. All in all, it seemed as appropriate an image as any to remember the Trips Festival by, so I turned on my heel and split as quickly as I'd come. And that was the very last time I sought out the company of any rock-'n'-roll stars whatsoever, the very last time until . . .

· · ·

"Looks like you fell in with a bad crowd, man."

Huh? Hoodat said dat?

Jerry Garcia, that's who; Jerry Garcia wading through the jackstrewn corpses carpeting the floor wall to wall, Jerry Garcia grinning down at me, his face swimming slowly into focus, his hairy aspect droll, almost elfin, Jerry Garcia reaching for the guitar case he'd stashed behind my chair about seven centuries ago when this night was young and so was I. All of which means, lemme see now, all of which means . . .

Son of a bitch, it's *over*! Three sets, three whole sets of the Sweetest Sound This Side of Pandemonium, five solid hours I've been cuddled up back here in icy congress with a cold tank while out front the Dead were raising a rumpus loud enough to wake the Living and set a multitude to boogalooing, and I've scarcely heard a sound all evening long, save the nitrous oxide whistling through the empty chambers of my mind. . . . I mean, great *Scott,* Front Page, you've got a *story* to write, fella, you can't be loafin' around back here on your dead ass when . . .

Prodded at last by my long-dormant conscience, goosed by good intentions, eyeballs bulging maniacally with the effort to Pull Myself Together, I am halfway to my feet when Jerry, who by now has retrieved his guitar case and made his way back to the door, turns and halts me with an upraised hand.

"What's your hurry?" he says, still grinning. "The tank's not empty yet, is it?"

I blink as this highly relevant bit of intelligence illuminates my socked-in consciousness, and when I look again, Jerry is gone, vanished like the Cheshire cat, leaving just the memory of his grin hanging in midair to mark his passing. And the next thing I know, I'm back in my chair, and somehow the hose is rising magically, like a fakir's cobra, from the writhing turmoil on the floor to meet my outstretched hand, and I am thinking, "Yeah, right, just another li'l toke or two for the road, and then I'll get a good night's sleep so I can come back tomorrow night all primed and cocked to . . ."

·   ·   ·

"An Evening with the Grateful Dead," Fillmore West, first set: the Acoustic Dead lead off, Bill the Drummer and the three guitars (all acoustic, no electronic augmentation) and Pig, his electric organ temporarily supplanted by an old upright piano—they open w. "Cumberland Blues," much fine bluegrassy gittar pickin', good downhome lyrix like "a lotta po'man got de cumberlan' bloooze, / he cain't win for looozin' "—sounds like it came straight out of Appalachia (didn't tho; Hunter wrote it)—Jerry sings it *just* rite, his husky tenor a power-thru-gentleness sort of trip, almost unnaturally soft but with a kind of lilting gulp that makes me think of Lefty Frizzell or the way Hank Williams sings "Honky-Tonk Blues"—JG's voice's sweetness belies its tuffness and is in perfect counterpoint to the uncompromising pessimism of Hunter's lyrix—seems to me the Dead are carrying their years in the meat-grinder racket really well, aging gracefully—Bobby Weir *still* has the face of a debauched Renaissance choirboy, beautifully modeled features, there are moments when he looks like a dissolute twelve-yr-old—when he does backup vocals for JG (or solo, as on "Truckin'" and several others) he sings in a voice not quite his own, the kind of voice that skims across the top of the glottis and comes out sounding like it never plumbed the depths of the throat at all—Pig's piano has that fine country-honkie-gospel kind of plinking barrelhouse gait that's perfect for the back-to-the-roots thing the Dead are into these days—Pig has somehow shed fifty, maybe seventy-five pounds in the five years since that night at Ben's Big Beat, and now stands revealed as what he was all the time beneath that S. Clay Wilson–ogreish exterior, a fierce-looking *little* guy in cowboy funk, boots and low-slung Levi's and oily leather sheepherder's coat, a battered Stetson with its rolled brim cocked so low over his eyes that his tough, pinched little face is barely visible above his scraggly goatee, Gabby Hayes with teeth—Phil Lesh almost never surfaces in the group but is always working behind everybody else, providing substance on bass, fleshing out vocals, clowning, goofing around with little hippy-dippy mouth-breather mugging trips, he looks to be the loosest of them all onstage—Bill Kreutzmann is darkly handsome, dour, brooding, solemn, looks "deep" and plays the same way, hunches possessively over his traps and seems almost to lose himself in his own rumbling-hoofbeats-in-the-middle-distance rhythms—he is *never* flashy; his drumming is as steady as the drone of a tamboura, a fixed point around which the guitars work their airy filigrees; tonight's the first time the Dead have tried a strictly acoustic set on the Fillmore audience, and when "Cumberland Blues" is over, a scattering of old-line Dead fans, missing the electronically amplified bedlam of yesteryear, holler, "Play louder! Play louder!"—but Jerry, smiling beatifically, steps to the mike and cools them out by explaining very gently, "No, no, man, you don't understand, this is the part where we play *soft* and you *listen* loud!"—then they do "New Speedway Boogie," "Dire Wolf (Don't Murder Me)," "Candyman," and two or three others, mostly from the *Workingman's Dead* album, then finish off the set with a reverently beautiful and altogether decorous rendition of that All-Time Number-One Sike-O-Deelik Space-Music Golden Oldie, "Swing Low, Sweet Chariot," everybody *loves* it, crowd really gets off behind it—a fine, rousing set, looks like a *good* night. . . .

· · ·

"I just play the way I play; I play what I like to hear. I don't really think about guitar players anymore, I think about music; I like music, you know what I mean? When I buy records, I don't buy guitar players, I buy . . . music. Because all those guys, they're just learning to play the guitar, just like I am, and I don't listen to them much, because that'd be like learning from me. You know? They've derived all their shit from the same shit I've derived all my shit from. No, I listen to the real shit if I'm lookin' for ideas musically, guitarwise and so forth; I go to the masters, not to the other students. Like Django Reinhardt or B. B. King, you know, guys who really play. But the main thing is that I play music because I love

music, you know, and all my life I've loved music, and I've gotten more and more into lookin' at the whole overall thing. And that's where I am now, doin' that. . . ."

. . .

Altamont is but one dark moment in the community's *total* experience, the first installment of the dues that we must pay for our deliverance. On the Big Trip, the poet warns, the pilgrims will encounter suffering as well as joy, and those who have no heart for the undertaking would do well to stand aside, because "this train's got to run today."

The song's thrice-repeated refrain, "I spent a little time on the mountain, / Spent a little time on the hill," bespeaks the poet's (or, if you will, the singer's) modest claim to have made a private, careful consideration, *hors de combat,* of the enlightened person's obligation in a time of public turmoil;[1] in fact, we *must* seek guidance within ourselves, since public advice—"Like some say, better run away: / Others say better stand still"—is likely to be hysterical and paralyzingly contradictory. And in the next quatrain that contradiction blooms into a full-blown paradox:

> Now I don't know, but I been told,
> It's hard to run with the weight of gold.
> Other hand, I've heard it said,
> It's just as hard with the weight of lead.

Metaphorically, these lines describe and define the two equally seductive—and equally treacherous—temptations that beguile the truthseeker, the Scylla and Charybdis between which he must thread his perilous course: on the one hand, Fortune, represented at Altamont in the opulent persons of the Stones, seen here as listing dangerously

1 A very literal interpretation of the refrain might also make reference to the fact that the Dead, scheduled to go on after the Stones, never actually played that day; thus they had ample opportunity to climb "the hill" overlooking the scene and see for themselves that things were indeed "gettin' out of hand."

beneath "the weight of gold"; and on the other, Violence, the way of the Angels, burdened as they are with chains and helmets and Iron Crosses and all their weaponry, the hardware of their sullen calling. Then too, of course, there is the more literal reading of the passage, in which the relative subtlety of the metaphor is overridden by the ominous, code-of-the-old-West caveat to the effect that he who is so foolish as to make off with his brothers' gold is subject to end up carrying their hot lead as well, cut down by the heavy-handed irony of a Fate against which any admirer of *The Treasure of the Sierra Madre* could have warned him right from the start.

Nor may we shrug off the events at Altamont as harbingers of a mere "change in style"; rather, the minstrel contends, the change is *substantive,* and the death of Meredith Hunter signals that when the pilgrimage arrived at Altamont it entered into new and hostile territory, the twilight of its own dark night of the soul. Yet "one step's done and another begun," and so the song, even as it grieves one emblematic death and dreads the miles and trials ahead, directs us to turn our eyes to the changes yet to come. For, the next verse reminds us, "Things went down we don't understand, / But I think in time we will"—that is, however weary we are of mistakes and wrong turns and, most of all, of the terrible burden of our desperate longing for the destination, we can only comprehend the meaning of present events—and of the judgments they pass—from the perspective of the next change.

And now, with the following quatrain—

Now I don't know, but I was told,
In the heat of the sun a man died of cold.
Keep on comin' or stand and wait,
With the sun so dark and the hour so late …

—an almost *literal* shadow sweeps across the trackless yellow landscape of the song, the specter of some nameless thing so unspeakably awful that its very shadow casts a deadly chill, a pall from which no escape is possible, no matter whether we "keep on comin'" or stand and wait." It is, of course, the specter of our own inhumanity, our selfishness, our passionless indifference, and now at last the lesson of the song—and of Altamont—is clear: the Angels are the dark aspect of ourselves, reflections of the beast that skulks behind our eyes; we created them as surely as we created the Rolling Stones, fashioned them all of the mute clay of our need for Heroes and Villains as surely as we created Altamont itself that fateful day. Thus we can no more excise the bloody-handed Angels from our midst than we can cut away some vital part of our own psyche, lobotomize ourselves.

Nonetheless, that hard lesson learned the hard way, our course remains set, fixed by the iron resolve of destiny, and there can be no turning back; we can only face up to "the lack … / Of any other highway to ride" and, as R. Crumb puts it, "keep on truckin'." True, we travel this treacherous road at our own risk, but…

· · ·

Bob Weir: "If you want something for nothing, go jerk off."

· · ·

Among the habitués of the performers' lounge backstage at the Fillmore is this tall, rangy, loose-limbed, spacy-looking young freak—the Sunnyvale Express, they call him—who, during the breaks, is never far from Jerry Garcia's circle of friends and admirers, usually toying idly with a guitar, just noodling, picking out disconnected phrases and fragments to underscore whatever conversation is going on around him, nothing special, here a bit of bluegrass, there a snippet of flamenco or a rock riff or what have you, anything at all, apparently, that comes to mind. It's obvious he's a Garcia fan, but there is about him none of that earnest innocence and humility that can do so much toward making even us hero worshipers a tolerable lot; rather, the Sunnyvale Express's whole bearing and manner bespeak the languid arrogance of a cox-comb, and a couple of times I've spotted him eyeing Jerry with a look of ill-disguised envy.

He is here again tonight with his old lady, an impossibly beautiful but otherworldly-looking redhead named (brace yourself) the Burning Bush, who paints her eyelids dead black like Theda Bara and wears antique crushed-velvet vamp costumes, the two of them lounging in an old thread-bare armchair near the couch where Jerry sits talking animat-edly to a rock-magazine interviewer. As I cross the big room toward them, the Sunnyvale Express disentangles himself from the several pale, entwining limbs of the Burning Bush, rises slowly from his chair, takes up his guitar, props one foot on the arm of Jerry's couch and announces, in a voice as som-nolent with dope as a sleepwalker's, "Now I'm 'onna play jus' like ole G'cia, here."

And with that he launches into what has to be accounted, at least on the face of it, one of the most dazzling virtuoso per-formances I've ever heard, clawing great fistfuls of sound off the bass strings even as he picks the high notes off with blind-ing music-box precision and delicacy, playing, as far as I can determine, no particular song but rather a kind of collage, a mosaic—all right, a *medley,* then—of those staccato riffs that are almost a Garcia signature, not chords but rushing runs of single bass notes in which each note is sonorously deep yet somehow clear, sharp, *bright,* never murky or muddy. Closing my eyes, I can at first almost make myself believe it is Jerry himself who is swathing my mind like a swami's turbaned head in layer upon layer of silken sound, but after a minute or so I begin to sense that for all its resonant vibrancy, the Sun-nyvale Express's playing desperately wants the very quality that Jerry's is richest in—call it density or warmth or even, if you must, soul—and that the only ingredient the Express can replace it with is a sour mix of envy and insolence and sullen mockery. His playing is technically perfect but as devoid of human feeling for the music as a player piano tinkling away on an empty stage; one whose prime interest is in listening to the real thing might as well attend a concert featuring Sammy Davis Jr. playing "Danny Boy" on the Jew's harp.

So it is no surprise to discover, when I look again, that the same old Sunnyvale Express is playing still. Just behind him, leaning forward in her chair, sits the Burning Bush, her dark-ringed eyes glazed with rapture, her right hand lost to the wrist between her lover's parted thighs, cupping and fondling his crotch in the upturned palm. And around them, on the couch and in the other chairs, Jerry and his friends sit listening and watching, their faces stonily impassive. When, after he's played for maybe five minutes or so, the Express senses at last the chilly indifference with which his efforts are being received, he abruptly stops playing, favors his implacable audience with an elaborately phlegmatic shrug and turns and drifts off toward the far end of the room, the Burning Bush floating along beside him, her busy hand now wandering aimlessly, crablike, across his narrow rump.

"Whew, that guy," says Jerry wearily, rising to go out front for his set with the New Riders. "He's like my own personal psychic bedbug." Then, brightening, he adds, "But you know, I *need* guys like him around; everybody does. I mean, they keep us honest, you know what I mean?"

· · ·

PHIL LESH: The Grateful Dead are trying to save the world.

· · ·

"I don't think of music as a craft, see. Like, when I'm writing songs, I don't sit down and assemble stuff. Because music to me is more of

a flash than a craft, so that somethin' comes to me and that's the thing I'll bother to isolate, you know, the stuff that nudges its way out of the subconscious and you sorta go, 'Oh!' and suddenly there's a whole melody in your head. And it happens just often enough to seem like a, you know, like a flow. I mean, I recognize the mechanism; I know what it is as opposed to everything else. And that ends up to be the stuff I can live with a long time, and that's a thing I think about a lot, too. . . ."

· · ·

So here we are, me and ole Wheat Germ, smack in the middle of your typical sunny Sunday afternoon in a small, semirural suburb in upper Marin County, and well under way is your typical softball game in your typical small-town municipal ball park: chicken-wire backstop, rickety wooden bleachers along both baselines, scrofulously barren infield, shaggy outfield—in short, your regulation government-issue I-see-Amurrica-playing scene as it is enacted every summer Sunday not just here in Marin County but from sea to shining sea, lots of good cold beer and good fellowship and good-natured umpire baiting . . . and here today among these particular devotees of the national pastime, an abundance of good vibes and good karma and the world's own amount of goooooood dope.

Because the curiously coiffed fifty or sixty fans in the stands here today are not your common, ordinary, garden-variety bleacherites, those dulcet-toned, undershirted cigar chompers and their frumpy Cowbell Annies who customarily attend to the umpire baiting on these occasions. Such undershirts as are in evidence this afternoon are brilliantly tie-dyed, and the ladies in the crowd, for all their electrified bride-of-Frankenstein hairdos, are almost unanimously pretty, not a frump in sight. Nor do those improbably be-

furred gents manning their posts upon the field of combat
bear more than a passing resemblance to the Mudville Nine's
anonymous opponents, nor is that the Mighty Casey at the
bat.

No, sports fans, the awful truth (may J. G. Taylor Spink,
up there in the Great Press Box in the Sky, be spared it!) is that
the freaks afield are Jefferson Airplanes to a man; and the big-
wigged fellow who just struck out, the one who looks like
John the Baptist, that's Jerry Garcia, guitarist extraordinaire
but a banjo hitter if ever there was one. And the umpire just
now being baited, that scowly little dude with the scraggly
chin whiskers and the red-white-and-blue backward baseball
cap, is either Augie Donatelli or Pigpen McKernan, choose
one.

So far, seen as I am seeing it through the blue haze of all
those joints that keep coming my way, it's been a genuine piss-
cutter of a ball game—which appraisal has, as the Great
Scorer is reputed to have written, naught to do with who's
winning (the Airplane, by about eleven to about six, nobody
seems to know exactly) or losing but solely with How They're
Playing the Game. For if the Great Scorer ever looked in on
this contest, He'd probably take His ball and go home, because these weirdos are simply having much more fun than
this moldy old sport was ever intended to provide. Most of
them play like the guys who always made the second string in
high school but never actually got in a game; lotsa hustle, lotsa
chatter on the benches and base paths, no end of hot-pepper
razzle-dazzle when they're chucking the old pill around the
infield, but complete and utter panic when they somehow get
themselves involved in an actual honest-to-God *play*. The
Airplane, for instance, has a beautiful, big-bearded guy
wearing bib overalls in the outfield who circles frantically under pop flies like a man with one leg shorter than the other,

hollering, "Me! Me! Me!" and waving his arms as though be-siegedbyaswarmofbees, but who, to my admittedly none too reliable recollection, has yet to lay a glove on the ball. And Jerry Garcia cavorts very impressively around the Dead's hot corner until he sees the ball headed in his direction, at which point he instantly goes into such gleeful paroxysms of excite-ment that he can't possibly execute the play.

What they lack in skill, though, they more than make up for in élan, jawing at Pig and guzzling beer in the on-deck cir-cle and squawking, "Whaddaya waitin' for—*Christmas*?" at batters who don't choose to swing at every pitch within bat's length of the plate. So that when, along about the fifth in-ning, Mickey Hart, sometime second drummer for the Dead, bounces one out of the park over the low fence in deep left field and a furious hassle ensues along the third-base line over whether or not Pig should have ruled it a ground-rule double instead of a homer—both teams storming up and down the base paths and gesticulating wildly and turning the air yet another shade of blue with good old-fashioned cussing plain and fancy—one understands immediately that behind all their histrionics, the players are taking enormous delight in burlesquing these hoary old rituals, and at the same time one senses, too, that behind *that* is a profound and abiding re-spect—*reverence,* even—for the very traditions they are pre-tending to make light of. Which in turn goes a long way to-ward explaining how it is that the Dead, who not long ago were plunging ever deeper into the howling wilderness of electronic exoticism, are now working almost exclusively within the relatively strict, fundamental forms of stay-at-home country music and blues. It may even help explain why Mickey Hart, after he has negotiated the knot of wrangling dialecticians around Pigpen and tagged the plate, trots di-rectly over to where I'm sitting with my ubiquitous notebook spread upon my knee and says, grinning proudly, "Listen, man, I don't give a shit what you write about my drummin', but you be *sure* and put that fuckin' homer in, OK?"

Anyhow, all those heady speculations aside, there remains one more disconcerting little distinction between today's contest and your run-of-the-mill Sunday softball game—to wit: that unwashed young chap over there, furtively but eagerly proffering first this freak, then that, something or other from the small round tin he's palming, is no peanut vendor. As a matter of embarrassing fact, he's none other than the noted Wheat Germ, my very own millionaire millstone, and judging from the withering scowls his attempts to peddle his wares have been drawing all afternoon, business is bad, exceeding bad. Evidently the Dead's and the Airplane's respective rooting sections prefer their tradesmen to come on—if at all—considerably cooler than Wheat Germ, who, his self-advertised six million dollars' worth of experience in these affairs notwithstanding, has already forgotten the cardinal precept of his chosen profession: *Nobody* loves a pushy pusher. Poor old Wheat Germ; even from where I sit, in the bleachers down near third, it's apparent that he's trying way too hard, buttonholing fans while they're trying to watch Paul Kantner strike out Jerry Garcia, spraying them with the humid spindrift of his enthusiasm, generally conducting himself in a manner likely to get him a reprimand from the Dealers' Association's Ethical Practices Committee if the word gets around.

Which is all the same to me, actually, except that as I ponder the obdurate sales resistance his cheapjack wheedling seems to be eliciting in the marketplace, it begins to occur to me that it just might not be in my best interest to associate myself too closely with this pariah in the present company. After all, despite the unarguable fact that it was my vainglorious boasting of Connections in High Places that brought him here in the first place—thereby making Wheat Germ in a sense the corporeal embodiment of my vanity, my alter ego incarnate—Oh, Christ, here he comes now heading straight for me, wearing the rueful hangdog look of a man who's just suffered putdown upon putdown; everybody'll see that he's with me and I'll never get within hollerin' distance of the Dead again and . . . it positively *behooves* me to maintain at all costs my credibility in the eyes of these subjects of my report to my vast readership; one might almost say I owe it to my public to cook this albatross's goose somehow, to sneak away from him or pretend I don't know him or offer to drive him to the bus station or . . .

We need guys like him; they keep us honest. Jerry Garcia's own true words echoing up from some lost recess of my memory, and even as I hear them, I hear, too, my own voice saying, aloud and straining to convey the heartiness I'm trying hard to feel, yet in a kind of secret harmony with Jerry's words, "Hey, listen, Wheat Germ, the New Riders are playin' at the Family Dog tonight, and I've got an extra ticket. You want to come along?"

And as his snaggletoothed grin chases the despair from his unlovely countenance, I am smote by yet another Cosmic Axiom, this one more or less of my own making: One man's pain in the ass is the next man's psychic bedbug. Dig it, dad, you never know when you might need one.

• • •

PIGPEN: Hey, Magazine, y' wanna know the secret of m' success?

ME (*eagerly*): Yeah, sure, hell yes!

PIG (*growling sotto voce behind his hand, mock-furtive as a Disneyland Foxy Loxy*): Take 35 percent off the top and *split*!

. . .

"Well, I think the Grateful Dead is basically, like, a good, snappy rock-'n'-roll band. I mean, that's its basic character. So when we do country stuff, for instance, people sometimes tend to think we've suddenly gotten very pure, very direct. But we don't actually do it very purely or directly at all, compared to, like, Roy Acuff, say. And if we're talking about country music, we have to compare it to those kind of guys. I mean, when we play it, it's still us. . . ."

. . .

"An Evening with the GD": fillmore west, second set, new riders of the purple sage: garcia on pedal steel, dave torbert on bass, david nelson on electric guitar, mickey hart on drums, and most of all, marmaduke, né john dawson, vocalist-lyricist-acoustic-guitarist, loverly little guy all decked out (unlike other deads and new riders in their shitkicker roughrider cowboy funk) in high-style western sartorial splendor, dude duds, hand-embroidered cowboy shirt, hand-tooled high-heeled boots, trimly blocked stetson atop incongruously long pale blond locks, a psychedelic roy rogers— they open w. the great dave dudley truckdriver song "six days on the road," leap blithely from that to the stones' dope-disease-and-dark-night-of-the-soul song "connection," then to "henry," a *very* funny rock-'n'-rollicker by marmaduke about the travails of a dope runner (". . . went to Acapulco / to turn the golden key . . .") who gets himself involved in a wild keystone kops car chase after sampling his own wares ("henry tasted, he got wasted / couldn't even see . . .")—crowd *loves* it, fillmore is jammed to the rafters with dead fans by now and they're unanimous in their enthusiasm for the new riders— marmaduke onstage is really something to watch, he's so fresh, so ingenuous, so enthralled by the whole rock-'n'-roll-star trip, even backstage he can hardly keep his hands off his guitar, and out front when the crowd shows it digs him he blushes and grins all over his face and practically wags his tail with delight—new riders do two more marmaduke songs, "dirty business" and "the last lonely eagle" (which yr. reporter, ripped again, keeps hearing as "the last lonely ego," but fortunately does not fail to note that garcia plays brilliantly on it despite the fact that he's only taken up the pedal steel seriously in the last year or so, none of that mawkish, whiny, hawaiian-war-chant rebop; his pedal steel, like his guitar, is crisp and intense, it *weeps,* of course—it wouldn't be a pedal steel if it didn't—but it's properly melancholy, never merely sentimental)—then marmaduke does a yodeler that I don't recognize (*yodeling?* in the *Fillmore?*), then they finish off the set by bringing the whole house to its feet with the stones' "honky-tonk woman"—as marmaduke, beaming happily, basks in the warm applause, it occurs to me that these guys rank right up there near the top of the lower order of eternal verities: rock-'n'-roll stars may come and go, but there'll *always* be the Sons of the Pioneers. . . .

· · ·

Backstage again and I've retreated to the remotest corner of the lounge to work for a few minutes on my notes on the New Riders' set. I'm just getting fairly deep into it when I begin to feel that creeping uneasiness that signals another presence, close at hand and watching me intently. I lift my eyes reluctantly from my notebook and find myself face to face with a small child, just a toddler, a little boy about a year old, standing there right next to the arm of my chair, his wide blue eyes fixed on my moving ballpoint. He has rust-red hair, brushed neatly flat, and a round, fair face upon which has settled an expression as solemn as a judge's. And he very definitely does

not, let it be said here and now for reasons that will momentarily become apparent, resemble Jerry Garcia in any way,
shape, or form.

"Hi, sport," I greet the boy, offering him the pen. "You
wanta write something?"

"Oh, Lord, baby, don't go bothering people that way,
sweetheart. Is he bothering you?"

The mother, presumably: a tall, slender blonde, very pretty
in a sort of pale, bloodless way, oddly brittle-looking somehow, a china figurine off some Victorian parlor's whatnot
shelf or perhaps, with her plaid wool skirt and cardigan
sweater and plastic barrettes and silk stockings and penny
loafers, Andrew Wyeth's Kristina. She seems, in every sense
that the phrase can conjure, out of time.

"No, he's fine," I reassured her, flipping a page in my notebook for the boy to leave his mark on. "Let him write; he
probably understands it all better than I do, anyhow."

"Are you writing something about the band?" she asks. I
own up to it and name the magazine I'm doing it for. "Oh,"
she says, "that's very interesting. Because Jerry Garcia, well,
he's, you know," she rolls her eyes significantly toward the kid,
who by now is assiduously inscribing his hieroglyphic auto-
graph in my notebook, "he's little Jerry's father."

Uh, beg pardon, ma'am, but, heh-heh, I could've *sworn*
you said . . .

"His true father, I mean. He's his true father."

My first flash is to those two lines from Jerry's song "Friend
of the Devil," the ones that go, "Got a wife in Chino, babe, /
And one in Cherokee . . ." But then I cop another quick peek
at the weanling at my knee, with his sober delft-blue eyes and
that red hair, and instantly the next lines of the song come to
mind: "First one say she got my child, / But it don't look like

me." Which is to say either that the girl is some kind of shakedown artist or that she is, as the quaint old phrase so delicately had it, bereft of reason. Because if this kid is Jerry Garcia's offspring, then I am Walter Winchell.

"And you know what?" she hurries on. "I came all the way out here from Stockton on the Greyhound just so he could see little Jerry, and I paid my way in tonight just like everybody else, and I talked the door guy into letting me come backstage and *everything,* and then when I said hi to Jerry and held up the baby to him and all, he acted like, you know, like he didn't even *know* us. Which I just don't understand what's *wrong.* I mean, I sure hope it's not because of something I've, you know, *done* or anything. . . ."

True father indeed. But this time I can plainly hear, through the rush of words, the faint rattle of hysteria that bespeaks a screw loose somewhere.

"I just hope he's not, you know, *mad* at me or something," she adds, bending to scoop up little Jerry and clutch him defensively to her breast, as if to demonstrate that nothing in the living world terrifies her quite as much as the thought of Jerry Garcia in a snit. "Because I certainly don't know what I could've, you know, *done*. . . ."

My pen slips from little Jerry's moist grasp and clatters to the floor. Rising to retrieve it, I offer her what meager reassurance I can muster. "I wouldn't worry too much if I were you," I tell her lamely. "Jerry's pretty busy these days. He probably just didn't . . ."

"I mean, we're *very close,* me and Jerry are. Like, you take the last time I saw him, last April I think it was, why, I just walked right up to him, right on the street outside this building, and said, you know, 'Hi!' And he said hi back and *smiled* and sort of patted the baby on the *head* and everything. And that's why I'm afraid he must be mad about something. Because this time he just, you know, walked right on by like he didn't even *see* us!"

The girl is beginning now to look as distraught as she sounds; her cheeks are flushed and several strands of hair have pulled loose from the barrettes to dangle limply at her temples, and her pale eyes well with tears. She is, as they say, Going All to Pieces, and as her fragile composure shatters, I can read in the shards a case history of her delusion that if not altogether accurate in every detail, will answer almost as well as if it were:

Two years ago she was a carhop in a Stockton A&W root-beer stand, and that night, summer before last, when she got herself knocked up, the redheaded Stockton College dairy-and-animal-husbandry major who took her and two six-packs out on the levee in his Mustang played the Grateful Dead on his eight-track stereo while he pumped drunkenly atop her in the backseat, and she heard, in midzygote as it were, not the redhead's sodden grunting but a true dream lover's voice, his honeyed lips just at her ear whispering what somehow seemed—even though she didn't exactly, you know, *understand* it—the sweetest, tenderest, loveliest thing anybody had ever said to her, ever in her life:

> Lady finger, dipped in moonlight,
> Writing 'What for?' across the morning sky . . .

Jerry Garcia, of course, ready, as always, with the right word at the right moment. And since from that night forward she never once saw or heard from the redheaded dairy-and-animal-husbandry major ever again, whereas she could hear from Jerry Garcia anytime she wanted to, merely by playing a Grateful Dead album on the $29.95 Victor portable stereo she'd bought on sale at the discount store with her first week's wages from the root-beer stand, we-e-e-lll . . .

"I mean," she whimpers wretchedly, "we don't *want* nothing from him, not one thing. But you'd think he could've at least reckanized his own flesh and, you know, *blood*. . . ."

Well, it occurs to me to observe, there are an awful lot of people around here tonight; most likely he really *didn't* see you. But then it also occurs to me that she is already quite clear on that technicality and that as far as she is concerned, it's altogether beside the point; according to her lights, a man is *obliged* to see and recognize the fruit of his own loins in *any* crowd, he *is*.

And anyhow, before I can utter the first word, the girl suddenly squeaks, "Oooo! There he *is*!" and takes off for the other end of the room, leaving me standing there dumbfounded in a leftover cloud of her tooty-frooty dime-store perfume, still biting the air and trying to think of something to say. She is headed, as you might expect, for Jerry Garcia himself, who stands at the far end of the lounge talking to Pigpen and Phil Lesh and Zonk the Gasman's handsome wife, Candace, and Bob Weir's beautiful, Garboesque girlfriend, Frankie; and as she makes for them, I see, over her shoulder, those great blue eyes of little Jerry's gazing back at me, grave as a lemur's stare.

The girl marches resolutely up to Jerry and thrusts the baby at him and announces herself—I can't hear what she says, but it's doubtless some such commonplace pleasantry as "Allow me to present your own flesh and, you know, *blood*—" And Jerry looks at her with an expression so blankly devoid of recognition that for an instant I'm afraid some hideous little slice-of-life drama is about to happen, that any second now she's going to whip out a .44 and start blazing away at Jerry or herself or Candace and Frankie or whomever a lady in her frame of mind might settle on as a fit target for her ire.

But when at last Jerry's countenance lights up with that fabled beatific smile and he says hello or whatever and bends to peer closely at the baby, then at her, and, still smiling, shakes his head, there is even in his denial of them such a palpable quantity of gentleness and generosity that she is utterly disarmed and undone. She blushes and shies and smiles back at him, and after a moment she shoulders the baby once more and goes on out, restored, into the main ballroom. As the door closes after her, Jerry turns back to the others and delivers himself of one of those exaggerated, palms-upturned, beats-the-hell-out-of-*me* shrugs and that's it, it's over, good karma has triumphed once more over bad, and playing lead guitar for the Grateful Dead is still quite as safe a calling as, say, being Eddie Wakefield and playing first base for the Philadelphia Phils in 1949. . . .

. . .

"Guys in other bands have that kind of stuff a lot; there'll be five or six chicks runnin' around all the time sayin' they're somebody's old lady, that kind of trip. But we don't get too much of that sort of thing; actually, we're all kind of ugly for that. Ugly but honest, that's us. Hey, there's a good title for you, 'Ugly But Honest.' A'course, we ain't all that honest, either. Maybe just 'Ugly' is good enough. . . ."

. . .

"an evening with the gd," fillmore, third set, full complement dead (garcia, weir, lesh, pig, kreutzmann, hart), full electronic amplification—they open w. "dancing in the streets," a motown-style rocker, follow that w. merle haggard's tender honky tearjerker "mama tried," then "it's a man's world" with pig doing a very creditable james-brown-in-whiteface, then buddy holly's "not fade away," working through their repertory the way a painter might put together a retrospective, displaying their influences, putting the audience through the same changes the dead themselves have been subject to—it is eclecticism in its very best and highest sense, and the audience, already thoroughly jacked up by the first two sets, is flashing strongly to it—the upturned faces near the stage, awash with the splashover of swirling colors from the light show, seem to glow with enthusiasm and delight, and each time the band takes up a different song there arises from out there in the dark a wild chorus of voices, dozens of them from even the farthest corners of the hall, whooping and howling and yipping like coyotes baying at the moon, aa-ooo-aa-ooo-aaaa-ooooo, a savage, animal, tribal thing one knows instinctively they do *only* for the dead, in *honor* of the dead—a christian missionary would get gobbled up in seconds in such a scene as this—now bob weir, looking like a full-color, slick-paper idealization of billy the kid on a dime-mag cover, sings "truckin'," hunter's leisurely, laid-back ramble about the vicissitudes of life on the road with the dead ("busted / down on bourbon street / set up / like a bowlin' pin . . ."), puts me in mind of those old-timey toddlin' tunes like "side by side," only with more substance, gene kelly and donald o'connor with soul—they follow that with two more hunter songs, "uncle john's band" and "casey jones," and by the time casey ("drivin' that train / high on cocaine . . .") is highballing down the track toward that fateful encounter with train 102, the crowd is on its feet and chugging up and down, it *is* the train, a great joyous surging mass of energy hurtling headlong into the uncharted darkness of the future—and it doesn't stop when the song ends but charges right on into "love light" with just the scantest pause to catch its breath, pig taking the throttle now, strutting around onstage with his tambourine whirring in his hand and his hat cocked low and mean, *dangerous,* snarling and fierce ("i don' want it all! / i jes wanna leetle bit!"), his exhortations as raw and lewd and laden with insinuation as a carnival kootch-show pitchman's hype ("git yo' hands outta yo' pockets and turn on yo' *love* light!"), and every now and then i seem to hear a line of such brazen, unbounded lickerishness ("dew *yew* lak ta fu-u-u-uckkk?") that i start and blink and wonder did he really *say* that?—and the whole thing builds and builds, ten minutes, fifteen, twenty, and now the audience is clapping to keep time, they have joined the dead en masse as one enormous synchronized syncopated single-minded rhythm section, taking up the beat from bill the drummer's tom-tom and making it their own, insisting on it, demanding it, and the dead are delightedly handing it over to them, one by one laying down guitars and drumsticks and leaving the center of the stage to pig and jerry, first weir, then hart and lesh, then even bill the drummer, leaving their posts to join the crew of groupies and quippies and buddies and wives and old ladies at the rear of the stage back against the light-show screen among the throbbing blobs, greeting friends and accepting tokes on whatever gets passed their way, beer or joints or coke or ripple, and just jerry and pig and the audience are left to mind the music, jerry's guitar weaving incredible intricacies in front of the rhythmic whipcrack of applause, pig chanting his unholy litany (". . . so come awn, bay-beh, baby please, / i'm beggin' ya, bay-beh, and i'm on my knees . . .") like a man possessed by a whole mob of randy, rampant demons, and now jerry too puts down his guitar and leaves, and it's just pig up there alone with his tambourine and his snarl (". . . turn on yo' *light,* all i *need* . . .") and his three-thousand-member rhythm section keeping time, *keeping* time, i've never before considered

("... huh! ...") what that expression really means, the crowd has undertaken to tend and cherish the beat until the band comes back ("... i jus' got to *git* sum, it's all i *need* ...") and resumes its stewardship, the whole arrangement amounts to a very special kind of trust, we are ("... huh! ...") not just audience but keepers of the flame, we are *of* the grateful dead, *with* them ("... got ta keep pooshin', all i *need* ...") and *for* them and *of* them ...

BLAM!

It's the crack of doom or the first shot of the revolution or, anyhow, a cherry bomb that Pig has somehow set off just at his feet. A cloud of dense gray smoke still boils up around him; no longer any doubt about it, he is plainly a satanic manifestation. And without my noticing them, the other Dead have stolen back to their places and taken up their instruments, and at the signal of the cherry bomb, the song blasts into life again, the decibel count is astronomical, the crowd is shrieking in one hysterically ecstatic voice, and the volume of the music is so great it swallows up the very shriek itself; by a single diabolic stroke, a multitude three thousand strong has suddenly been struck dumb. The din is enough to wake even the moldering spirits of those moribund old poots who once set myriad toes a-tapping in the hallowed hall. I can almost see them now: Vaughn Monroe and Wayne King the Waltz King and Clyde McCoy and Ginny Sims and the Ink Spots and Frankie Yankovic and Ralph Flanagan and the Hill-toppers and Kay Kyser and His Kollege of Musical Knowledge and Horace Heidt and His Musical Knights ... a whole host of phantoms, troupers to the last, crawling out of this old wormy woodwork and rising up from the rankest, dankest depths of memory to join the living Dead for one last encore. Just *listen* to the racket. Bill the Drummer's heavy artillery is pounding at my temples, and Mickey Hart is laying into his four great shimmering gongs until the pandemonium itself is all atremble with their clangor and my back teeth taste of brass, and Lesh and Weir are ripping furiously at the faces of their guitars, and the crowd is screaming as if that enormous palpitating blood-red blob of light behind the band were the flaming dawn of doomsday, and Jerry's guitar is winding out a shrill silvery coil of sound that spirals up and up and up until, whining like a brain surgeon's drill, it bores straight through the skull and sinks its spinning shaft into the very quick of my mind, and Pig, a rag doll buffeted by hot blasts of ecstasy gusting up from three thousand burning throats, flings himself into a demented little Saint Vitus' dance of demonic glee and howls the kamikaze cry of one who is plunging headlong into the void, the last word beyond which *all* sound is rendered as meaningless as silence . . .

YEEEEEEEEE-
o-o-o-o-oowwwwwwwww!

•   •   •

. . . True, we travel this treacherous road at our own risk; but could we ever have supposed it might prove otherwise? And if the absence of "signs" and "dividin' lines" and "rules to guide" guarantees a hazardous journey, it also promises times when this heaven-bound ride is indescribably wild and sweet and free; things *will* get "out of hand"—"*always*"—but even that inevitability has its compensations, so long as we are among friends.

Still and all, "if the horse don't pull, you got to carry the load"—that is, if the communal vehicle and the full power of the community's combined energies will not bear one safely through, then the whole burden of care and growth must rest upon oneself. And, the minstrel cautions, it may well be that none of us is capable of that effort, that the whole enormous enterprise will come to nothing. But this is a time of

testing, of pitting our strength against all the forces that oppress us—
our guilt and our despair, our selfishness, our failures and our fear of
failure—for, "one way or another," relief *must* come, these gloomy
times *must* pass, the darkness *will* give.

Thus "New Speedway Boogie" is at once a sober—if highly subjective—study of a violently traumatic moment in the course of human
events, a desperate prayer for deliverance, and a hymn of hope. And
when those final fervent lines—

> One way or another,
> One way or another,
> One way or another,
> This darkness got to give.

—come echoing and reechoing down like "Excelsior!" from the
heights, it also becomes an anthem quite as stirring, in its own somber,
introspective way, as "Onward, Christian Soldiers."

· · ·

*"When I talk about musicians, I'm talkin' about people who make
music, not just people who are technically perfect. Music bein' That
Thing Which Gets You Off. I mean, that's just my definition of
that word. And when you're playin' and really Gettin' Off that
way, it's like when you're drivin' down a road past an orchard, you
know, and you look out and at first all you can see is just another
woods, a bunch of trees all jumbled up together, like there's no form
to it; it's chaos. But then you come to a certain point and suddenly—zing! zing! zing!—there it is, the order, the trees all lined
up perfectly no matter which way you look, so you can see the real
shape of the orchard! I mean, you know what I mean! And as you
move along, it gets away from you, it turns back into chaos again,
but now it doesn't matter, because now you understand. I mean,
now you know the secret . . ."*

Endnote

As its title suggests, I originally intended to include "Grateful Dead I Have Known" in *Famous People I Have Known,* but over the years the book (which wasn't published until 1985) slowly took on a narrative structure that just wouldn't comfortably accommodate the Dead.

But even though *Playboy* gave me an award for it and feted me in a style to which I could easily have grown accustomed, I've long wished for an opportunity to reconcile some of the differences between the *Playboy* version and the original, particularly to restore to the text the mock-scholarly "Brief Exegesis," which *Playboy* understandably felt was perhaps a little much for its readership.

(I'm much obliged to Cia White Holdorf—who later became, for many years, my wife—for invaluable help with the analysis of "New Speedway Boogie.")

The Dead, alas, have proved to be as mortal as the rest of us. Pigpen, as everybody knows, gave up the ghost many years ago and was succeeded on keyboard by Keith Godchaux, who died, and then by Brent Mydland, who died—a calamitous chain of events that almost begins to suggest some weird *Phantom of the Opera* knockoff: "Dead Hand at the Keyboard," say, or "The Organ's Revenge."

For some reason, whenever I hear of the death of someone with whom I have felt a close personal connection, I always remember the lines from that old folk song about the hound dog: "When Old Blue died, he died so hard / He shook the ground in my backyard." But when Jerry Garcia died, he shook the ground in just about *everybody's* backyard. His death hit me like a two-by-four between the eyes. Although I hadn't seen him in more than twenty years, Jerry had remained, through his music, a constant presence in my life;

Workingman's Dead alone provided the background music for a huge chapter of my life story.

Mountain Girl continues to be one of my favorite people, a woman of great gusto and spirit, great good humor, great intelligence, and great—no, monumental—beauty. She lives now with her longtime boyfriend, a big, handsome guy named Bill, on a little ranch in Oregon's Willamette Valley, breeding, of all things, donkeys.

Rumor has it she's writing a book. Only a jackass would miss that one.

A REVIEW FOR *Rolling Stone* (APRIL 1972) OF A STRANGE AND
WONDERFUL BOOK.

Ed Sanders's *The Family*

WITHOUT A DOUBT the trials will continue. For
Justice demands it. And only when all these affairs are known
and exposed can the curse of ritual sacrifice, Helter Skelter
and satanism be removed from the coasts and mountains and
deserts of California."

Okay, hoo dat said dat? John Mitchell? Dan Smoot? Rev.
Donn Moomaw? Your mother?

Wrong; Ed Sanders said it. Ed Sanders the former Fug,
founder of *Fuck You: A Magazine of the Arts,* which was one of
the seminal (yes it *was,* too, bad pun notwithstanding) underground publications of the early sixties, Ed Sanders the
author of *Shards of God: A Novel of the Yippies* (Grove Press,
1970), a fiery, fiercely surreal study of the Chicago Democratic
convention of '68, a cosmodemonic mindfuck of a novel in
which hero Abbie Hoffman assumes godlike proportions and
leads his barbarian hordes in a triumphant siege of "Dr. Hil-
ton's Honk Palace"—*that* Ed Sanders. And what's more, especially in light of the fact that those lines quoted above are
Sanders's final word on Manson—that is, they are the very

last lines of this curious and remarkable book—there can be no doubt that they accurately represent his perception of his subject.

Not, I hasten to add, that there's anything at all untoward in that; the case against Manson is so tight that Sanders's verdict could hardly have been otherwise. What *is* startling is not the judgment itself but the language it is couched in— that voice-of-doom bombast and fustian that is more often affected by Bible-banging law-and-order politicians than by wild-eyed anarcho-syndicalist Yippie peace creeps—not the verdict but Sanders's clarion call to the Forces of Repression to execute it.

Nor is this aggressive moralizing (of which the quoted passage is but one of countless examples) the only disconcerting quality in this book. For another, there is the fact that Sanders's prose is riddled with the most amazing assortment of solecisms and editorial oversights ever assembled between covers since Eisenhower's *Collected Speeches* went out of print. Our sensibilities are everywhere assaulted by such mind-bogglers as "over the mountains, such as it is" and "a small little [house]" and "the Colorado border in Riverside County, California," and "an Indian who murdered and tortured a white man" and "light green in color"—so many such *lapsus linguae,* in fact, that one catches oneself wondering seriously if they are actually *deliberate,* if Sanders has cunningly planted them throughout the book as a kind of peculiar comic relief amidst the Manson carnage.

Far more serious, though, is the astonishing number of loose ends left dangling and red herrings left uncaught in Sanders's account of these unhappy affairs. For example, he devotes one entire chapter to the nefarious doings of the England-based satanic cult that calls itself the Process, a sorry and contemptible lot indeed but one with which Manson seems to have had only the most tenuous connection. (He is "alleged" to have participated in the ritual torture of a homosexual "cult-lad" in 1968; also in 1968, he supposedly patronized a San Jose leather shop operated by a Process member; and—the clincher, presumably—during Manson's trial he "carved an inverted swastika that looks remarkably like the Process symbol into his forehead.") Then too there is the matter of Madame Jean Brayton, whose Ordo Templi Orientis Solar Lodge (a sado-vampire cult to which Sanders links Manson only by the flimsiest kind of hearsay) also rates an entire chapter, at the end of which she and her unholy minions disappear into the wilds of Mexico, never to be heard from again—at least not in the ensuing 250-plus pages of Sanders's book.

And how about the shooting of black drug dealer Bernard "Lotsa Poppa" Crowe, who after allegedly burning some member of the Family in a dope deal, seems to have taken a Manson bullet in the belly in the presence of several witnesses and was hospitalized for several weeks, apparently without the police even bothering to inquire, either of Crowe or of the witnesses, as to the identity of his assailant? And what are we to make of Sanders's account of the police raid (in quest of stolen cars, runaways, and what-have-you) on the Spahn ranch on July 27, during which Manson supposedly "told the officers that he had people scattered throughout the hills with guns trained upon the officers and that on [his] command the police could be wiped out," with what must have been the enormously satisfying result that five carloads of California's Finest promptly turned tail and split and *stayed gone*? There is, of course, no shortage of evidence of police incompetence in the Manson affair, but gee *whiz*, Ed . . .

Also, while I'm about it, I expect I ought at least to note in passing what is perhaps the most startling assertion in the book, presented here precisely as it is in Sanders's text (that is, utterly without amplification or clarification): "It is known that the Esalen Institute is extremely uptight over the fact that Manson visited there [the weekend before the Tate-LaBianca murders]. In fact, this writer received an oblique snuff-threat from someone representing Esalen Institute." As Sanders is fond of remarking after his descriptions of Manson's own least charming peccadilloes: Oo-ee-oo.

Yet despite all its inadequacies and excesses, its indiscretions and inaccuracies, *The Family* is an immensely readable book, an important book—even, if you will, a *necessary* book.

In the first place, although Sanders is certainly not in any ordinary or conventional sense a *good* writer, he is always an interesting one; his prose, almost perversely clumsy and uneven as it is, tantalizes us with its very unpredictability so that we find ourselves reading him as we might watch a drunken tightrope walker, incredulous at his imprudence yet fascinated by his crazy, lurching grace. Sanders's tone, even in the most hair-raisingly dramatic moments of the book, yaws giddily from arch ("Then Sebring lunged for the gun and Tex waxed murderous and shot Jay in the armpit.") to stark ("He stabbed her several times in the left breast through the brassiere. Screams. Stabs. Aorta. Death.") to sneering ("Sadie ripped her shirt on the barbed wire. Tsk, tsk."). His language, even when it deftly, almost playfully, parodies officialese ("Officers Whiteley and Guenther . . . proceeded to drive up to Inyo County to secure possession of Kitty Lutesinger."), even when its smirking and insinuating tone borders on fatuousness ("The legend [has it] that during the gobble the girl went nuts and, all in one incision, bit in twain Manson's virility."), nonetheless insistently bespeaks the intensity of Sanders's revulsion and outrage at Manson's ghastly work.

But finally, it is as plain, old-fashioned journalism that *The*

Family triumphs over its own shortcomings and eccentricities and emerges as a real achievement. In large part it owes its success as reportage directly to Sanders's refusal to make psychological or sociological or political apologies for Manson— no underprivileged-child jive, no handwringing hype for prison reform, no dead-piggies-is-good-piggies radical lunacy. Ed Sanders is a latter-day Cotton Mather; he believes in evil as a *literal* reality, and he abandons all those shibboleths and pacifiers in favor of a passion for detail so fierce it sometimes seems obsessive.

Limiting himself strictly to the years of Manson's coming of age as a villain, from July 22, 1955 (busted: L.A., car theft), to December 1, 1969, the day the LAPD flourished its trumpets and gave forth the glad tidings that it had broken the Tate-LaBianca case and collared a fiend of Miltonian dimensions, Sanders pounds away at us with a relentless barrage of facts, opinions, rumors, hearsay, and street skinny that details the career of this devious, vicious little man who aspired briefly to the throne of the Prince of Darkness himself, until he was laid low by a hubris as mean and nagging as Richard III's. Horrified, we watch as Manson advances from sneak thief and pimp and bad-check artist and jailbird, eagerly dabbling in "magic, warlockry, hypnotism, astral projection, Masonic lore, Scientology, ego games, subliminal motivation, music, and perhaps Rosicrucianism" among his "gobble-mates" in prison, to street musician to panhandler to acidhead gigolo and love loony to harem master to would-be warlock to would-be shaman to the stars (Dennis Wilson of the Beach Boys, Doris Day's son Terry Melcher, Angela Lansbury's thirteen-year-old daughter Didi, that whole fast crowd) to would-be star himself (the Family's recording of Charlie's song "Garbage Dump" is indescribably amazing; he coulda been a contender) to commandant of a pack of savagely cruel, thrill-seeking desert rats in stolen dune buggies, a junior Lucifer tyrannizing the devil's spawn, the demented riding herd on the deluded.

And as Manson's hideous little blood-and-porn extravaganza inexorably plays itself out, like a low-budget production of *Day of the Locust,* as Manson plots the apocalypse behind the sleazy false fronts of the Spahn Movie Ranch or trains his malevolent troops against the backdrop of the blazing, vacant fastnesses of Death Valley, as Los Angeles slowly cooks in its oily languor while its bored, vapid jet-set sensualists themselves toy idly with such foul diversions as satanism, ritual sacrifice, and sadomasochism, we can hardly resist concluding that here is a world about to receive the comeuppance it is asking for, that man, taking his cue from God, creates the devil in his own image. Or, to quote Sanders's touchstone line in *Shards of God,* "the vomit vomits into the vomit."

Is *The Family* a bad book? Well, maybe it is, maybe it is. But it's also the very best bad book I've ever read.

Endnote

Okay, it's pop quiz time. Identify the following:

1. Dan Smoot
2. Rev. Donn Moomaw

(We'll assume you recognize John Mitchell and your mother.)

Answers: Dan Smoot, a former FBI agent, and Rev. Moomaw, a former pro football player, were notorious right-wing blabsters of the time, the Liddy and Limbaugh of their day.

Where are they now? *Sic transit gloria.*

I wrote "Another Great Moment," like its companion piece, especially for this book. It has not been published previously.

Another Great
Moment in Sports

Now feature this, if you can:

Eddie McClammerham, the Wayward Youth with the Tony Curtis forelock, is all grown up; he boasts a family, a ponytail, and a tenuous grip on a lectureship at Stanford University. And he has declared himself an implacable foe of the war in Vietnam, against which he is, on a certain brilliant Palo Alto spring morning in the late 1960s, smack in the midst of the most massive and potentially most volatile political demonstration ever launched here on the campus of his nominal employer, the Harvard of the West, where the ghost of Herbert Hoover, stern and dour, still stalks the ivied halls, looking like a cartoon of himself in a Democratic newspaper.

Well, maybe not all that implacable. I was thirty-six years old, you understand; my forelock was already somewhat grizzled and was beginning to resemble Everett Dirksen's more than Tony Curtis's; and I had five hungry mouths to feed, of which the largest, if not the hungriest, was my own. And jobs at Stanford University—especially menial little part-time temporary numbers like the one I had been clinging to for years—were hard to come by and easily lost; we untenured incendiaries skated on ice as thin as our political convictions.

The target of this particular demonstration was a small, nondescript building called "the Hanover Avenue Facility" of the Stanford Research Institute, a think tank that did a great deal of contract work for the Department of Defense and with which the university itself, under fire from antiwar zealots, had recently and rather sententiously severed its connection—at least to the less than excruciatingly painful extent of officially changing the institute's name to "SRI." Actually, all of the really important defense work was carried on at SRI's sprawling complex of offices in Menlo Park, a couple of miles from Stanford, but the organizers of the demonstration had chosen to hit the Hanover Avenue Facility because it happened to be conveniently situated just off the campus—reminiscent of the old joke about the drunk who lost a dime in a dark alley and then was seen searching for it under the streetlamp at the next corner, where the light was better.

The fact is, I didn't much want to be a party to this demonstration anyhow. In the first place, in order to throw our inconsequential bodies on the line and stop the Odious Machine, it was necessary that we gather in front of the Hanover Avenue Facility at the unseemly hour of 6 A.M., so that we could liberate SRI's oppressed and benighted slave-laborers as they arrived for work. Now this is 6 A.M. in the *morning,* folks—a time of day when according to my limited experience, the very air outdoors is fouled with noxious morning vapors, and sensible people are snug in their beds at home.

I'd been involved in all manner of rallies, sit-ins, teach-ins, and countercultural soirees, most of which had at least started off as very tame affairs; if they later grew a bit . . . raucous, it happened spontaneously, in response to the circumstances of the moment—as when, for instance, our estimable vice president Hubert Humphrey came to campus to deliver a speech defending the war and, with his sophistries and hypocrisies, turned an ill-disposed but perfectly peaceable audience into a raging, slavering mob that would have spanked him soundly and sent him to his room if it could've laid its collective mitts on the slippery old scamp.

Once upon a time, and not all that long ago either, there'd been something called the Peace Movement, comprised largely of soft-hearted, soft-headed liberals not unlike myself—We Hapless Few, as it were. But now the Few had become Many, and the Peace Movement had become the Resistance, and at Stanford its leadership had devolved into the hands of the most bellicose, doctrinaire Richie Rich revolutionaries on campus, a sort of foreshortened Rainbow Coalition that arced all the way from the Red Guards to the White Panthers, with a bland, colorless mass of liberal softies in the middle, holding up the whole airy illusion like the meringue on a moose-poop pie.

So we are gathered, perhaps three hundred strong, just after sunup on the little crew-cut front lawn of the Hanover Avenue Facility, to receive our marching orders. Our leaders, in their undergraduate wisdom—egged on by a single Maoist English professor and a pack of hectoring grad students and junior faculty—have been defiantly bearding the local constabulary, via the media, on a daily basis, vilifying them as pusillanimous porcine poltroons and hinting darkly that they will be subjected to all manner of unspeakable indignities if they dare to interfere with our amiable pursuits—with the predictable result that behind one of the nearby buildings is a small army of angry cops in full riot gear, complete with rifles mounted with tear-gas grenades.

Not to worry, though, because each and every one of us

devilishly cunning anarcho-syndicalists is (supposed to be) equipped with a trusty Wet-Hankie-in-a-Baggie Tear-Gas Neutralizer Kit. (Mine is in the hip pocket of my low-rider bell-bottoms; I'm crossing my fingers that it won't start seeping at some unseemly moment.) According to current counterculture folklore, a wet bandanna tied burglar-style about the lower face will turn away tear gas like a soft answer turneth away wrath—both very shaky propositions, as events will all too shortly demonstrate.

About a block from where we're now assembled, Hanover Avenue ends at Page Mill Road, a major traffic tributary, and half a block from there Page Mill meets El Camino Real, the principal business artery of the entire bayshore side of the San Francisco Peninsula; at the morning rush hour—coming right up—it's one of the busiest intersections in the area, and the perfect spot to administer a dose of urban gridlock to the local body politic.

To that purpose, Our Leaderships are just now informing us, they have dispatched a small squad of Bolshevik gremlins to prank with the morning traffic. (Sure enough, I can already hear from over at the intersection the plaintive beeping of the disgruntled early-bird commuter.) This tactic, we are assured, will distract the police and render them puny in the face of our righteous indignation, even as it secures forever our place in the minds and hearts of The People.

Beep, beep.

· · ·

Actually, the troubling aspects of this demonstration emanated not so much from the leadership as from the followership, of which I was a charter cipher. After all, we were supposedly smart folks, here at the Harvard of the West; if we were being led astray it was our own damn fault.

But for the last few months it had been just about impossible even to identify the leadership, never mind making an impression on it. Indeed, as best I could determine, there *was* no leadership. Oh, strings were being pulled behind the scenes, no doubt, and there were always plenty of officious types running around barking orders ("Awright, People! Go immediately to your Affinity Group!"), and no end of passionate—not to say loud—speechifying, theorizing, and philosophizing. Sometimes, at meetings and rallies, the air would fairly ring with the clangor of clashing dialectics.

And out of this unseemly discord would somehow emerge the policy du jour. For ours was what we proudly called a Participatory Democracy, which seemed to mean that tactical decisions were arrived at spontaneously, by unanimous impulse, with all the scatterbrained coherence of the flight pattern of a flock of grackles. Participatory it certainly was, but I have no idea why we called it a democracy; I don't recall ever once voting on anything, or even being asked for my opinion (although I meekly volunteered it now and then). Just showing up seemed to be all that was required.

Beep, beep, bee-e-e-e-eep!

. . .

Tresidder Student Union is situated near the center of the Stanford campus; its "front yard," so to speak, is White Plaza, an open space officially designated the campus Free Speech area. Tresidder even has a front porch of sorts, a broad, sunstruck stone patio with tables and chairs, a loafer's paradise where my friends and I used to drink coffee and talk politics till the very air turned pinko.

Meanwhile, if there was a rally going on out on White Plaza, the political invective would be flying as thick as Frisbees in the springtime, and when there was no rally in progress, the likelihood was that the male student firebrands would assemble on the plaza for the purpose of playing, of all things, football, that most Philistine of undergraduate pursuits. They weren't going at it seriously, of course—just tossing the ball around. But there was an almost poignant irony in the very notion of these dedicated, passionate young un-Americans—in the context of the times, not a term of opprobrium but a badge of honor—engaging in this all-American pastime.

The irony did not, I think, escape its perpetrators. For the long-haired beardnik eggheads were actually pretty handy with the football—good enough, at any rate, to impress the passing Stanford coeds and make the frat boys reconsider some of their fondest preconceptions. It was a diabolical subversive act, this frolicsome chucking about of the old pigskin, a cleverly disguised Bolshevik recruitment commercial.

Among the regulars was an undergraduate activist I'll call Norman, as unlikely a candidate for gridiron glory as you'll encounter anywhere. A declared Maoist with a minor in overthrowing the state, Norman was a tall, pallid, somewhat overweight kid who looked as if he'd spent his entire life pearl-diving in the library. But there must've been a quarterback bottom-feeding in his gene pool, because he could indisputably throw the football—great, soaring, spiraling rainbow passes that found the intended receiver with uncanny accuracy.

Norman was equally prominent among our so-called leadership. He was a forceful speaker, he had dat ol' dialectic down pat, and he was brave; in each of the two sit-ins I'd been a party to, he was the first to enter the building and one of the last to leave. Somewhere I'd heard he was the scion of a Chicago family of working-class Jewish socialists, which alone would make him an anomaly in the Stanford WASPs' nest and probably go a long way toward explaining why, despite his pudgy, unprepossessing exterior, he seemed tougher than his movement peers, readier for action, more serious and at the same time more exuberantly revolutionary. Unlike all too many of the rest of us, he wasn't rebelling *against* his parents, he was rebelling *with* them.

· · ·

Anyhow, on the morning of the Hanover Avenue Facility action, it's no surprise that Norman—looking rather dashing, actually, with his wet bandanna tied fetchingly around his forehead and, for some unfathomable reason (it's not a bit cold out here), a black leather glove on his right hand—is once again making his presence felt. Right now, he's standing atop the front steps of the building, speaking through a bullhorn, laying out for us the tactics the lead grackles recommend this morning. We are to divide ourselves, it seems, into two groups: the "peaceful protesters" will go across the street and trudge up and down the sidewalk carrying peace signs and singing "We Shall Overcome," while the "militant cadres" (the Maoist English professor is nowhere to be seen, but his language is still very much with us) will link arms in a human chain across the building's entrance, heroically interposing their own personal bodies between the SRI war machine's wretched wage slaves and their cruel masters. There is little question which group Norman intends to ally himself with.

For me, however, the decision's not quite so obvious—because, you see, there are all those cops. They've moved out into the open now; over my right shoulder I can see a noble phalanx of them formed up military-style on the greensward between our building and the next, maybe as many as a hundred cops all decked out in side arms and bulletproof vests and those spooky helmets with the Plexiglas face mask, the front ranks bearing their grenade-launcher rifles at the ready, the rear ranks armed with black nightsticks the size of baseball bats.

Over my left shoulder, in the meantime, a monumental traffic jam has been a-building. Smack in the middle of it I can see the long yellow hump of a school bus, sitting crosswise in the intersection of Page Mill and El Camino. Someone says that one of our gremlins crept up under its hood and made off with the distributor cap.

The din is tremendous: an angry cacophony of car horns, police sirens, and bullhorns. Over where the cops are gathered, the rising sun glints menacingly off all those face masks; the riflemen are doing some sort of thrust-and-parry drill with their grenade launchers, while the rest of the troops, rarin' to crack some Commie noggins, smack their palms impatiently with their nightsticks.

Now, I have the heart of a lion, as is well known in literary circles; nonetheless my feet, those shameless cowards, march straight across the street and fall in with the peaceful protesters, who are shuffling along like a chain gang, as if they've already been busted, beaten, jailed, and nominated for martyrdom. In my mortification, I humbly take up a sign emblazoned with the ubiquitous peace symbol—appropriately (in my case) nicknamed "Footprint of the American Chicken"—and begin slogging the line.

But after fifteen or twenty minutes, I know that if I have to mutter one more chorus of "We Shall Overcome," I'll be in danger of doing something awful that will bring down contumely and disapprobation upon the entire worldwide peace movement. Sincerity is a virtue, but these folks have OD'd on it; they should continue this march straight down El Camino to the local detox center. So I ask the guy in front of me—a divinity student, wouldn't you know?—to hold my peace sign for a minute, and head back across the street, to jump-start the Revolution.

The police have cordoned off Hanover Avenue to automobile traffic, so the street teems with demonstrators. Norman has taken charge of the bullhorn again and is making what must be a terrific speech, judging from the number of *"Right on, man!"* points the crowd awards him every time he bellows, "ALL POWER TO THE PEOPLE!" There are a couple of TV news outfits on the scene, and flashbulbs are popping everywhere, like daytime fireflies.

The tension—like the racket—is almost palpable. The very air is thick with it; just crossing Hanover Avenue is like walking into a powerful psychesonic headwind. There's a line of cars stretching out of sight up Page Mill Road behind the campus, and the word is that traffic on El Camino is already backed up for miles, and right now every single one of those cars is blowing its infernal goddamn horn. I quite literally cannot hear myself think; I am giddy with fear, yet reckless abandon fills me like an inspiration. As I make my way through the crowd, I spot a guy I know, a poli-sci grad student named, let's say, Ronnie, in the human-blockade line. I break in next to him and lock arms against the boobarian hordes.

Ronnie, as it happens, is a fellow Kentuckian. Like me, he is strangely alight this morning with revolutionary zeal; his eyes are blazing unnaturally. He looks a little crazy.

"Ed McClackerty," he shouts above the din, "today I found out what I am!"

"Far out," I holler back. "What are you, Ronnie?"

"Ed McClackerty," he cries—and now he disengages his right arm to thrust his fist exultantly at the heavens—*"I'm a street-fightin' man!"*

"I like a man who knows what he is," I tell him politely. But the noise drowns me out.

Approaching us now is a nondescript little gray gent in a coat and tie—obviously an SRI lackey, poor devil—trying to go to work, he explains in a middle-European accent. No no, brother, we respond in several dozen voices, no work today, today we stop the war in Vietnam! I don't have nossing to do vith that, he protests, I study traffic patterns in Sunnywale! Nonetheless, we turn him away, and as he goes off, grumbling, I ask Ronnie (at the top of my voice) how many other war criminals they've turned back this morning.

"Oh," he shouts cheerfully, "just him. He was the first one. The rest all went in the back door."

Say what? I glance behind me and, sure enough, there beyond the plateglass doors are half a dozen SRI types—*inside* the building, mind you—standing around watching us as though we were already on the evening news. And then at that moment who walks up behind *them* but the little traffic-pattern guy we just turned away!

Slowly the scales fall from my eyes, and when they do the first thing I see is that this blockade is an absolute sham, and we're about to get our heads cracked open for the crime of . . . loitering.

Mumbling something (at the top of my voice) to the street-fightin' man about needing to take a leak, I pull out of the line and plunge back into the crowd, which has become even more restive; passing through it is like pushing through the directionless shove and tug of heavy surf. Bullhorns are blaring, but no one seems to be listening. A few people are hastily tying on their wet bandannas, but many more, having confronted the awesome reality of the juggernaut that's about to descend upon them, aren't even bothering. The rousing bravado of an hour ago has mostly vanished; suddenly everyone looks apprehensive, and there's a potent miasma of impending panic on the air.

Down at the end of the block, where Hanover meets Page Mill, some kind of rumble is in progress; over the heads of the crowd I can see revolving blue gumball-machine lights, and people are craning for a look. Behind me, a woman screams. I hear the muffled *whumpf* of what is, I will realize momentarily, the launching of the first tear-gas grenade. It lands on the street somewhere off to my right—*thwok*—at the fringes of the crowd. More screams, more *whumpf*s, more *thwok*s. My first thought is to seek what I imagine to be the relative safety of the peaceful protester ranks, but I reach the street in time to see those good souls disband in wild disarray, a hissing, fuming grenade having just landed *thwok* amidst them, like a missive from Old Man Hate himself. So much for the soft-answer defense.

The human blockade, meanwhile, has proved itself all too human; like the peaceful protester brigade, it has hastily disassembled itself and melted away into the milling crowds. Already a poisonous fog hangs over us; every stifling whiff of it is a malediction, a dire promise that something truly evil is about to happen. To my right, a chant goes up: "WALK, DON'T RUN! WALK, DON'T RUN!" Instantly, people start running; behind them, the police are on the move. For a long moment I stand there rooted in—again appropriately—the middle of the road, immobilized by uncertainty and fear, as the crowd surges around me, moving down Hanover in the direction of Page Mill.

"WALK, DON'T RUN! WALK, DON'T RUN!"

I try to obey, but once I finally start moving I find it utterly impossible not to run. As I yield to that imperative, I notice that the runner on my immediate right, maybe eight or ten feet away, is young Norman, he of the grenade-launcher throwing arm. He is still wearing his black glove, the mystery of which is about to be revealed to me.

For at that moment a tear-gas canister—they're about the size of a sixteen-ounce can of Colt .45—lands precisely between Norman and me; sizzling venomously with noxious gases, hot as a two-dollar pistol, it bounces on the pavement once, twice, then rolls to a stop as Norman catches up with it, reaches down and scoops it up—with that gloved hand, of course—executes a full 360-degree spin without missing a beat or a step, and heaves the canister in a long, spiraling lateral trajectory straight through a big plateglass picture window on the second floor of the Hanover Avenue Facility. In the final instant before grenade meets glass, the stricken face of a woman appears at the window, then vanishes as the missile punches through and a dense cloud of tear gas fills the room within.

So you might say that Norman has been preparing all his life for his Clear Moment, sacrificing hours of reading Marx in the library to work on his forward pass so that he'll be ready when the time comes, planning for that nanosecond in history that will mark the convergence of the hot grenade, the glove, and the plateglass window. And when it arrives, there is only one thing to do, which he does, and only one way to do it: perfectly. Which he does.

We're all in full retreat now, stampeding down Hanover with the canisters *thwok*ing here and there, hurrying us along. At the intersection, the convoy of patrol cars I'd noticed earlier has arranged itself so as to force us up Page Mill, away from El Camino; there are also a dozen or so cops lined up across the road, in full riot regalia, truncheons at the ready. As we round the turn, my recent acquaintance the divinity student, running flat-out like the rest of us but still doggedly carrying my peace-symbol-on-a-stick, cuts a little too close to the police line and instantly gets keelhauled and cold-cocked for his audacity. The last I see of him, he's facedown on the pavement, one cop standing over him while another cuffs his hands behind his back. Beside him on the roadbed is the over-sized footprint of the American chicken.

We have the right lane of Page Mill all to ourselves, but the left lane is bumper-to-bumper early-morning grumpy-to-start-with commuters who have been, thanks to us, immobilized for the last hour and fifteen minutes. Most of them appear to be reviling and defaming us behind their rolled-up windows as we mush along, gasping for breath in the mephitic air. Actually, though, their presence benefits us, inasmuch as the police, with all those witnesses on hand, are obliged to hold their wrath in check. They can't even drop more tear-gas grenades into our ranks, because if one of those big suckers went a little astray, it could put one helluva dent in the hood of some solid citizen's El Dorado.

The "Walk, don't run!" strategists are at our heels again, but this time we have the luxury of heeding their advice, because the cops are at *their* heels now, and the cops are walking too. Not at what you'd exactly call a leisurely pace, though; this is a forced march. They advance relentlessly, and we're still pickin'em up and puttin'em down at a furious rate. Intuitively, I understand that if I were to stumble and fall, those walk-don't-run nags would walk right over me and leave me there like roadkill for the cops to work over and walk over in their turn, as they'd done so obligingly with the late divinity student.

("Late" doesn't mean the poor guy's dead; it just means I'd bet my ass he changes his major at the soonest opportunity.)

Off to our right, after we've progressed a few hundred yards up Page Mill, is a broad, open field of brown grass, and a handful of our number have peeled off from the Bataan death march and are over in the field calling and beckoning to the rest of us to follow them.

"No!" scream our self-appointed consciences, as in a single voice. "Stay together! Stay on the road! Walk, don't run!"

"Come with us!" cry the schismatics. "Come this way!"

For the third time this morning—the third time before breakfast!—I find myself on the horns of what is essentially the same dilemma, although this time it seems to have no moral dimension whatsoever: I simply have to decide—*right now*—whether my own best chance for survival is in numbers or in flight.

Flight wins! Suddenly I'm scrambling down into the little gully between the road and the field, on my way to freedom! Hey, that's it, I'll just keep on running, I'll run all the way to Canada! Unfortunately, however, I've forgotten all about the First Law of Revolutionary Physics, which is that tear gas is heavier than air. Stepping down into that little ravine is like plunging into the Love Canal; my own breath suffocates me, my eyes are blinded by my tears, I'm seismically disoriented, and I experience an attack of claustrophobia that would deck an exhibitionist. Weeping and gasping and choking and wheezing and reeling and lurching, I scramble out again, a far, far wiser man.

I am, I discover when I get my bearings, right back where I started—on Page Mill Road, surrounded by my chastened fellow insurrectionists. The difference is, they aren't going anywhere; the police have stopped advancing, and we, it seems, have retaliated by halting our retreat.

Let that be a lesson to them! All power to The People!

. . .

The demonstration was over. The cops stayed where they were until they got the traffic moving again, and then they allowed us to straggle back onto campus, a few at a time. There was a halfhearted attempt to rally our troops in White Plaza, but most of us just wanted to go to Tresidder and rinse the tear gas out of our eyes and sit down to a cup of coffee and a doughnut.

The revolution was over, too—at least as far as I was concerned. I was dog-tired, and I'd enjoyed all the amenities of it I could stand. I wasn't just temporarily tuckered out, either; this weariness ran deeper than that: it was positively existential. The time had come to tune out, turn in, and drop off. I would revolute no more forever.

Fast-forward now about twenty years, to the late eighties. I'm in the Louisville airport, seeing someone off, when I notice this handsome, middle-aged young man in a pin-striped suit, Gucci loafers, and a belted raincoat, carrying a swanky leather briefcase and trying very hard to look important. It is, of all people, Ronnie, the street-fightin' man.

I identify myself, and he remembers me. We chat for a couple of minutes; then he glances at his Rolex and says he has to catch a plane. Well, I tell him as we part company, it was good to see you, Ronnie. Where are you off to?

"D.C.," he says, turning to go. "I'm a lobbyist for the Humana Corporation."

O the clear moment.

Endnote

Since I only finished writing this piece about fifteen minutes ago, I don't have a whole lot to add. So I figured I'd just sublet this space to some other worthy purpose—such as, say, the publication of "Ed McClanahanski's Manifesto on the Rise and Disastrous Triumph of Creative Writing as an Academic Discipline," which goes something like this:

I've said that when I inherited Bern Malamud's class at

OSC, my pedagogical role model, stylewise, was Bob Hazel—in honor of whom, on my way to the first class meeting, I slipped into the faculty men's room and took off my necktie. It was the beginning of a long career in academic stealth and subterfuge. Whenever and wherever I taught over the ensuing thirty years, I wanted my writing classes to feel like snug little subversive cells within the institution—liberated zones, as it were. We were coconspirators, my students and I, against the Forces of Oppression, in the insufferable persons of those musty old stupids who ran the rest of whatever English Department I was currently associated with.

And for the longest time, it worked like a charm. In the beginning, in the context of the stuffy, uptight late-Eisenhower era, any class in which students were enjoined to seek Truth and Beauty through—as needed—profaning and blaspheming, not to mention trashing Mom and Dad and all they stood for, was bound to prove popular. Later, at Stanford in the sixties, I expanded the syllabus to include radical politics, drug experiences, and tales of sexual liberation. Ah, the atmosphere was heady, friends, I'm here to tell you! My classes were almost always oversubscribed; undergrads prostrated themselves in my path on registration day, petitioning for admission. Like Bob Hazel before me, I strode the campus as a god!

Okay, a demigod. There's no denying I owed a certain portion of my popularity just to the air of palsy-walsy informality I cultivated in the classroom. The camaraderie was genuine, though; my students and I really *did* become friends, and many of them in turn became part of the parade of missing links that trooped through my Palo Alto household during those entertaining years. I was a pretty damn good teacher, too, in my fashion; my students really wanted to write well, not so much for me as for their classmates—which was, of course, exactly as it should be.

Little did I suspect, however, that I was even then sowing

the seeds for the collapse of Western civilization. For in those days, I'll remind you, a C was still a pretty respectable grade among undergraduates. So on the first day of class each term, when I told my students (speaking in hushed, conspiratorial tones, you may be sure) that I certainly didn't intend to punish them for having no talent and that if they'd just produce the requisite number of pages of fiction—no matter how woefully inept—they couldn't possibly get below a C, the students were positively jubilant. It instantly made the prospect of writing creatively look a lot less intimidating and freed them to try their wings.

Now I don't mean to suggest that I invented grade inflation; you have only to check out Dr. Havighurst's assessment of my maiden short story near the end of this book to see that every creative-writing teacher since the dawn of time has been forgiving in the grades department.

But by the late 1980s, every college teacher of *any* description, in every discipline from Flower Arranging to Bidness Administration to Mechanical Engineering, thought he or she was a creative-writing teacher! They *all* dressed down and did first names and had forelocks, they *all* inflated grades! A's were suddenly (to borrow a phrase from Wendell Berry's grandmother) as common as pig tracks! We'd been co-opted!

Making matters even worse was yet another truly terrible idea of which we forward-looking progressives had all been much enamored back in the olden times: Students' Final Teacher Evaluations. SFTEs are these harmless-looking little questionnaires that the teacher is required to hand out in class at the end of each term, soliciting the student's (anonymous, of course) personal opinion of the educational experience he or she has just endured. ("Does the instructor come to class on time?" "Is the instructor well prepared?" "Rate this course on a scale of 1 to 5 . . .") In other words, not only had the faculty copped out, for all practical purposes, on its solemn responsibility to grade the performance of the students but now we were letting the students grade *our* performance! The monkeys had taken over the zoo!

Originally, the SFTEs were strictly between the instructor and the students; the department administrators merely gathered up the questionnaires, held them in a sealed envelope until the term grades were in, then returned them to the instructor to read in private. This was privileged information; no self-respecting administrator would have *dreamed* of peeking into those envelopes.

But by the late 1980s, administrators were not only reading the damn things, they were actually making personnel decisions on the basis of these fink sheets! You could get fired or passed over for tenure on the strength of some postadolescent twerp's opinion of the way you held your mouth. The sort of shared confidence and trust that I'd always nurtured so carefully in my classes was now utterly out of the question; threaten to tack a "minus" on some kid's A, and the little snitch was liable to rat you out—for tardiness, say—on the next SFTE.

In the spring of 1989, on the last day of the last class I would teach, I handed out my SFTE forms for, blessedly, the last, last time. "The university says I have to give you these," I told my students rather grimly, "but no power on earth can make me read 'em." And I didn't; later, when the department secretary sent them to me, I round-filed the parcel without a second thought—just as I had done for years.

But there were, as a matter of fact, an unusual number of good writers and smart people in that class, and among the best and smartest was a grad student named . . . Tom Marksbury! We'd become friends and (briefly for both of us, thank goodness) bachelor running mates while he was in my class,

and in the years since then I've acquired an almost insupportable burden of respect for his intelligence and acumen. So a
couple of years ago, when I was going through a stack of
manuscripts that had turned up in an old file cabinet (preparing to send them to the Centre College Library in Dan-
ville, Kentucky, where my—ahem!—papers are stashed), I
came across several odds and ends that I just couldn't quite
bring myself to put into deep freeze until I'd given them one
more airing. Naturally, I thought of Tom; let him share *my*
burdens for a change, I figured.

"Hmmm," Tom mused aloud one day, having plugged
away at my runic scribblings for a week or so. "Y'know, I
think there might be a *book* in this."

Tom and I live thirty miles apart, but I distinctly heard
him say that. After lengthy negotiations between his people
and my people, we partnered up and produced the conglom-
erate you see before you.

But to this day I have to wonder what the little fink wrote
on that SFTE.

I WAS COMMISSIONED TO WRITE THIS PROFILE OF PORT ROYAL, KENTUCKY, FOR AN *Esquire* SERIES CALLED "WHY I LIVE WHERE I LIVE." IT WAS REJECTED ON THE GROUNDS THAT IT WAS "NOT UPSCALE LITERARY NEW YORK ENOUGH FOR THIS MAGAZINE." (GO FIGURE.) THE PIECE WAS PUBLISHED IN *The Journal of Kentucky Studies* (FALL 1985).

Where I Live

emplacement, site, location, position, situation, station,
substation, quarter, locality, district, assigned place, pitch,
beat, billet, socket, groove, center, meeting place, focus,
birthplace, dwelling place, fireside, home, place of residence,
address, habitat, location, premises, building, mansion,
house, spot, plot, point, dot, pinpoint, niche, nook, corner,
hole, glory hole, pigeonhole, pocket, compartment, confine,
limit, confined place, prison, coffin, grave
"Place," a found poem,
discovered in my thesaurus

WHERE I LIVE NOW—and where I hope to live as long as I live anywhere—is in a comfortable old white frame farmhouse on a two-lane road a mile or so outside a little Kentucky River town called Port Royal, in what I like to call South-central Northwestern Kentucky, not far (not far enough) from Louisville.

I grew up in South-central Northeastern Kentucky, only about eighty miles east of Port Royal, but I took the long way around to get from there to here. I came by way of Oregon, California, and Montana, my principal stops during a twenty-year ramble through the West, riding the Visiting Lecturer in Creative Writing circuit, following my nose, my muse, . . . and sometimes, my muse's nose.

In fact, I was back on the road again when I landed in Port Royal almost ten years ago and came to a screeching halt. I had recently worn out my welcome as Visiting Lecturer at yet another western university, and my wife Cia and I had then embarked upon what was surely one of the most feckless endeavors in the history of freelance literary enterprise: we were banging about the country in an old VW microbus, trying to put together a book about honky-tonks—which, we were discovering, is something like trying to write about mortuaries when you're full of embalming fluid. By the time we got to Kentucky, we'd had about all the beer, bad country music, and bar-stool philosophy we could handle. We were coming down with a serious case of the honky-tonk blues, compounded by a touch of motion sickness.

Our plan had been to visit my old friends Wendell and Tanya Berry at their farm near Port Royal—Wendell being, of course, the noted Kentucky poet, novelist, essayist, and ecology curmudgeon, who has been a denizen of these parts almost all his life—and to put up for a few weeks of R and R in the vacant tenant house on Wendell's uncle Jim Perry's farm, just down the road. The little house had seen better days, but after all those weeks in the VW it seemed to us extravagantly well appointed and as roomy as all outdoors. And the location was just grand—a pretty river at our doorstep, a garden on the riverbank, a Cinemascope view of the valley without another house in sight. It was the perfect spot for a pair of road-weary nesters to set up housekeeping, and we knew right away that it was going to figure in our future, if we could just manage to survive the present.

Survive we did, although in the process Wendell's estimable Uncle Jim learned the hard way never to let a Visiting Lecturer get a foot in the door; we lived, rent free, in his tenant house—still my all-time favorite residence—for the next five years, until our burgeoning family obliged us to seek larger accommodations. My writing career hadn't proved to be quite as moribund as I'd once thought it was, and with a little help from our friends we bought the house we live in now, out on the other side of town. The McSquatleys were digging in for the long pull.

As urban complexes go, Port Royal doesn't amount to much—a clutch of forty or fifty neat, modest houses on the bluff above the river, a couple of stoutly Protestant churches, a grocery store, a branch of the county bank, a post office, Miss Mary Gladys's junktique store, a garage, and the H&H Coal Company and Drug Store, which has sold neither coal nor drugs for a very long time but does turn a lot of trade in an astonishing variety of feed and seed, soda pop, hardware, rototillers, farm supplies, building supplies, work clothes, housewares, chain saws, candy bars, lawn mowers, wristwatches, gas and oil, instant coffee, microwave mystery-burgers, and conversation. The H&H—or as it's known far and wide in Henry County, "William Van's," after its proprietor, William Van Hawkins—is Port Royal's answer to the Louisville shopping malls that have sapped the economic vitality of this and a hundred other small towns around here; if William Van ain't got it, you don't need it, and chances are you're better off without it.

Port Royal is unincorporated, so it is graced by no city hall, no mayor, not even a constable. But keeping the peace (except at Halloween, which seems to last in this neighborhood from Columbus Day till around Thanksgiving and is apparently celebrated by every sporting young buck under the age of about thirty-seven) generally presents no problem, not since Henry County voted itself dry back in the thirties, and Coondick Garrett closed his poolroom.

We still have our fair share of reprobates, you understand: for instance, there's the local gent we'll call Pisswilliger, who in his youth, spent a few seasons as the star attraction of a carnival sideshow and nowadays occasionally entertains the clientele in William Van's by munching lightbulbs and razor blades—mere appetizers, Pisswilliger hints, for the live chickens and varmints *tartare* he'd dined on when he was big in show business.

And how about old Freck, the village inebriate who wandered into the Baptist church one Sunday morning while the preacher, a young seminarian, was expounding on the text "Can these bones live?" from Ezekiel 37:3. Freck made his way unsteadily down the aisle and installed himself in the front pew, where, evidently contemplating the ravages to the soul of a life misspent, he set up an increasingly audible moaning and groaning whenever the preacher drove home a point. As the seminarian warmed to his theme, he made of his text a sort of refrain, sonorously intoning, as a tag line to each paragraph of the sermon, "Can these . . . bones . . . live?" Each time he posed the question, Freck would answer with a lugubrious groan. "So once again," the preacher declared at last, "once again we must ask ourselves the biblical question, 'Can these . . . bones . . . live?'" "No way!" cried Freck, in a voice thick with remorse and Mogen David. "No way!"

Then there's the widow lady down the road a piece, the one whose woodpile is said to grow miraculously larger each year as the winter progresses. . . .

But in the main, the two hundred or so citizens of Port Royal and its immediate environs are surely the swellest, sweetest, most upright, most generous, least suspicious two hundred folks assembled anywhere this side of heaven's gate—as evidenced by the fact that when a certain disreputable-looking old dropout and his child-bride (actually she was twenty-seven, but next to me she looked a whole lot younger) pulled into town, travel-bedraggled and as poor as Job's turkey, everybody was . . . *nice* to us! They helped us plumb and carpenter and get the resident watersnake out of the cistern and winterize the house and cut firewood; they gave us credit at the garage and the grocery store and William Van's; they invited us to supper, to church, to hog killings and homemakers' meetings and poker parties; in the spring they helped us get a garden in the ground; they brought us fruit and vegetables and eggs and milk and fresh-caught catfish and even, now and then, a squirrel or two. When our babies came along, our neighbors helped us welcome them, and a few years later, when Cia miscarried and we lost our twins, they helped us grieve.

Country people are more trusting—therefore more generous and kinder—than megalopolitans, suburbanites, and other backward races because, if you'll pardon the tautology, they're more secure. Here in Port Royal, we're always among friends. One tries to pull one's weight, of course; for a while there I cut tobacco and bucked hay and forked manure and castrated calves like a very son of the soil. But in the ledger where such accounts are kept, we'll never get our books to balance because our friends just keep right on being good to us.

Not that folks hereabouts don't set great store by their independence. Consider, for instance, my exemplary friend and nearest neighbor Kelsie Mertz, a farmer, trapper, beekeeper, occasional fiddler, and pretty fair Sunday painter, who takes his independence very seriously: ask Kelsie to sell you one of his pictures, and he's liable to tell you to go paint your own if you like it so damn much. "Some people," says Kelsie indignantly, "think that if you've got something nice, *they* ought to have it!" Just so.

The operative social principle, though, is *inter*dependence. Around here, *every*body (my incompetent self excluded) can carpenter a little, or plumb, or wire, or weld, and since we don't have ready access to the service industries, we all rely on our resident geniuses, such as my friend Sherman, the Oral Roberts of backyard auto mechanics, who can heal what ails your car by the merest laying on of hands, or Red Meder, who's not only an artiste with a welding torch but also a dead ringer for both Phil Harris *and* Forrest Tucker and a wonderfully entertaining cusser besides. We even have our own local whole-systems analyst—the jackleg plumber Wendell told me about who, after examining a neighbor's queasy septic tank, solemnly opined that the tank's indigestion had arisen from the owner's failure to chew his food properly.

This part of the country has its problems, certainly. For openers, the imminent collapse of the federally administered tobacco price-support program (when Howard Metzenbaum's your enemy and Jesse Helms is your best friend, you got troubles, pal) threatens to turn a lot of lovely and productive farmland back into a tangled wilderness. In the northwest corner of the county, there's a chemical factory that sometimes seems to bubble as ominously as a witch's cauldron, and since we have no zoning laws, other similarly amiable industries are doubtless eyeing us and licking their chops. We have too many poor people and, probably, too many rich ones too. Our schools, like everybody else's, are understaffed and overadministrated. And Louisville's pernicious suburbs are creeping inexorably in our direction; not ten minutes ago I heard a radio report of a traffic accident in the neighboring county "on the corner of Radiance Road and Rainbow Drive, out in the Heidi Springs subdivision. . . ."

Ah, but the compensations! Our TV reception's not too good, and we almost never have to go to the movies. John Y. Brown Jr. and Phyllis George have moved to New York, and that's been a great comfort. There are no sushi bars in Port Royal, no Volvos, no Hairless Krishnas, and hardly any joggers. We have more cows than people—a social order in perfect balance. The world our children grow up in will be circumscribed, but they'll know it inch by inch; their society will be small, but it will last them all their lives. As long as they behave themselves, they'll never run out of friends.

Cia and I haven't honky-tonked in years. My personal romance with country music ended the night I dropped in for a beer at the Pit Stop Bar & Bait Shop (formerly the M&M Disco & Bait Shop) up in Carrollton, across the county line, and heard a song on the jukebox tenderly entitled "You Fuckin' Jerk, You Piss Me Off." I went home and wrote my own song, about a couple of drifters who find each other, fall in love, and come to rest in Kentucky. I'll spare you the rest of the lyrics, but the chorus goes kinda like this:

> All the roads in the world lead to home, sweet home;
> They all lead the other way, too.
> Some have to stay, and some have to go,
> And some are just passin' through.

No more passin' through for us; the McSquatleys are here for the duration. The fast lane is no place for a '67 VW microbus, anyhow.

Endnote

I would have had a great deal more to say in "Why I Live Where I Live" about my famous friend and neighbor Wendell Berry—who was, of course, exactly the reason why I lived there in the first place—except that writing about Wendell in a venue like *Esquire* would've almost automatically constituted an invasion of his hard-won privacy—which is not to say that I haven't done so with impunity on other occasions.

Wendell and Tanya Berry have been my friends for more than forty years. Wendell and I got to know each other in graduate English classes at the University of Kentucky in the fall of '56; Tanya Amyx, his fiancée, was a senior English major. I was still doing my shades-and-cycle-boots thing, and Wendell was—oh, my—*formidably* straight. Treetop tall and as sober as an undertaker, always gaily decked out in a starched button-down and a narrow necktie and a cardigan sweater, he scared the peewaddin out of me at first; it was like the young Abe Lincoln had just walked in and caught me pretending to be the young Tony Curtis. And young Tony was three years *older* than young Abe.

Still, however warily, Wendell and I liked each other right away, and it wasn't long till I discovered the gleeful, goofy Wendellian grin that lurked just behind all that exterior gravitas. We've had some grand times together over a lot of years:

Like the 1958 Kentucky Derby party where, during a walk in the country after what could have been his fourth (my sixth) mint julep, the coltish young Wendell undertook a six-foot broad jump over an eight-foot creek and landed up to his argyles in backwater.

Or our glorious four-day canoe trip down the Kentucky River a few weeks later that same spring, and the night we spent along the way in the old fishing camp that, a few years later, would provide Wendell with the title of his landmark first book of essays, *The Long-Legged House*. Or another four-day trip we took up the Ohio in 1961 on my father's towboat, the *City of Maysville*. (We put in a great deal of time in the wheel house, where the pilot, a burly, whiskey-voiced old scapegrace named Cap'n Bill, regaled us with highly improbable tales of his sexual prowess. "You know how much I get?" he'd growl, squinting like a pirate. "All I can stand!")

Or the time in San Francisco when, after an uproarious martini-enhanced dinner at a big Fisherman's Wharf restaurant, we were crossing the Golden Gate Bridge and Wendell said to the guy in the tollbooth, as he forked over the toll, "Thank *you*, sir! This certainly is a mighty fine bridge!"

During the years my second family and I lived next door to Wendell and Tanya, he and I logged countless hours of working side by side—housing tobacco, bucking hay, fencing, killing hogs, forking manure, and even (the juxtaposition is intentional) teaching college English. Best of all, though, were the wintry days we worked with Wendell's team of Belgian draft horses, cutting firewood in the woods up Cane Run.

The winter of '77 was especially bitter and protracted; we had snow upon snow upon snow, weeks and weeks of relentless cold. First the ponds froze, then the creeks, then the Kentucky River, and before the siege had ended there were ice-skaters on the wide Ohio for the first time in almost sixty years.

Three or four afternoons a week, Wendell and I would take our chain saws and the Belgians and Wendell's little border collie Zip into the woods, where we'd fell the trees we wanted and limb them, and then use the horses to drag the logs into the clear to be worked up into firewood. Following those great, gorgeous Belgians as, snorting and farting and straining at the traces, they tramped through the picture-perfect snowy woods, the little black-and-white dog nipping at their heels, their breath coming in puffs of white vapor as though they had steam engines inside them . . . Well, it was better than taking an afternoon stroll through a Currier and Ives print—unless you persuade Wendell Berry to tag along with you.

Not even counting all I've learned from him about writing and literature, Wendell has been my mentor in a thousand ways. (I daresay I've taught him a thing or two as well, but we needn't go into that.) Almost daily, as we worked together, he showed me or told me all manner of stuff I desperately needed to know about trees and plants and farm animals, about the ways of weather and the seasons, about handling tools, about stringing fence and building rock wall—and along the way he generously clued me in on the history and the mores of the community he'd lived in all his life, into which I was striving to insinuate myself.

Under Wendell's tutelage, I became that prized commodity in farming communities, a Pretty Good Hand. ("Y'know, Wendell," I told him one blistering August day while we were hanging tobacco in a ninety-eight-degree barn, "my dad always wanted me to learn how to do this kind of work, but I don't think he meant for me to start when I was forty-five years old.") The knowledge he imparted sustained me and my family for years, and I'm eternally grateful for his priceless help and his enduring—some would say persevering—friendship.

As for Tanya, everybody knows what a beautiful, gracious, warm, caring person she is, so here's a flashback that reveals a side of her that her countless more circumspect admirers will never mention:

Once, during our long-ago days at the university in Lexington, Tanya and I and a grad school pal of mine named

Charlie Mahan (now long since gathered unto his fathers) were having lunch together at the Paddock, a student hang-out just off the UK campus. Tanya had to eat and run in order to make it to her one o'clock class. As she was hurrying off, Charlie turned to me and murmured almost wistfully, "*Damn,* she's sexy!"

"Where I Live" describes a life that, as fate would have it, I no longer live. I include it here as a tribute to Port Royal and to all the friends and neighbors who meant so much to me during the years I spent there.

AN AFTERWORD TO THE GNOMON PRESS 1997 REISSUE OF *Famous People I Have Known,* "FURTHURMORE" ALSO APPEARED IN *Wild Duck Review* (DECEMBER 1996). THE ORIGINAL *Famous People* ENDED WITH AN ACCOUNT OF MY INADVERTENT NONPARTICIPATION IN THE VOTER REGISTRATION STRUGGLE IN MISSISSIPPI DURING THE "LONG, HOT SUMMER" OF 1964. ("I COULDN'T EVEN *find* THE DAMNED CIVIL RIGHTS MOVEMENT," I'D CONFESSED IN *Famous People.*)

Furthurmore

ONE AFTERNOON in the early summer of 1964—the very summer in which I would later ride to the rescue of the civil rights movement—I stood in Ken Kesey's front yard under the California redwoods, way out there on the westernmost lip of the land, and wistfully waved good-bye as Ken's psychedelically retrofitted 1939 International Harvester school bus lumbered off eastbound up Highway 84, the Good Ship Further—"Furthur," if you're a purist—adorned stem to stern with luridly amorphous abstract expressionist psyche-doodles and psychedribbles, Ray Charles's "Hit the Road, Jack" blaring from the loudspeakers mounted on the poop-deck, and all my most audacious pals—the Merry Pranksters, they'd lately taken to calling themselves, Ken and Faye and Jane and Babbs and Hassler and Chloe and George and Hagen and them, and the Real Neal (Cassady, that is) at the Wheel—gaily waving back from every porthole, setting sail across the trackless wastes of America for the World's Fair in exotic, unspoiled New York City.

You dip! chided a still, small voice within me. *You missed the boat again.*

No no, I reassured myself, you're a family man, you got responsibilities. Besides, bless their hearts, those nitwits will get busted before they're halfway to Burlingame. Go home and work on your novel, family man, think of your wife and babies, think of your adoring public. Think, you self-absorbed hedonist, of the civil rights movement!

Well, if you've read this far, you know how all that turned out: the civil rights movement muddled through without me, and while my adoring public waited another nineteen years for that novel, I became a family man . . . twice over.

Which means the still, small voice had it right: I'd missed the boat. The nitwits didn't get busted (actually they *did,* but that came later), and as everybody who read Tom Wolfe's *The Electric Kool-Aid Acid Test* knows to the point of distraction, the bus trip turned out to be one of the signal adventures of a gloriously adventurous decade. Ken's loose assortment of proto-hippie sybarites had, almost inadvertently, administered to America its first national contact high, and they came home to California fired with missionary fervor.

They purposed, these new-minted zealots, nothing less than to turn on the world—Heads up, world!—and thereby to show it to itself in a whole new light. The issue of their resolve was an ever-burgeoning series of Bay Area parties called the Acid Tests, hosted by the Pranksters, featuring Day-Glo decor and strobe lights and throbbing-blob light shows—all Prankster innovations—and the cacophonous rock of an unheralded group by the improbable name of the Grateful

Dead, and—ah yes! the refreshments!—God's own plenty of the infamous Electric Kool-Aid, liberally spiked with LSD.

Heads up, world!

Do I hear someone out there muttering that all this seems a bit . . . well, old hat? Permit me to remind you, friends, that in the mid 1960s the chapeau was brand spanking fresh-off-the-rack new, and that the Acid Tests spawned the great Trips Festival at San Francisco's Longshoremen's Hall in early 1966, and that the Trips Festival begat—but you know the begats as well as I do.

Meanwhile, after a few more adventures (so thoroughly chronicled by Tom Wolfe that there's no need to recount them here), Ken did eventually have to do a little jail time. Then he and Faye went back to their native Oregon and set up housekeeping on an old dairy farm in the shadow of Mount Pisgah, near Springfield and Eugene.

So tempus fugited relentlessly onward, and suddenly we've eased into the 1990s somehow, and Ken has this new book out entitled *The Further Inquiry,* a sort of recapitulation of the original bus trip in the form of a screenplay about a purgatorial mock trial of the late, much-lamented Neal Cassady (who died under mysterious circumstances in Mexico in 1968), to determine whether his spirit is suitable for admission into heaven.

To promote the book, rumor has it, Ken has resurrected the bus and reassembled as many of the old crew as are still (as Lord George Buckley used to say) sensible to the pinch, and is preparing to embark on one last trip across the country, destination the Smithsonian, where he plans to donate Furthur to posterity, that generations yet unborn might see in it a model for liberating themselves from the constraints of some still undreamed-of Twenty-First Century Eisenhower Era.

Now, by the time reports of these goings-on reached me in

Port Royal, in the waning days of the summer of 1990, I was in a bad way. Earlier that summer, my marriage, which I'd naively supposed was indestructible, had blown up in my face as abruptly as a letter bomb. I survived, but I had suffered major collateral damage, and so far, the progress of my convalescence was not encouraging.

So anyhow, there I am—or there, at any rate, is what was left of me—shell-shocked and bewildered amidst the rubble of domestic cataclysm, forlornly wondering wot-the-hell-next, when—*mirabile dictu!*—here comes the bus again!

Shall I do it this time? Shall I submit my aging but still serviceable person to the rigors of this unprecedented second chance, mayhap to drown my sorrows in Electric Kool-Aid? Hey, you betcher sike-o-deelic ass I shall! Make room for one more geezer, pals! Hit the road, Jack!

. . .

"The bus," Ken is fond of saying these days, "is like Zapata's horse"—which, he will remind you, ran off into the hills when its master (Brando in the movie) was cut down in ambush. According to Hollywood-enhanced legend, the noble steed roams there to this day, awaiting the first shots of the next revolution and the coming of the new Zapata—or the return of the old one.

Could be. Certainly, *some* variety of magic or miracle of regeneration has been at work here, if the bus that now stands gorgeous and gleaming in Ken's barnyard is the same one I'd last seen moldering into the ground on this exact spot back in 1985. The original Furthur—the Ur-Furthur, if you will—though it was painted and repainted so often that the paint itself became a sort of carapace, an inch thick in spots, always had a rather murky, haphazard look, as if it had been assaulted by a band of renegade finger-painters.

(Indeed, my own daughter Kris, who in 1964 was four years old, still remembers slapping on one of the first daubs, in the company of her favorite childhood playmate, the Keseys' daughter Shannon.)

But this 1990 incarnation is a Furthur of an altogether different hue, an hallucinogenic little cream puff featuring everything from a man-sized Sistine Adam to a spotted owl to a radiant Sun God to Pogo to a school of surreal fish to the obligatory Grateful Dead death's head to Oz-inspired lions and tigers and bears to Buddhas to totem poles to seagulls to the Silver Surfer—an eye-popping panorama of intertwined images and icons, all rendered in meticulous detail ("Holy shit!" marvels a tiny Tin Woodsman, standing agog on the Yellow Brick Road), all varnished to a shimmering high gloss, all interrelated to an extent that declares, in no uncertain terms, that what you see is the product, Gulley Jimson–like, of a single, unifying vision—Ken's, of course—yet in such a wild array of styles and techniques as to make it abundantly apparent that every artistic talent within hailing distance had a hand in this paint job. Earl Scheib need not apply.

So is this *the* bus, or a ringer? More to the point, does it matter?

"Mr. Kesey," sniffed a Smithsonian spokesparty on the phone, "is running around Oregon in something he *calls* the original bus, invoking the Smithsonian's name without our permission. We are *not* interested in reproductions, facsimiles, simulations, or counterfeits of any description whatsoever."

One is tempted to inquire whether the Smithsonian's interest might be piqued if Mr. Kesey offered to have himself stuffed and mounted on the bus as a hood ornament. And one might also wonder, idly, whether the Smithsonian is familiar with that ancient Prankster caveat "Never Trust a Prankster."

But one bites one's tongue and bides one's time, awaiting Mr. Kesey's rejoinder, which isn't long in coming.

"Are we dealing with the body," he snorts, "or are we dealing with the spirit? Because that's what the bus is, see, a spirit, not a bucket of nuts and bolts. Giving this bus to the Smithsonian would be like putting your balls in a golden chest and sending them to the Queen. It'd be a nice thing to do, but it would be a mistake."

This whole stunt is just a hustle, then? Just another book tour, tricked out in love beads and bell-bottoms?

"That's like saying I put on the Acid Tests to promote Tom Wolfe's book. On these book tours, the publishers want to kiss the bookstore owners' asses, and they want the writers to be their lips. I'll never sell enough books on this trip to make any money. But the bus isn't a *thing*, it's an *event*, it doesn't work until it's full of people, and music, and it begins to warble, and reverberate. It wouldn't be *right* to turn it into a relic, an artifact! The Smithsonian has talked itself out of this bus!"

• • •

Intending to take full advantage of the therapeutic, restorative, recreational, and literary possibilities in this adventure, I had contrived to present myself at the Kesey farm almost two weeks before the scheduled date of departure, Major Magazine press card in my hatband, ready to ride scribe.

(Actually, I wasn't ready for much of anything, with the possible exception of a winding-sheet. Stricken I was, and down in the mouth to a disfiguring degree, alone and palely loitering. Fate had deposited me on the Keseys' doorstep like so much soggy wet-wash, still warm from the Maytag of life.)

Ken and Faye have made their home for many years in a capacious hay barn on a sixty-five acre farm in the Willamette Valley, a few miles south of Springfield. It's been a haven to me since the days when I roamed the west on the Visiting Lecturer in Creative Writing circuit, searching for some modest little sinecure to call my own. More than a few of the grandest times of my life were had right here, over the years—some of the craziest poker games (Ken's favorite call is "Dukers, Jukers, and One-Eyed Pukers Wild") and craziest conversations (Mad Genius Paul Foster: "Since the number of people now alive is greater than the total of all now dead, it follows that death has been reduced to a 50 percent probability. And since the world's population is still increasing, the odds are inevitably going to improve . . .") and craziest psychotropic cocktail parties (one memorable Kentucky Derby Day a thousand years ago, we started out on silicone shoe polish fumes, worked up to psilocybin, and ended up knocking back a few schnapps juleps) . . . In short, a hard place to be unhappy in.

Still, being of a resolute and determined nature, I managed to suffer pretty good during those two weeks, although there were a couple of moments when I was in grave peril of enjoying myself just a little.

In the mornings, say, drinking bottomless cups of coffee at the big round cluttered dining room table that is to the Kesey Corporation what the War Room is to the Pentagon, sitting there with the soft autumnal Oregon sunshine streaming through the windows, sharpening our wits with a taste of Colonel Kesey's finest prankweed while we plotted strategy for the Great Smithsonian Shuck-Off. It was at one such session that I was elevated from (self-appointed) Dean of the School of Subjective Journalism to the exalted post of Minister of Misinformation, from which vantage point I was to fire salvos of obfuscation at the Smithsonian via the public press—which, it being a slow season for stories about fun and frivolity, was eating this one up.

(Hello, AP? This here's the Reverend Mackrelham, Minister of Misinformation, with the latest sound bite from the Kommandant! Headline: KESEY SCORNS SMITHSONIAN OFFER! *Lead:* "The Smithsonian says it wants to 'restore the original bus,' scoffed the redoubtable Sage of Oregon today, striking a defiant stance. 'I told 'em, Okay, fine, let's paint it yellow!'")

(Hello, CNN? This here's the Imam Hammerclam, Mullah of Misinformation, with the latest . . .)

Actually, I wasn't all that great at this line of work. In print, see, I can lie with the best of 'em—what's a writer who can't lie?—but I've never been any good at the old one-on-one shuck 'n' jive. My heart pounds so loud you can hear it over the telephone, my voice cracks as though I'd been called to the principal's office, my face flushes as if . . . well, never mind. Also, you have to be fast on your mental feet in the PR biz, nimble enough to stay a step or two ahead of the curve—whereas I am notoriously retroactive in the snappy riposte department, generally coming up with the right thing to say about two weeks after the appropriate moment.

I was no Marlin Fitzwater, that's the point.

Nonetheless, we were being besieged by the very targets we besieged: all the local papers—the Portland *Oregonian,* the Eugene *Register-Guard,* the Roseburg *Gazette*—ran big feature stories as a matter of course; *People* was in touch, and *Newsweek* and *Time;* the San Jose *Mercury-News* sent its ace reporter Lee Quarnstrom—himself an old inner-circle Prankster—to ride with us and do a series of pieces for national syndication; the *New York Times* and NPR were scrambling aboard. The popular press, I was discovering, is like a music box; *anyone* can play it.

We spent one entire day (don't ask why) fashioning, out of Mylar and bent sticks and helium balloons and Day-Glo tape and good old Yankee know-how, our very own flying saucer, which, that evening, we managed to get airborne to an altitude of about forty feet, and then somehow inveigled the local TV station (call letters KEZI, believe it or not) into putting it on the eleven o'clock news. They ran it as a "Martians Invade Kesey Farm to See Bus Bound for Smithsonian" sort of thing, an antidote to all those ominous stories about the preparations for the looming war in the Persian Gulf. Nobody seemed to notice that the diameter of the flying saucer was exactly that of the Keseys' dining room table.

So an unconscionable amount of fun was being had, and this was truly a hard place to be unhappy in.

Hard—but not impossible.

· · ·

Mount Pisgah, altitude around four thousand feet, rises as bold and tawny as a dromedary's hump amongst the lesser hillocks in the broad Willamette Valley. At its summit, about an hour's determined hike from the farm, is a modest memorial to Ken's and Faye's son Jed, their youngest, who was killed at twenty when the University of Oregon wrestling team's van fell off a Central Washington mountainside in a snowstorm in 1984. (Properly speaking, it really isn't a memorial at all, since it doesn't even bear Jed's name; rather, the Keseys and their friends caused it to be placed there as, in Faye's words, "a gift from Jed.") The marker replicates, in bronze, a basalt outcropping about the size of a stout tree stump, maybe four feet high, topped by a bronze bas-relief of the valley that spreads itself tremendously before it. From the farm, you can see the marker, a fleabite on the dromedary's hump; from the marker, you can see the farm, distance rendering the big red barn a microscopic Monopoly hotel. The top of Pisgah is a serene, beautiful, melancholy spot, and during those sunny au-

tumn days before the trip, I oft betook my wounded and solitary self up there to sit with my back resting against Jed's
reassuringly sturdy gift, and commune with dat ole debbil
Mr. Mortality.

Three months earlier, just one day after my smug little pipe
dream of a world had suddenly come crashing down about my
ears, I'd made another, far more desperate journey west, that
time to my dear California friend KC's place, in the hills
above Palo Alto. Just minutes after I arrived, very much the
worse for the wear, someone phoned KC with the news that
his own close friend Drew, whom I had also known and liked,
had gone home from a party the night before and, despondent
over the recent collapse of his marriage of nineteen years, put
a bullet through his head.

Now a coincidence like that will tend to stick with a person
for a good long while—which is why I was still thinking
about it three months later, on Jed's mountaintop in Oregon.

I don't mean that I was contemplating following Drew's
example, but rather just that his death had brought me to a
whole new, intimate knowledge of how, assailed by a confusion of grief and disappointment and pain and despair and
(oh yes) guilt, a person could do such a thing. I couldn't have
done it myself—but I wouldn't have minded too much if
someone else had done it for me. In a story of mine called
"Finch's Song" there's a beleaguered character whose gloomy
ruminations perfectly reflected my own frame of mind:

"By little and little," I had written, "Finch's dread of his departure from this mortal coil had at last almost entirely given
way to a deep, inchoate longing to begin the journey, a longing
not so much to die as merely to be . . . elsewhere, to be *taken,*
to join those shadowy legions known as The Departed."

Jed Kesey and his sister, Shannon, and older brother,
Zane, along with their half-sister, Sunshine, had grown up

with my first set of kids, Kris and Cait and Jess. As adolescents, they'd spent whole summers together at the farm; I seem to recall that Cait was sort of sweet on Jed one summer. He was a fine, high-spirited, handsome boy—"a lightfoot lad," as Housman has it—and his loss was perhaps the first my children had suffered out of their own generation. From Pisgah's heights I could see his gravesite, just beyond the barn far below me. I wished with all my heart that he and I could trade places, that Jed were up here on the mountain with his whole unlived life opening out before him, and I were burrowed deep beneath the Oregon sod, two thousand miles from the home I could no longer love.

Lee Quarnstrom, yet another indispensable old friend, arrived two or three days before the bus was scheduled to embark. One morning, Lee and I were sitting at the dining room table drinking coffee when Lee suddenly stood up and looked out across the barnyard toward Jed's grave and said, "My son was shot dead on the street on Fisherman's Wharf eight years ago. He was eighteen years old. I think about it every day."

Death, needless to say, is a fact of life: Enis and Neal, *sic transit gloria.* Gordon Fraser, that sweet man. My old Maysville drinking buddy LouJack Collings, felled by a stroke at forty-one. Dear Fred Nelson, a suicide in his midforties. Lanky and Bobby Sky and good old Page Browning, three Prankster pals of mine who'd checked out early. Jed. Drew. Lee's boy. The marriage that was supposed to outlive, by an eternity, the two mortals who were party to it.

After Drew's death, I wrote a little poem, another first for me. If I can be said to have a strong suit, poetry is certainly not it, so mine is doubtless a poor effort, and I offer it here in all humility. It's called "The Hosts," and, of course, it's for Drew:

With our mind's eye
We watch over our departed guest,
Anxious to see him safely home.
How brief the visit,
How long the vigil!

. . .

The bus, the man said, is not a thing, it's an event. Hoo boy, I'll say it is. On a shakedown run to Portland the day before the big trip is to begin, while Ken is signing books in a big downtown bookstore, the bus is fairly mobbed by a traffic-blocking throng of Furthurphiles of every stripe and vintage, hippie graybeards and thistle-headed punks, literary duffers and yuppie culture-mongers crowding round to glom the magic, all thirsting powerfully for the merest taste of Old On-the-Bus, that ineffable elixir from an age when everything and anything seemed not merely possible but likely.

I spot a couple of old friends among them, and get off and mingle a bit. After a few minutes, though, I find myself inexorably drawn back on board.

"When you first get on the bus," Ken had told me just that morning, "it seems dangerous, and everything outside seems safe. But after you've been on it for a while, that turns around, and the bus is where you want to be. The danger is outside."

Danger or no, inside the bus is definitely where one wants to be. Wonderfully wired for sound, with walls all Day-Glo whorls and swirls, and carpets and cushions enough for a pasha's tent, it is deliciously cozy, like being inside a colossal translucent Easter egg. This is the absolute domain of artist and dedicated Prankster Roy Sebern, who decorated it, and who is its guardian and protector, and will climb your frame if you come in without wiping your feet. The Secretary of the

Interior, we have dubbed him. And before long, I become almost as protective of that sweet space as Roy is. To be On The
Bus, I am already discovering, is to be inside a work of art; the
real pleasure is in looking out and observing the gratification
and delight of the viewers. Thinking about that, I begin to
understand what makes the Mona Lisa smile.

Aside from several energetic second-generation Pranksters (who cheerfully undertake, thank heavens, to do most of
the real work on the trip), our basic crew is largely of the
geezer persuasion. "In 1964," Ken reminds us as we make our
way south to San Francisco, "we were young people, trying to
turn on the old. Now we're old people, trying to turn on the
young." What he doesn't say is that this time we are also dam-
aged people, most of us; death and divorce have touched our
lives, and pain and loss and failure.

"And when we show up in this bus," he goes on, "the kids
see that we've made good on a promise, and they're *lifted* by
that, it makes sparks go off in their hearts, and strengthens
them." And the little pep talk makes sparks go off in geezer
hearts, and lifts and strengthens us as well.

In Berkeley, where we spend a day campaigning for our old
friend Wavy Gravy, who's a candidate (though not, it turns
out, a successful one) for a seat on the city council, Ken
waxes political:

"There's a battle for constitutional rights going on," he declares, "and it's called the War on Drugs. But it's not over yet,
so don't stop fighting. Give the government enough rope, my
daddy used to say, and it'll step on its dick every time. They
have no more right to tell us what we can put inside our heads
than they have to tell women what they can do inside their
bodies. *This*"—he points to his own great bald noggin—"is
our last stronghold! Don't let them take it from us!"

And a day or two later, at a reading in San Francisco, he re-

gales a large, enthusiastic audience with a riff that is fast becoming a Kesey classic, his advice-to-writers exhortation:
"You writers, one of these days you'll be walking along, and
suddenly you'll look up and there, across the street, will be . . .
God! And he'll say, '*Co-o-o-ome to Me!* Come to Me and I will
make the words fly into your ears like little bluebirds and out
of your mouth like honeybees! Come to Me and I will get you
a grant from the NEA, and a good review in the *New York
Times*! Co-o-ome to Me!' And it's the job of you writers to
say"—now his fist comes up, with a defiant middle finger
standing at attention—"it's your job to say, 'Fuck you, God!
Fuck you!'" As always, it brings the house down.[1]

These thunderous admonitions, though, are the exception, not the rule, on this trip. "There's nothing complicated
about what we're doing," he explains gently the next day to a
group of sweet-faced coeds we've happened upon on the
Stanford campus. "The bus is like a kite, or a sunset, or fireworks, or a tree in the fall. You go by and people smile, and
you smile, and that's it. But it's enough."

• • •

Enough? Well, maybe—for most folks. But there are afflic-
tions that no amount of kites and sunsets can assuage,
wounds too deep for any soothing balm. Amongst countless
loving friends both old and new, I was incurably, inconsolably
lonesome and heartsore; awash in a cornucopia of diversions,

1 I first heard Ken deliver himself of his advice-to-writers dictum in 1988,
in a speech at the University of Louisville. The person I was with at the
time—who was then showing serious symptoms of acute sanctimonious-
ness—objected to his remarks, on the grounds that they were blasphemous.
I disagreed, but for years was unable to articulate my reasons. This troubled
me until a few months ago when during a reading of "Furthurmore," it suddenly dawned on me: That's not God, that's the Devil! And not only are the
righteous *permitted* to say "Fuck you!" to the Devil; indeed, they're *enjoined*
to say it!

I clung to my unhappiness like a drowning man clutching a concrete lifesaver.

But first, about those diversions: I never saw any Electric Kool-Aid on this trip, but there was some very interesting orange juice circulating from time to time. (Lee Quarnstrom complained one night on the road about all those transparent purple bunnies hopping across the Interstate. "Hallucinations are shy," Ken reminded him. "But if you entertain them, they'll bring all their friends, and then they're hard to get shut of.") Then too, there was the Wavy Gravy campaign ("A rubber chicken in every pothole! Put a *real* clown on city council!"). And a Halloween party at which Huey Lewis showed up as an Elvis impersonator. (Hey, you don't believe me? I got pictures!) Paul Krassner, the *Realist* editor and sometime stand-up comedian, came on board, firing zingers from the hip. ("Used to be, you'd go to a rock concert, and some total stranger would walk up and hand you a pill, and you'd take it without a second thought. These days, we've got the Tylenol killer. That's why I never take any legal drugs.")

On the aforementioned night of the transparent purple bunnies, I even roused myself out of my torpor long enough to get off a pretty good one-liner of my own. But modesty forfends—so I'll let Lee tell it for me:

"The lowest point so far," he wrote in one of his syndicated pieces, "was at Dunnigan, north of Vacaville, where we finally stopped, at 3:30 A.M., after a night of Prankster music and hallucinations, to get some sleep in a crummy flat place just off the freeway. Here were a dozen or so of us jammed sideways in the bus, bodies bent and twisted between coolers and cameras and other trappings and paraphernalia, the whole joint reeking of the vaporous effects of the elk-and-bean chili we had eaten at a stopover dinner with friends up in the Oregon Vortex, none of us really comfortable enough to sleep. As we lay there, mind-goblins dancing out at the edges of our vision, each of us feeling just damned miserable, McClanahan, in a send-up of the Old Milwaukee beer commercial, said loudly:

'Y'know, fellas, it just doesn't get any better than this!' "

Meanwhile, I too plugged doggedly away at my scribblings, laboriously (or so it seemed) taking notes for my Major Magazine assignment, but my heart wasn't in it; I still had some loitering to do, the paler the better. Old friends abounded, popping up like transparent purple bunnies (Peter Najarian! Mountain Girl! Vic! Jane! Stark Naked![2] Bob Hunter! Chloe! Jim! Page Stegner! Candace!); new friends (I think particularly of Wally and Roseanna and Roseanna's beautiful mother Regina, who opened their splendid Marin County home to this roving band of superannuated hipsters, flipsters, and finger-poppin' granddaddies[3]) raised my spirits amazingly. But some essential portion of me was still . . . elsewhere, and couldn't be reached.

The day we campaigned for Wavy Gravy was one of those picture-perfect California fall days, all golden sunshine and cerulean skies with little white clouds like puffs of smoke from God's own hookah. A three-man Dixieland ensemble was tootling merrily away on the little caboose platform at the rear of the bus, and a small army of Gravyites in big flappy shoes and outsized polka-dot pants and goofy hats and Bozo wigs and rubber noses surrounded us as we rolled slowly through the winding, flower-bedizened streets of the Berkeley hills, cheering on groovy ole Gravy as he stood atop the bus in all his clownery, making madcap—or just plain mad—campaign speeches over the loudspeaker. ("Yup, I always wanted to assassinate Nixon with a ballpoint pen, so I could

2 d. 1993.
3 With another bow to Lord George.

say, 'Eat Bic, Dick!'") Yet even at the daffiest, dizziest apex of the hijinks, hard truths obtruded.

"See that church over there?" Lee said to me quietly, amidst the merriment. "My son's funeral was in that church."

Later that day, during what might be described as a pre-emptive nonvictory party at Wavy's Hog Farm commune in downtown Berkeley, I happened to be in the kitchen with Lee and Ken while the party roared in the other room. The two of them stood there by the kitchen sink in a broad beam of late afternoon sunlight, the featured players in what was—and is—for me a deeply moving tableau.

"Up in the hills today," Lee told Ken, "we went past the church where my son's funeral was held."

"You never get over it," Ken said softly.

"Yeah," Lee said. "And you never want to."

"Right," said Ken. "It's how you keep them with you."

Compared to grief, I was beginning to discern, dying is a breeze.

·   ·   ·

Mutiny! On only our eighth day out, at the University of the Pacific in Stockton, while Ken is in the auditorium doing a reading and signing books, a lawless minority of the crew commandeers the bus and mysteriously disappears it some-how into the California night, leaving only its chalked out-line and the cryptically disarming old Prankster motto NOTHING LASTS inscribed on the pavement.

There are rumors they've absconded to Reno to blow the booty they discovered in the hold, but the more likely story is that they took the backstreets out of Stockton, paused some-where north of town just long enough to hide Furthur's exu-berant exterior under a quick coat of water-soluble powder-blue church-bus anonymity (with "Mount Pisgah School for the Dumb" emblazoned on the sides), and hightailed it back to Oregon—perhaps the only mutiny in maritime history planned down to the last detail by the captain of the ship.

What, then, was the point of it all? If he never intended to complete the journey, if he had no intention whatsoever of presenting *any* bus to the Smithsonian, or even of driving this cherry new edition to D.C. just to give the stuffy old Institution's leg a well-deserved pulling, if, fer Crissakes, he wasn't even interested in promoting and selling his own book, why did Kesey go to the huge bother and expense of setting out on this foredoomed misadventure in the first place? Why assemble a crew and call in the media and assert his considerable presence upon the public consciousness once again, when he knew from the word go that the end of the line would come, God save us all, in Stockton?

As those who love Ken and know the history of his endeavors have long since come to understand, his purposes were, as ever, many and varied, great and small, selfless and self-serving, artistic and political, cosmic and comic, complex and simple-minded.

But my own short-form answer goes something like this: He wanted expressly to effect a reappearance of Furthur (remember Zapata's horse?) in this time of terrible national ennui, a time when the revolutionary spirit of the sixties seemed moribund, extinguished, buried beneath the rubble of the recent past.

And it worked. Wherever we took the bus, from the shopping mall in Roseburg, Oregon, to the streets of Berkeley, it was greeted by smiles of recognition, honking horns, upraised fists, and more V signs (okay, peace signs, if you insist) than I'd seen in twenty years. On a cold, windy weekday midnight, in the parking lot of a convenience store on the outskirts of Weed, California, it instantly drew a crowd of admirers; in Portland and Berkeley and San Francisco and Palo Alto, it drew sweet, mild-mannered little mobs. Even to those unfamiliar with its fossilology, Furthur seemed— seems—almost immediately to suggest personal liberation, artistic freedom, gaiety, joy; everywhere one sensed an almost palpable wonder in the air and felt oneself present at the rebirth of a frail, nascent kind of hope.

"We have to reestablish the whole idea of *trust* in this nation," Kesey declared in that rousing speech in Berkeley. "The war is not on drugs, it's on consciousness. If Jesse Helms wants to lock horns with God, I can take him up there and introduce him in twenty minutes. But it won't be the Southern Baptist God with the big voice and the white beard, it'll be the God of the stars and the lights and the planets and the colors. The government says we should Just Say No. But I think we should just say . . . Thanks!"

My most treasured memento of the trip is a snapshot of myself (taken by David Stanford, Ken's editor at Viking) sitting atop the bus as we cruised down the coast highway toward Santa Cruz. The blue Pacific's on my right, the wind is in my face, and I look happier than I'd been in months.

Which reminds me: Thanks, Ken. Thanks a million.

• • •

And so it ended. I came back to Kentucky and faced up to the grim realization that even in Port Royal, the more things change, the more they change. I spent a miserable, restless winter trying to come to terms with living alone in the big, empty farmhouse that echoed mercilessly with ten years' worth of memories. The weeds had taken the garden, the neighbors' dogs had taken the sheep, the possums had taken the chickens—except for four wretched roosters who'd so far survived the watches of the night by huddling together in the top of a hickory tree. Otherwise, the livestock consisted solely of my old yellow, jake-legged tomcat, Sunset, who'd lived there as long as I had and who somehow seemed, that winter, to be exactly as sad and lonesome as I was. I contemplated writing one more country song—"Four Roosters, a Tomcat, Old Grand-Dad, and Me"—but the title pretty much said it all, so I never got beyond it.

During the winter, the possums picked off the surviving roosters, one by one, and the Major Magazine cut my three thousand allotted words to three hundred and ran it as a photo caption under an immense depiction of Ken in some sort of pirate getup, clowning around. It's time I stopped writing about this guy, I told myself; after all, it would be nice to be the protagonist of my own life story.

There was one more shining bus-trip moment, though: I was talking to KC on the phone one evening in the dead of that dismal winter, burdening him yet again with my miseries and megrims, when he asked me if I recalled crossing the Golden Gate Bridge in the bus, back in the fall.

I did remember it, vividly, because there had been a little group of people, gaily dressed as if they were celebrating something, gathered on the pedestrian walkway in the middle of the bridge, and when Furthur came toddling along they all got wildly excited, waving and jumping up and down and applauding and so forth; some of them, as I recalled, even threw flowers. But why did he ask?

Well, KC explained, that was a group of Drew's friends and family. They were gathered there that morning, more than three months after his death, to cast his ashes into the bay and say one last good-bye. And when the bus happened along at just that moment, they unanimously (and, no doubt, quite correctly) took it as a blessing, a benediction.

Just say Oh Wow.

By the time spring came creeping in at last, and the crocuses had pushed their little elfin heads up through the snow, I knew I'd never make it through another winter in that house. So I put it on the market and, to my surprise, sold it almost immediately. Then I went to Lexington, sixty miles away, where I had family and friends beyond number, and found a cottage that seemed ideally suited to be a disconsolate old bachelor's pad. I closed both transactions on the same day, around the middle of April 1991, and began to plan the move.

Two weeks later, on the first Saturday in May—which every Kentuckian knows from birth is Derby Day—I went to a Derby party near Lexington, and there I met a tall, beautiful Belgian piano teacher named Hilda, who had the bluest eyes and the brightest smile and the prettiest ways I've ever been struck dumb by.

She also had, as I discovered on our first date, a monumental Great Dane—Lisa—not to mention a grand piano the size of a two-car garage. Nonetheless, after we'd seen each other a few times, I'd regained my eloquence sufficiently to persuade her that we could all fit very nicely into this no-longer-disconsolate bachelor's humble pad.

"Sunset," I confided to my feline associate one mellow cocktail hour around the first of June, "everything's about to change again. We're gonna move to town and live with two tall, beautiful foreign ladies. And Sunset, old top, you're gonna love it!"

Sunset said he'd drink to that.

Hilda and I were married on the last day of July 1991, on the very spot where we'd met three months earlier.

Lisa and Sunset hit it off famously as well and were a loving couple until three summers ago when Sunset became, alas, a widower.

Lexington, Kentucky
June 1997

Endnote

In late September of 1997, Ken had a stroke. Faye hustled him to the hospital very quickly, and the damage was minimal: temporary paralysis of his right arm and hand. By coincidence, Hilda and I had planned an early October visit to Oregon. We thought of canceling, but Faye wouldn't hear of it.

So we went, and by the time we got there, five or six days after the stroke, Ken was already back home—"walkin' around barkin' orders," as his daughter Sunshine had warned us on the phone, which is to say that he was very much himself.

"So how you feelin', bro?" I asked rhetorically, by way of a greeting.

"As my dad used to say," he answered, grinning, "I feel like somethin' a coyote threw up over a cliff."

Still Kesey after all these years.

MY FIRST ATTEMPT AT A FULLY REALIZED, ADULT SHORT STORY, FOR
DR. HAVIGHURST'S CREATIVE-WRITING CLASS IN 1952, IN RESPONSE TO
HIS ASSIGNMENT: A STORY WITH FLASHBACKS.

Fear and Hope
and a Gutter

Every step seemed to bring his face nearer the sidewalk, his feet farther from it. As he lurched forward, the cracks in the concrete slid fast and faster beneath him, and he came to believe he was actually flying. The wet sidewalk reflected rhythmically flashing red signs, and though he could not muster the strength to look up and read them, he knew they all said the same thing: BAR-flash-WHISKEY-BY-THE-DRINK-flash-BAR-flash. The streets were empty and the bars closed at this time of night, but still they kept their goddamn signs going, just so you wouldn't forget about them by opening time tomorrow morning. As if anybody could.

Then the legs buckled beneath him and he pitched forward blindly. He groped frantically for something to hang on to, his hands clawing the air, finding nothing. The edge of the foot-high curb grazed the left side of his face and smashed into his groin at once, and he drew his knees up to his stomach in pain as his body slid gently into the gutter.

Lying there, his cheek resting on the moist coolness of the brick street, he waited patiently for the pain in his abdomen to subside. It left him, finally, and all that remained of it was an overpowering urge to vomit. He gagged several times but succeeded only in tying his guts into knots, nothing more. Giving up, he lay quietly, his sides heaving with exhaustion.

God, he thought, the old-timer *said* it would get to this, where not even the stuff you drink down here can put you all the way under. He said it just kills your body, but it leaves your mind alive to think. He said when you get that far gone, there's no chance of pulling yourself together. You can't go anywhere but down. Wonder what it was that made it so much torture for the old-timer to think? Jesus, it's not the thinking that gets me, it's those damned dreams that drive me off my spinner. The same dreams, always the same three dreams! And every time I have them, my guts shrivel up a little more, and another little part of me dies and rots away while it waits for a decent burial! Twenty-four years old and I'm a walking corpse, drunk on fear with a whiskey chaser!

He rubbed his hand over his sallow, unshaven jaw, and he wondered if it showed in a man's face when his soul was dying. Feeling the loose, sagging flesh beneath his matted beard, he decided that it did. This set him to thinking of the three dreams, and he forgot the rotgut whiskey that even now churned in his belly, the cold nights spent in other gutters, the long days without food. He remembered only the three dreams as the terror of his existence. His shoulders jerked uncontrollably, and he could feel the whiskey beginning to creep at last from his belly to his brain.

He pressed his palms against the bricks and tried to lift himself, in a last desperate effort to get on his feet and walk until he had shaken off the drowsiness that fogged his mind. But he saw at once that it was useless. His body was a dead weight and seemed to be a part of the gutter. It was like trying to lift the whole street from its bed. He sank back, exhausted. A tiny trickle of water ran past his face. "No use. No use," he sighed aloud, and the little stream swirled into a black, steel-barred cave in the side of the gutter. He heard it splashing into the sewer below, and the sleep came.

I

A small, towheaded boy stood in the dark hallway, clutching a stuffed giraffe in his left hand, rubbing his tear-streaked face with the sleeve of his blue flannel pajamas. An occasional frightened sob shook his body, and he wanted to scream out that he was afraid of his dark, lonely room, of the storm that shook the trees outside his window, of the creaking noises the floors of the big house made.

But he knew no one would come to ease the fear, because no one was there to come. It was like last night, and the night before that, and almost every night since he could remember. No one was there.

He heard a car door slam, and he ran back to his room and got into bed as fast as he could. Feet stamped on the porch, and the front door opened. The boy was glad he had gotten back in bed before they came in, because if his mother caught him up she would be mad, and his father would look at him with his cold eyes—not saying anything, just looking.

He listened as they came up the stairs. His father stumbled on the top step, and his mother giggled. Then they went into their bedroom and closed the door. They never looked into his room.

For a fleeting, joyous instant he thought the pressure on his back was the hand of his father, come to look into his room after all, to make sure that everything was all right. Then he realized that what he felt in the small of his back was the sharp stab of a knee. Knowing what it was, he didn't even bother to look around. Furtive hands searched his pockets, and he felt his flat, dog-eared billfold being lifted from his hip. Hell, he thought, that guy can look all night, and he won't find any money on *me*. The knee was lifted, and the billfold fell into the gutter. A voice above him muttered, "Sonofabitch!" Youthful footsteps moved swiftly down the sidewalk, and the signs flashed on and off and on and off.

II

The lean, loosely muscled youth stood tense in center field, thrusting his fist into the greasy, web-fingered glove on his left hand. A thousand miles in front of him, the pitcher rubbed rosin into his hands, the runners on second and third made little jerky hops of impatience, and the batter scraped the dirt with his spikes.

The center fielder rubbed his sweating hands across his chest. "Come on, Sam!" he murmured. "Don't lose this guy! One more strike, and it's the state tournament for old RHS!" The pitcher, as if in answer to the plea, went into his windup, kicked high, and reached toward the plate.

At the crack of the bat, fear caught in the throat of the center fielder. Beads of sweat laced his forehead as he watched the ball sail in a wide, slow arc over second base. Circling nervously below the falling ball, he heard the sigh of relief from the stands, as they realized he was there waiting to make the catch.

He shaded his eyes and watched the ball grow from a white dot in the blue sky into a huge globe that was sure to crush him. Almost in self-defense, he stuck up his glove, and the ball caromed off the padded thumb and bounced on the close-cropped outfield grass. The winning run had long since crossed the plate, and the sigh of relief became a groan. As the center fielder trudged slowly toward the infield, the loudspeaker announced the single word "Error."

He choked, strangling on the muddy water that was flowing an inch deep in the gutter. The rain was falling in sheets now. He raised his head in time to see the billfold swept away, riding the crest of the raging little flood. The water swirled into the cuffs of his pants, tugging at his clothes, until he could almost picture himself following the billfold down the gutter, down and down and down.

III

Standing there in front of Auburn Hall, the spring sun warming his back, he thought of what he was going to say. Damn it all, she's so terrific, what can a guy like me say to make her want to tie herself down? Two years, almost two years since I met her in freshman registration line, and still no more to it than just going steady. Well, if I'm ever going to ask her, it's got to be today, else I'll chicken out again.

The bell rang, and as he watched the steady stream of students pouring through the doors, he felt the old fear rise in him again. Then he saw her, her blonde hair catching the gold of the sunshine as she stepped from the shadowy doorway. Watching her move toward him, he decided for the ten thousandth time that she was beautiful. Not pretty. Not attractive. Just beautiful, that's all.

"Hi, Hope."

"Hi, Al."

"Let's go for a walk. It's too nice a day to stay inside."

"Gosh, I'll buy some of that! I could hardly keep my eyes open in that class."

Walking across the campus, they talked idly of the little events of the day, and he wondered what it was about her that made him forget the fear that hung over him like a cloud. Seemed like even when things were really rough, all it took was a look or a word from her to make everything okay. He dropped her books in the grass before a tree-shaded bench. They sat down, and he took her hand.

"Look, Hope, there's something I got to tell you, something I've known for a long time. We've been dating pretty steady for two years, and, well, I guess by rights you know a lot more about love than I do, I mean with your parents and all, but—"

"Wait, Al. I think I know what you're going to say—correct me

if I'm wrong—and I don't want you to say it. We've had wonder-
ful times together, and I was hoping we could keep it that way.
Why spoil it by getting serious? I'm really sorry you feel this way.
If you want, we can keep on dating, or even going steady, but
nothing more than that. I hope you understand, Al. I'd better go
back to the dorm now."

She picked up her books and moved quickly down the walk.
Watching her go, a bitter smile twisted his lips as he wondered how
she ever came to be named Hope.

Dawn slowly overtook the fast-fading darkness. One by
one, the windows of the tenements glowed with the light of
bare bulbs, and grotesque heads, bristling with steel curlers,
passed back and forth before the lighted squares. A man in a
leather jacket and jeans, with a lunch pail under his arm,
walked slowly along the street, too sleep-laden to mind the
driving rain. Seeing the heap of clothing in the gutter, he
thought at first to go on about his way. "Just another drunk,"
he muttered.

Then he noticed that the gutter was almost half filled with
a boiling torrent of water. He quickened his steps till he was
at the gutter's edge, and grasping the body by the shoulders, he tugged it up over the curb and onto the sidewalk. He
turned it over, and a bloated yellow face, wearing a sardonic
smile on the blue lips, met his stare.

"Lord God!" the man said aloud. "What a way to die!
Drownded in a gutter!"

Endnote

Dr. Havighurst kindly overlooked a dangling mod-
ifier or two ("Watching her go, a bitter smile twisted his
lips . . ."), along with some of the lamest dialogue ("Hi,
Hope." "Hi, Al.") in the history of human speech, not to

mention the lamest interior monologue ("The same dreams, always the same three dreams!") in the history of human cogitation. But "drownded" (which I thought was really cool) proved too much for him; it garnered an "sp?" in the margin.

Here's what Dr. Havighurst wrote on the last page of my gloomy little manuscript:

> *There is a grim and graphic detail in the foreground of this story that makes it real. But the man is never as real as the street and the gutter, and the cutbacks are not very effective. The relation of the baseball episode to this downhill life is not clear—and it has no significance in itself. The campus scene is fairly life-like, but it can hardly be regarded as leading to death in a gutter.*

c+

Wendell wrote this piece in 1971 as an introduction to an early version of *Famous People I Have Known*, which was never published in that form. So I've blithely turned his old introduction into a sort of afterword—but be warned: Wendell gets the afterword, but I get the *last* word.

Ed McClanahan
of Brooksville:
A Recognition

by Wendell Berry

Convention expects one to assume a stance of critical cunning at the start of such a piece as this, as if to assure the knowing world that one is not the dupe of friendship, that one is capable of "objectivity" and the other intellectual virtues of our age. And so I may as well begin by admitting that I am incapable of being objective about either Ed McClanahan or his work. I can only speak of him as a compatriot and a beloved friend. To those who may be put off by such a display of subjectivity, I can give the assurance that Ed has his faults, some of which would no doubt repay scrutiny.

But this will not be an attempt at criticism. It will be a testimony and a recognition.

I first knew Ed when he came as a graduate student to the University of Kentucky in the fall of 1956—a tall fellow who usually wore a Levi's jacket and pants (which failed somewhat to meet in the middle), boots, sunglasses, and a lot of long wavy black hair swept back over his ears in a ducktail. It was a getup straight out of the small Kentucky towns of our young manhood, and it had as explicit a social intention as a debutante's chiffon evening gown. It declared that this was a man who gave not a damn for the world of debutantes and chiffon gowns, who aspired to "live fast, love hard, die young, and leave a beautiful memoree." It suggested that on many a Saturday night he had tooled his Ford dangerously fast into the curves of the hill roads of Bracken and Mason Counties, driving with one hand, a can of beer in the other, left elbow draped nonchalantly out the window. But this was also a student of literature and, as we soon knew, an aspiring writer who had already attended a number of other universities in quest of his art. What to make of it all? Here was a *literary* honky-tonker, a man who no doubt led a secret mental life as reckless and dangerous and free as a Saturday night roadhouse, a man who, given sufficient weariness and sorrow, might drink himself to death on beer—a project I believe he may have undertaken several times in his youth but invariably lived too long to complete.

Also at the university at that time were James Baker Hall, with whom I had already been friends for two or three years of nearly constant discussion of the few books we had managed to read, and Gurney Norman, the youngest of us, who sometimes turned up at English Club meetings in a uniform and crew cut, the Billy Budd of ROTC. Among the four of us in the years that followed there would develop a mutuality of experience and interest, indebtedness and dependence, plans and delights that I can only call brotherhood, an elastic trapezoid of common ground that keeps us joined however far apart we go.

To none of us could the 1956 version of Ed McClanahan have seemed very strange, though we all must have wondered what to make of it—much as we all must have wondered what to make of the 1956 versions of ourselves. Only now, after so long a time, does it occur to me how thoroughly provincial a figure Ed was, as we all were in those days, and how much our story since has been a drama of American provinciality. For we were perhaps the last generation (only for a while, I hope) of American provincials—the last for whom provinciality was possible. We grew up under local influences just before television and the consequent homogenizing of the national consciousness.

But ours was not an innocent provinciality such as that of the Aran Islanders, say, at the time of Synge's visit. From childhood ours had been an increasingly self-conscious provinciality—an *ordeal* of provinciality. For two or three generations before us the people of Kentucky, like those of the rest of the country south of the Ohio River, had been learning, with the help of outside "educational" influences, to think of themselves as *different*. They had been made aware preeminently that their speech was different—and moreover that it was inferior to "standard American." Into the speech of well-meaning people in our part of the country there came a hesitancy and a tone of apology, especially in the presence of strangers. Those of weak character who had traveled a bit were apt to put on the accent of some more elegant place, like Cincinnati. Few in our generation made it to college without having encountered, at home or at school, some authority who made one uncomfortable with the sound of one's own voice. We had been picked at not only for our grammar but for our accents, our flat *i*'s, our failure to enunciate -*ing* at the ends of our words. Our native speech was being destroyed in our very mouths—or so it was hoped. We got the point: Kentucky was a cultural appendix to the urban Northeast. That Allen Tate and Robert Penn Warren were Kentuckians I learned to my astonishment only after I was in college.

And so in 1956 Ed, like the rest of us, was deeply involved in this very complicated provinciality, defiantly affirming it in some of its aspects, defiantly repudiating it in others, and the gestures both of affirmation and repudiation were helplessly provincial. It might seem no more than honest, for instance, to look and sound as country as you felt you were. On the other hand, there was no use in pretending that you were not sick and tired of certain aspects of your local inheritance. If you defiantly held to some of the identifying local ways, you had to know that you were both declaring and inviting scorn. However you might suffer and despise certain people's contempt for provincial life, you yet hungered to know what they knew and to go where they had been. It was a character-splitting self-consciousness that made for a considerable amount of awkwardness both in your thinking and in your bearing toward the world. This is not, I hasten to say, an exercise in omniscience. I am guessing to some extent; looking back, I believe that I see in Ed some of the conflicts and uncertainties that I felt then in myself.

I am aware that the word *provincial* is usually applied as an insult. I am also aware that remembering the work of such provincials as Henry David Thoreau and William Faulkner, people thus insulted may rest somewhat at ease. But there is no use in being a chauvinist of terms. I would rather the word would bear no judgment at all; let it refer merely to a condition that some of us have had to deal with. I have used it so prominently here because it is in thinking of him as a provincial that I can best apprehend what I believe to be the accomplishment of Ed McClanahan. Provincialism, I think, is a permanent condition. If one begins provincial, then one is apt to end so, however changed. It cannot be got over—except hypocritically. More or less like the rest of us, it seems to me, Ed began helplessly provincial, became stubbornly and defiantly provincial, and is now provincial by conviction and rebirth. But he is not *simply* provincial. He got around a good deal during his school days, and for the last thirteen years he has lived in the West, mostly in the San Francisco Bay Area. He is a migratory provincial. And in his wanderings he has looked at the world with a provincial eye. When you have been raised in a place that the rest of the country has almost by premeditation paid no attention to, you can never quite get over being someplace else. When you go to a *famous* place, the unexpectedness is most clamorous and enduring; your mode of communication becomes a startled letter home: "Dear Mom, Well, here I am in —————— that you have heard so much about." You sit down occasionally and count up the famous places you have been or the famous people you have met. And you are amazed. Who would believe it?

But provinciality is not just an interesting social condition. In modern times it has also come to be a moral predicament, attended by dangers that are apparent enough to the qualified; and the fewer provincials there are, the greater the dangers become. There are two:

You may become a *phony* provincial. If you are from our part of the country you can become a fake southerner. Once you make it into the society of northerners you will find that you come from the South and that it is Solid. People who have seen *Showboat* will presume to know who you are better than you do: "Well, shut my mouf, honey chile! Wheah yawl

fum?" Or some learned party next to you at dinner will want
to know: "How is it that so many of our most brilliant writers
have come from the South?" You can surround yourself with a
certain air of romance just by keeping still and allowing it to
be assumed that you have been a cotton picker.

Or you may become a phony urban sophisticate. You may
contrive an accent, manners, dress, demeanor, and conversational interests that imply that you were born as far as may be
desirable from home. You can sound like your daddy was a
television announcer. Country people in Kentucky are familiar with those who leave home with burrs in their hair and
come back talking like Yankees, with the hauteur of those
who have seen the Beyond.

Either way—by generalizing and mythifying your origins
or by denying them—you are cut off from your history and
from the springs of your character. Your deepest identity
turns rancid and useless in your very being, like a meal soured
on your stomach.

Ed McClanahan has avoided both dangers. The life of the
places he has gone to has appealed to him strongly; he has
taken part in it too wholeheartedly and generously ever to be
mistaken for anybody he is not. And he has refused to take
part—and to speak of his experiences—as anybody but who
he is. He is a trustworthy reporter of the life he has seen precisely because his voice is as far as possible unlike that of the
anonymous, displaced mouth that speaks to us out of the public media. It is his honesty, and his generosity, that he lets us
know not only what he is talking about but precisely *who* is
talking. This is *not* a recording.

Given the stresses of contemporary provincialism, we can
find it no surprise that Ed is a stylist—a man intricately aware
of how he sounds, meticulously attentive to the nuances of
diction, rhythm, syntax. He has to be, for every sentence is

burdened not only with what it has to tell but with an attitude
toward itself that is invariably complex, the cultural burden
that our time has placed upon the provincial consciousness.

Consider, for example, the title story, "Famous People I
Have Known." The subject is patently provincial. The piece,
at ground level, is an exploitation of an inescapable provincial
voice: that of a boy from Brooksville, Kentucky, saying,
"Wow, look where I have got to! Who would believe it?" But
the *attitude* toward that homely voice is intricate enough to
make the language almost baroque. The voice is given a certain amount of credit; a certain value is placed upon its innocence. But the attitude is also skeptical and ironic. Incorpo-
rating this complexity of attitude, the language transcends its
autobiographical occasion; it assumes the force of social criticism, and of a sort of tragedy.

Who would believe it? the provincial asks in wonder at
himself. And the migrant, out of his broader experience, can
only come up with a sad, small truth: almost anybody. For in
these media-ridden days, "famous people" have become, in
my grandmother's phrase, as common as pig tracks. Glamour
is an illusion. The *grand monde* that lives so much upon the
ridicule and at the expense of our private worlds is a bubble or
a dream. Those who return to the province infatuated with
the Beyond are deluded. The only life we can have is our own.
What do all our encounters with the great and the glamor-
ous—with "history"—add up to? Only to ourselves, as we
are, as we have become. The Ed McClanahan who rubbed
shoulders with these great is still no more—though happily
no less—than Ed McClanahan. That is the sort of realization that assures a man of his mortality and makes him an
artisan.

This is written from the point of view of a resident provincial. It was Gurney Norman who helped me see that one of

the duties of a writer is to return from his experience, however far out it may be, to report what has happened to him. That is what Ed has done in these pieces. And as one who often stays at home and waits for such news, I understand and appreciate him in that way. As the single residential provincial of our brotherhood, I have occasionally felt myself somewhat out-numbered by those of the migrant sort, but I have grown ever more grateful for their news.

Such a bringing back of news has a double function: one must be both an adventurer and a craftsman. One must have the courage and the curiosity to leave the home ground. But one does not leave merely to become lost; the value—at least the negotiable, the public value—of the adventure lies in the return. One must have craftsmanship equal to his courage; there must be skill enough to get home with the news.

Ed's language is his compass and map. It is not something novel and shallow that he learned at the extremity of his trip and will use to impress us stay-at-homes if some accident should bring him back. On the contrary, it incorporates the knowledge of the whole journey. It lies behind him in all the passages and turnings of his travels and is with him, like the string an explorer unwinds as he goes into a cave. If it sounds like it has arrived on the Palo Alto scene in the early seventies, it also sounds like it began in Brooksville in the early thirties. Because of that, on all his returns, in all the messages he sends back, I hear the voice of a man I am de-lighted to recognize.

Endnote

Famous People, like *The Natural Man,* was a gleam in my eye for many years before it became, in 1985, a reality. In 1971, when I published a piece by that title in *Esquire,* I was al-ready planning the book. But in the ensuing years, Wendell's

"Recognition" fell through the cracks somehow, and I'd forgotten all about it until it surfaced when I cleaned out that old file cabinet. How I had managed to forget it I'll never understand, considering that Wendell's were perhaps the kindest words anyone had ever said about me.

The only thing is, I still don't know what he could possibly have meant by that reference to my "faults." I never noticed any goddamn "faults."

autobiography of a voice

PERHAPS THE SIMPLEST and most maddening question we can ask of anyone doomed to be a writer is "Where'd you learn how to talk so funny?" Sometimes the answers are complicated. Sometimes a map in the form of a Möbius strip is the only thorough reply.

The particular stretch of cartography laid out in this book belongs to Ed McClanahan. As we track the twists and turns in the long arc of his development as a stylist, we can catch the slow feed of voice as it reveals itself. "I always told myself that if I could just putter around with this stuff long enough, I could eventually get it to work," he says.

The evolution of "this stuff"—the gradual refinements, the sudden liberations, the working and the waiting and the cajoling of self into the song it always wanted to sing—continues to bedazzle me. For those of us who need a little extra time to get our abilities in sync with our best intentions,

McClanahan's personal victory offers some kind of collective hope. A lot of promising writers fall by the wayside for a lot of different reasons. Ed has kept his promise.

For starters, then, consider a couple of moments from the long and happy life of an American writer.

1964: The gods that be at *Esquire* magazine are paring their fingernails and looking for pawns. They behold one Edward Poage McClanahan, a young, largely unknown Kentucky writer, and they declare him elect. Perhaps this is due to a novella he has under contract, written with all the reflex nihilism and energy of youth and called, loftily, "From a Considerable Height." It might have something to do with Ed's managing to cobble together a good run of riffs for Rust Hills at a cocktail party. *Esquire* has an argument to make, a much-needed one, a contention that what we had come to understand as the "contemporary" literary situation post-1945 or so has shifted, that the old lions are yielding ground to strange new creatures; it's a recognition that literary power (an oxymoron if there ever was one) perpetually plunges forward and shifts sideways and doubles back on itself like a snake. Ed McClanahan suits their purposes.

They scoot the gamepiece of his name to an arbitrary location they designate the "Red-Hot Center" of American writing (as opposed to "Squaresville," where abide the likes of Clifton Fadiman and Orville Prescott). "Little ole unpublished me," Ed recalls in *Famous People I Have Known,* "suddenly wallowing right in there cheek to jowl with the biggest fish in the biggest pond of all: Mailer! Styron! Baldwin! Salinger! Bellow! And . . . McClanahan?" There he squirms, traduced, for all of American writing to see. The novel the world awaited would not appear for nineteen years.

1992: Ed announces to my wife, Brenda, that he intends to shed the responsibilities of composition. Two books he has every right to be proud of and he has had his say. The screen that glows around the clock in the little office in the front of his house will be turned off tomorrow. The office itself will henceforth be stripped of prose and other adornments—the tie-dyed curtains, the photos of family and friends, the fetishes and souvenirs and what Ed calls "my hillbilly tchotchkes," the knickknacks and awards and the framed original of the book cover R. Crumb did for *Famous People*—all the casual reminders that sustained him through the prolonged distillation of that prose. Forty years of detritus and glory will be cleared away to make, perhaps, a formal guest room. Brenda and I try, without much luck, to hide our apprehension.

What happens outside these misleading parameters—between, that is, the false start and the ersatz finale—is the story. And the story is still very much in progress.

In the time between that premature canonization and the publication of his first novel at age fifty-one, McClanahan came to view the "red-hot center" as a crucible, a furnace. "I guess it was the best and worst thing that could have happened to me. The goddamn red-hot center just got hotter and hotter until I felt like I was frying in it. There was a letter in the very next issue of *Esquire* demanding to know who the hell I was and what I had to show for myself."

What he *would* have to show—but not until 1983—was that novel. By the midseventies, after internal adjustments aplenty, the novella "From a Considerable Height" had grown into an unfinished novel titled *A Hell of a Note*. For a few weeks there in 1980, he was fondly referring to it as *Stepeasy*. Then, just prior to the ides of March of 1981, it experienced yet another wrenching transmogrification, this time from first-person to third-person, and emerged as *The Natural Man*.

By 1985, in what looked—deceptively—like rapid sequence, McClanahan introduced us to *Famous People I Have Known,* a lyric poem masquerading as a memoir, one of the most romantic landmarks of what we used to call the New Journalism. The centerpiece of *Famous People* had appeared in *Playboy* eleven years earlier. Not so much a profile of as a meditation on the late Little Enis—Lexington, Kentucky's self-appointed "All American Left-Handed Upside-down Guitar Player"—the *Playboy* piece represented a breakthrough for McClanahan's fiction as well, as Enis became both his muse and avatar (see "Empathy Follows Sympathy"), helping him to set *The Natural Man* free at last. In Enis, he had found just the right note—pitched halfway between humble disbelief and go-for-baroque braggadocio, for the "Ed" he was inventing and refining, the "Ed" who would take us to the nexus of celebrity and anonymity.

In 1996, more than thirty years after the "red-hot center" nearly cooked his goose and just four years after Ed swore, in Faulkner's telling phrase, to "forever break the pencil," a collection of three long stories called *A Congress of Wonders* appeared. Each of them had been incubating for . . . yes, more than thirty years. Ed had made an abortive attempt to write a version of "Juanita and the Frog Prince" as early as 1953. "Finch's Song"—which Ed once told me stemmed from wanting to "play all the notes I could reach on the instrument, take it to all the places it could go"—began in 1962 as another novella whose inherent problems were reflected in its title, "Consider the Lilies, How They Grow." "The Congress of Wonders" had apparently been tugging at Ed since he haunted the carnivals that passed through the small Kentucky hometown of his boyhood.

So all three of these books were, in a very real sense, well under way long before McClanahan got tossed into that center. The fictions and the life proceeded apace, a work in progress.

What had to come was the voice, and this book is the autobiography of that voice. Ed has given us a time tunnel, and wandering through it we can trace the convolutions of a point of view in process, the development of an attitude, the evolution of a style. Like Lyndon Baines Johnson, baring to the camera's eye the scars of his surgery with a wink and a flourish, Ed wants us to see how it was done.

Pay every attention to that man behind the curtain.

. . .

Ed and I met in 1978, when I was an undergraduate, under the most awkward circumstances imaginable. He was interviewing for a position teaching fiction at my college; the operating fiction at same was that the students had some say in the appointment. Ed was still five long years away from finishing *The Natural Man;* I was twenty-one and, literarily speaking, a true sophomore. But his eyes were shining with the joy of good work, and he showed me fifty pages of the book. He did me the enormous favor of appearing to take me seriously, a charity he has extended to this day. It seemed to matter what I thought of it.

I thought it was perfect, of course, just perfect. Ed never got the job, probably thanks to my impassioned recommendation, but after graduation I stayed in touch, and what an education it was to watch him tinkering away at his dissatisfactions with the nuances of that book, working it, polishing it, never seeming in the slightest impatient with it, recognizing that nuance is all, that every syllable has to count. He showed me his Enis essay, and I could see how much strength he took from this thing that he had gotten absolutely right. He showed me how much you have to trust yourself, how hard on yourself you need to be, how much fun you need to have. He taught me how much the discipline and the play really do matter.

Now I find myself in the classroom trying to hand these lessons down. "Creative writing" courses have been much and not altogether unfairly maligned—even, as we have seen, by a certain former teacher of mine—yet they strike me as being at the very least a benign means of producing better *readers*, to train more empathetic and critical and curious operators of texts. In the long run, like everyone else, Ed McClanahan had to teach himself how to write. But he got and gave a lot of help along the way. It will always be a relay; it has never been a race.

. . .

Ed's close friend Gurney Norman sees writing as a journey into what he calls "the long dark tunnel into self." *My* Vita, *If You Will* is an honest run at a cross-section, an X-ray of what one of those long dark tunnels looks like from inside. When I suggested to Ed that an assemblage of some of his uncollected work might suggest the points of departure, the arrivals, the passage into that work, we began to see new ways to focus on the flash, the accretion, the silences, the steady gains. What we wanted to avoid was a bundling of incoherence best summarized as "Here's a whole bunch of stuff we found in the attic." What we wanted to catch was the process itself, the false starts and the breakthroughs, the slow accumulation of voice, the other people—teachers, colleagues, friends—who helped along the way. We wanted to make a sort of documentary in prose, I guess, that could employ long shots and dissolves and still frames and flash-forwards to tell the story behind these stories. What we wanted was context and sequence.

We hope the endnotes provide that. They are palimpsests hot off the press. First designed to hold a few stray anecdotes in one location, later nothing less than interstitial tissue, the endnotes just kept growing, and we realized Ed had a chance to fill in the empty spaces on the vita, the absences, the really interesting stuff that is always the trickiest to explain in the job interview. Now Ed's realized voice narrates the documentary, telling the story of the discovery and the paring away and the ongoing reinvention of his idealized voice. "You lucky bastard," I was moved to say when the memories really started flooding in. "What you've got here is the perfect opportunity to excavate your own ruins."

. . .

Maybe shit just happens, but magic takes some marinating. It's instructive (and a double caution) to look at the progression of early fictions included here. "Fear and Hope and a Gutter" will have to speak for itself; I can't hope to improve on the words of kindly old Dr. Havighurst. "The Cynic" forces its sensitive and misunderstood protagonist into the perhaps too-efficient narrative strategy of stealing a look in the mirror to admire his premature dissipation and callow world-weariness, a projection of the young author's still-unearned despair. "The Cynic," however, is a much better story. The atmosphere and setting are better modulated, the dialogue is well observed, and the matchstick men create a moving and accidentally almost hopeful image. As effective an exercise in apocalyptic wishful thinking as any wild-child-come-lately is apt to vent tomorrow, the tale still hints somehow at the lightness and generosity, the *earned* sentiment, yet to come.

McClanahan's "Postcard" hails us from Italy, yet it really comes from the venerable tradition of American innocence colliding with European experience, a line moving from Hawthorne through James to Tennessee Williams. You can tell our emerging stylist has been doing a lot of reading and a lot of writing since his earliest efforts. The work is careful and focused; the young man won't be caught raw-faced in the mirror this time.

Still, a somewhat forced "maturity" and "sophistication" have been laminated onto material Ed is not completely comfortable with, material not completely his own. We can see the standard of the writing rising, but the writing itself seems designed to please someone else's standard. The teacher is still looking over his shoulder.

"The Little-Known Bird of the Inner Eye" represents the breakthrough into what we can now see as the beginning of his mature work. In Freddy, we can see most clearly the origins of Finch Fronk, the embattled protagonist of "Finch's Song," which Ed says is his favorite single piece of writing; here too is the genesis, perhaps, of that most pitiful and proud of his characters, the "morphadyke" oracle, Jo-Jo of "The Congress of Wonders." The sentimental grotesque and robust baroque are on full display, and the humor is beginning to creep in. (It is startling, given the admixture of comedy and pathos that infuses McClanahan's later work, how often pathos dominates early on.) With "Little-Known Bird," he moves beyond apprenticeship. He can stand back and declare: This is mine, this has got my personality and my style all over it; for better or for worse, no one else could have written this.

"The Greatest Writing Ever Wrote" and "The Harry Eastep File" are lost chapters from *The Natural Man,* vital to appreciating that book fully and the changes it is, in effect, still generating for Ed. "Greatest Writing" suggests what the first-person point of view he abandoned at the last minute would have been like, but it also offers an extended, hilarious version of the theater marquee rewrite scene—Ed's very own *ars poetica*—that was truncated in the final product. And just as "Greatest Writing" looks back on what might have been, the two short pieces in "The Harry Eastep File" anticipate what will be, for they are to furnish the capital, the seed money, for Ed's next novel, *The Return of the Son of Needmore*.

. . .

McClanahan's prose has such urgency, so much forward momentum, unfurls itself in such a rushing torrent that it appears to be spontaneous, composed all of a piece. It is not. His stories are fictions of calculated impulse and arrested immediacy, long-time balancing acts of conjure and risk and grace. Yet, ensculpted and bejeweled as it is, this is not the "lapidary" prose of the mandarin. There is nothing bloodless about it. It is available to those of us who have to breathe the less rarified air of the everyday. It is beautiful, and it is of use.

I expect Ed would be rightly suspicious of being called a poet, but poet he is, if only in his preoccupation with language and rhythm, with making something beautiful. With making music. His sentences meter and scan, they whirl and tumble in fluid control to conclusions both mathematic and unexpected, and then—just as Emily Dickinson asked—they click shut like a box.

Ed claims an old back injury prevents him from carrying a tune. This hasn't stopped him from singing; rather, it has forced the music underground into the prose itself. He says he writes in order to read his stuff aloud, and to hear these lyrics performed by the man who wrote them is to recall the same phrasings from the rise and crawl of Ed's everyday conversational rambles—phrasings that are mellifluous, pointed, self-aware, loud, vulnerable, cultivated, raunchy, gentle, acerbic, wise. Like the shaman Doctor Rexroat, who has stalked into most of Ed's fiction at one point or another to disorder and control the fates and furies, that voice is a bit of a cross between a backstreets preacher, a confidence man who has bought into his own bill of goods, and Mr. Magoo on nitrous oxide.

Reviewers have invoked the names of everyone from S. J. Perelman to Eudora Welty in their attempts to nail down Ed's signature, but as with any really original stylist, the name of anybody else will miss the mercurial mark a little bit every time.

My best shot: It's as if, between divided allegiance to the great southern voices—not just the usual suspects like Welty and Faulkner and O'Connor but also the beguiling trashiness of Erskine Caldwell—and the sentiment and irony and manners of the great Victorian voices, the satisfying and moving fussiness of Austen and Dickens and Trollope, Ed decided to split the difference. You end up with something like the day the hogs ate Little Dorrit.

Because it is Ed's voice, damn it, and while you can trace where it came from, you have to marvel at everywhere it's been.

· · ·

If Kentucky is the beginning and the culmination of Mc-Clanahan's work, what came in between were California and the 1960s. Throughout the rich cluster of reminiscences here, he finds much to celebrate, much to mourn, and more than a little to deplore. Elegies abound, and valedictions, laudations of the ones who prevailed, who made it through the darkness and the most serious kind of fun. In these pieces, Ed limns a sort of natural aristocracy of freakdom, from Neal Cassady through Jerry Garcia, remembering Richard Brautigan and Paul Krassner and Ed Sanders (and one Charles Manson), the circles in which he spun, the plethora of luminaries he managed to bounce off of, the stories only he can tell.

If the mythology of the counterculture has a progenitor, it is surely Neal Cassady, the original missing link, connecting Beats to freaks while disconnecting everything in sight, the not-so-straight continuum from Kerouac to Kesey, so evocative and so hard to understand. Ed's "Dirge" for Cassady is the most alert writing I have seen on what has been looking lately like an exhausted subject, catching both the man and the machinations behind the myth.

And if the mythology has a surviving warrior king, it would have to be Kesey, always Kesey, as the Merry Pranksters—who started out as a small circle of friends but now look something like a generation—wind their long strange trip into the nineties with "Furthurmore." Here is Ed's poignant rumination on whatever happened to life as we used to know it, what we thought we had, what we only believed we lost, what we are never going to get back, and what we have really held on to all along.

Then there is his legendary "Grateful Dead I Have Known," published here for the first time in its entirety. For my money, this is where the voice McClanahan had been training really started to sing, where he finally broke through into the riskier, more flamboyant style that would steer him through the books to come, the books he had carried in his head all that time. The three books on his shelf, complete. To which we can now, joyfully, add a fourth.

• • •

Way back when, around the time Ed taught the little-known bird to fly, he found himself to his delight dragging home from a long day at the freshman composition mill and writing a little for himself, working "at a white heat, sometimes five hundred words a night" on "From a Considerable Height." Five hundred words is about two pages. Two pages, double-spaced. But two pages as sustained as he could get them, at the highest pitch he found it possible to hold. Two pages suggesting possibilities rich enough to build on for years until he could finally get them just so.

Nowadays, especially as he wrote the abundance of new material for this book—all the endnotes and two brand-new pieces, "Great Moments in Sports" and "Another Great Moment in Sports"—Ed composes with the same sureness but with a newfound ease, a seamlessness, a certainty he never knew while presiding over the slow, fecund permutations of the earlier work. He subjects the language to the same old pressures but achieves a brand-new flow-to-yield ratio. He seems to have his ear right up to the tap.

He writes . . . well, faster. He has slowly and stealthily stolen up on that trick he likens to "performing brain surgery on yourself." So look for that new novel any minute now. Because the lights are on in the little office in Lexington, and Ed McClanahan, the man behind the tie-dyed curtains, is hard at it, pushing words around, trying to turn them into magic. He is sixty-five years old and he is writing the next one. He is singing.

Tom Marksbury

Printed in the United States
by Baker & Taylor Publisher Services